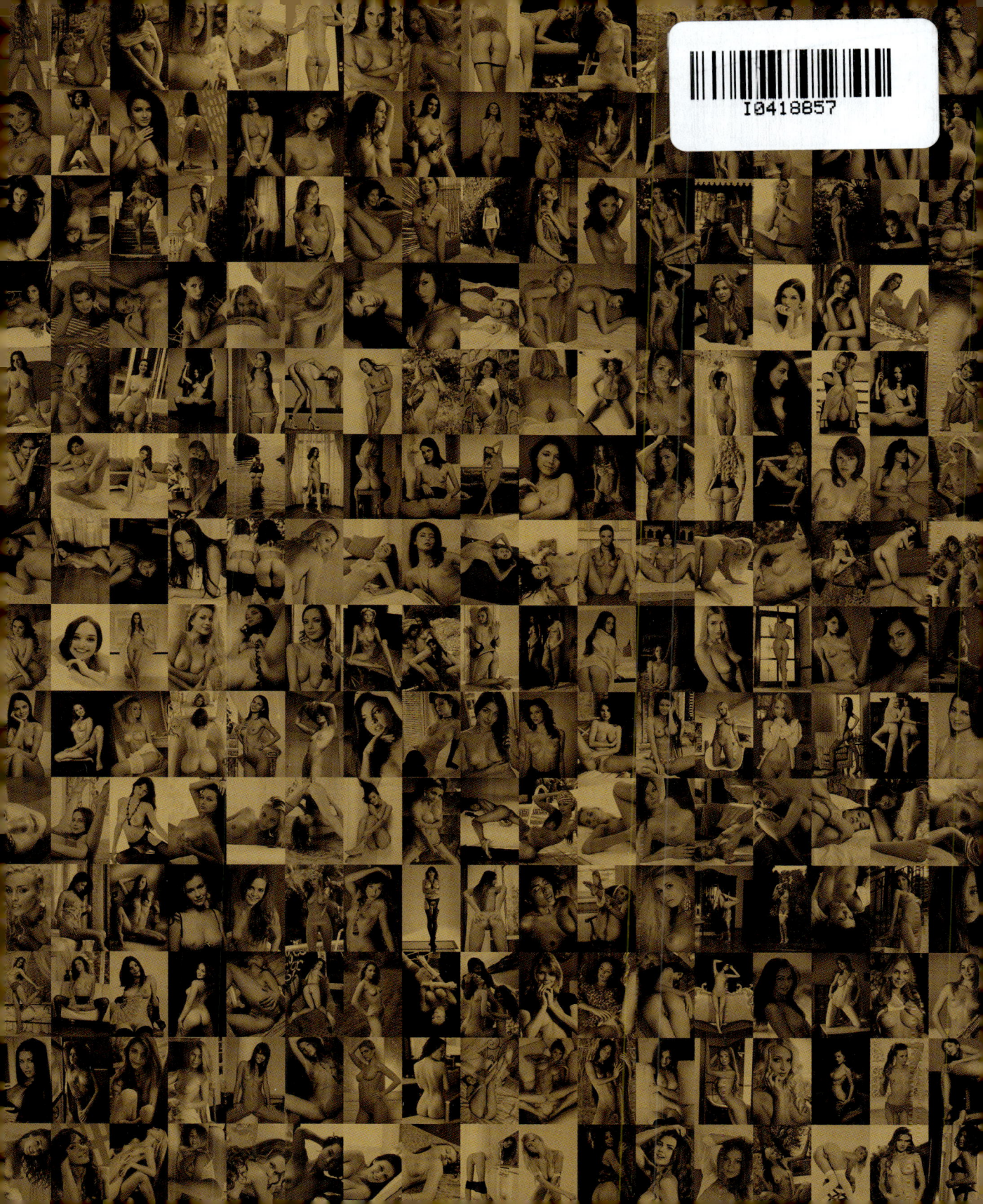

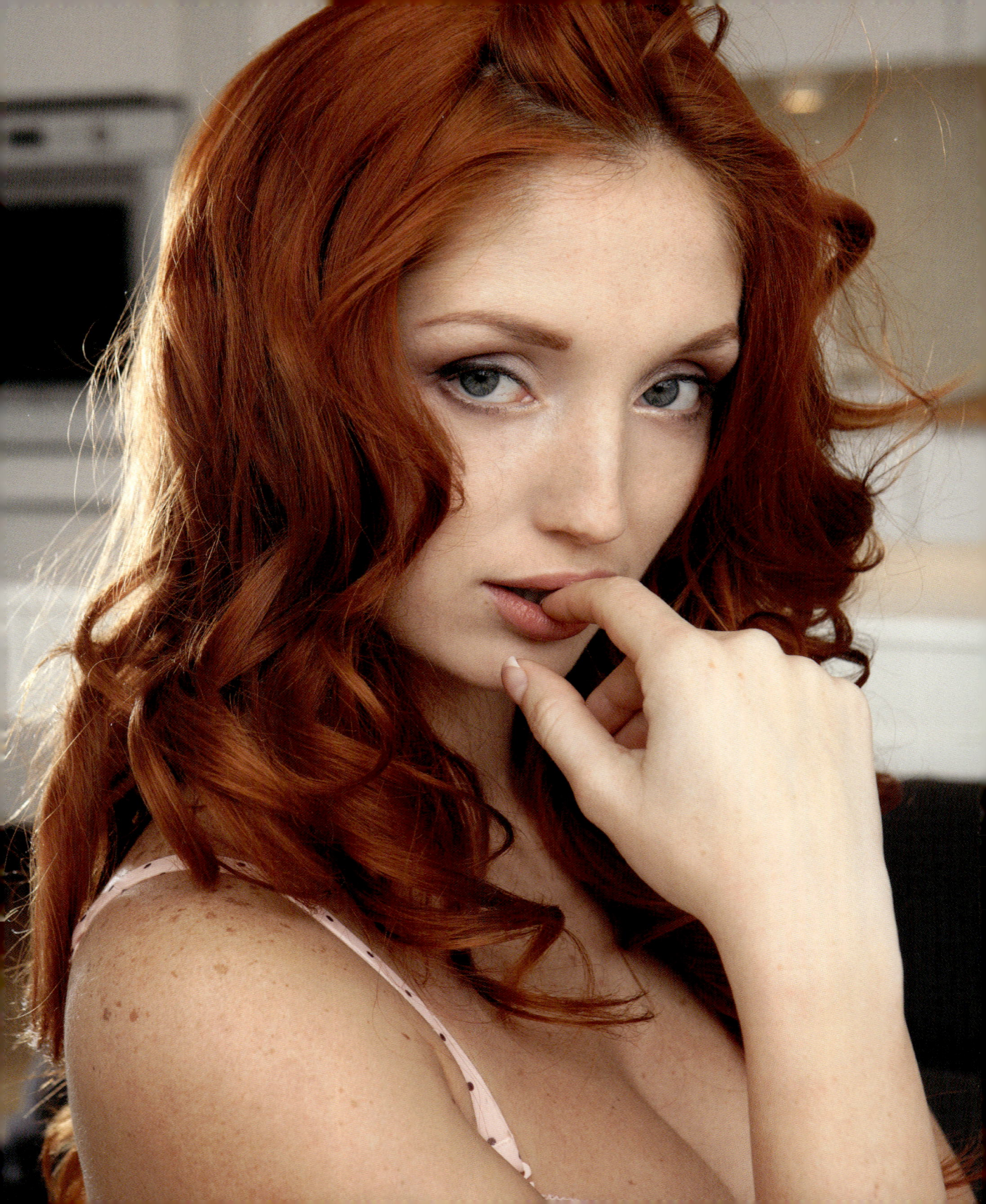

TOP MODELS OF
MetArt.™.COM
WHERE FLAWLESS BEAUTY MEETS ART

MICHELLE H

COLLECTED AND EDITED BY ISABELLA CATALINA

EDITION Skylight
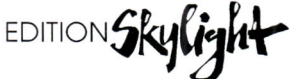

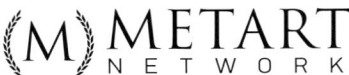

First edition 2025
Copyright © 2025 by Edition Skylight

EDITION SKYLIGHT
Rosengartenstrasse 13B
CH-8608 Bubikon / Zürich
Switzerland
info@edition-skylight.com
www.edition-skylight.com

ISBN 978-3-03766-705-7

Bibliographic information published by Die Deutsche Bibliothek
Die Deutsche Bibliothek lists this publication in the
Deutsche Nationalbibliografie; detailed bibliographic data
are available in the Internet at http://dnb.ddb.de.

Printed in Bosnia and Herzegovina

RED HAIR, BIG BEAUTIFUL EYES AND AN UNMATCHED APPETITE FOR SEX!

Stunning redhead **Michelle H** is one of our most popular Metart models. At the time of writing, Michelle is rated #48, with a rating of 9.15 based on 3,943 votes, with 253,598 views and 5,111 followers. She has appeared on many other sites in the Network: The Life Erotic, Errotica Archives, Rylsky Art, Eternal Desire; and on Domai, Goddess Nudes and Erotic Beauty as Nalla. Most notably, she has starred in several very hot girl-girl movies on Viv Thomas, working with director Alis Locanta; while on SexArt she is a major star, with 27 photosets to date, three girl-girl movies (one with top model Nancy A and one with Sybil A) and an unforgettable boy-girl movie, "The Port". She's a sultry goddess, but with a gorgeous smile that makes her altogether more approachable. And then, there's that stunning figure, with big, beautiful natural breasts and a perfect ass. It's not just her looks that have made her so successful though; she's a smart and ambitious girl, who brings her unique vision to her own movies. We are blessed with many talented female directors throughout the Metart Network, but Michelle is the only one who is still active as a model for other artists while also shooting her own movies – and sometimes appearing in them herself. Her work as Red Fox here on Metart, on Metart X, and particularly her kinky, fetish flavored films on The Life Erotic, suggest she is a creative force to be reckoned with. Here's hoping she'll be appearing on both sides of the camera for a long time to come.

ROTE HAARE, GROSSE SCHÖNE AUGEN UND EIN UNVERGLEICHLICHER APPETIT AUF SEX!

Die atemberaubende rothaarige **Michelle H** ist eines unserer beliebtesten Metart-Models. Zum Zeitpunkt der Erstellung dieses Artikels ist Michelle auf Platz 48, mit einer Bewertung von 9.15 basierend auf 3.943 Stimmen, mit 253.598 Ansichten und 5.111 Followern. Sie ist auf vielen anderen Seiten des Netzwerks erschienen: The Life Erotic, Errotica Archives, Rylsky Art, Eternal Desire; und auf Domai, Goddess Nudes und Erotic Beauty als Nalla. Vor allem aber hat sie die Hauptrolle gespielt in mehreren sehr heißen Girl-Girl-Filmen für Viv Thomas, mit dem Regisseur Alis Locanta; bei SexArt ist sie ein großer Star, mit bisher 27 Fotosets, drei Girl-Girl-Filmen (einer mit Topmodel Nancy A und einer mit Sybil A) und einem unvergesslichen Boy-Girl-Film, „The Port". Sie ist eine unersättliche Göttin mit einem umwerfenden Lächeln und dieser atemberaubenden Figur, mit großen, schönen natürlichen Brüsten und einem perfekten Hintern. Es ist aber nicht nur ihr Aussehen, das sie so erfolgreich gemacht hat; sie ist ein cleveres und ehrgeiziges Mädchen, das ihre Vision in die eigenen Filme einbringt. Wir sind gesegnet mit vielen talentierten Regisseurinnen im Metart Network, aber Michelle ist die einzige, die noch als Model für andere Künstler tätig ist und gleichzeitig ihre eigenen Filme dreht – und manchmal selbst in ihnen auftritt. Ihre Arbeit als Red Fox hier auf Metart, auf Metart X, und vor allem ihre fetischlastigen Filme auf The Life Erotic zeigen, dass sie eine kreative Kraft ist, mit der man rechnen muss. Wir hoffen, dass sie noch lange auf beiden Seiten der Kamera aktiv sein wird.

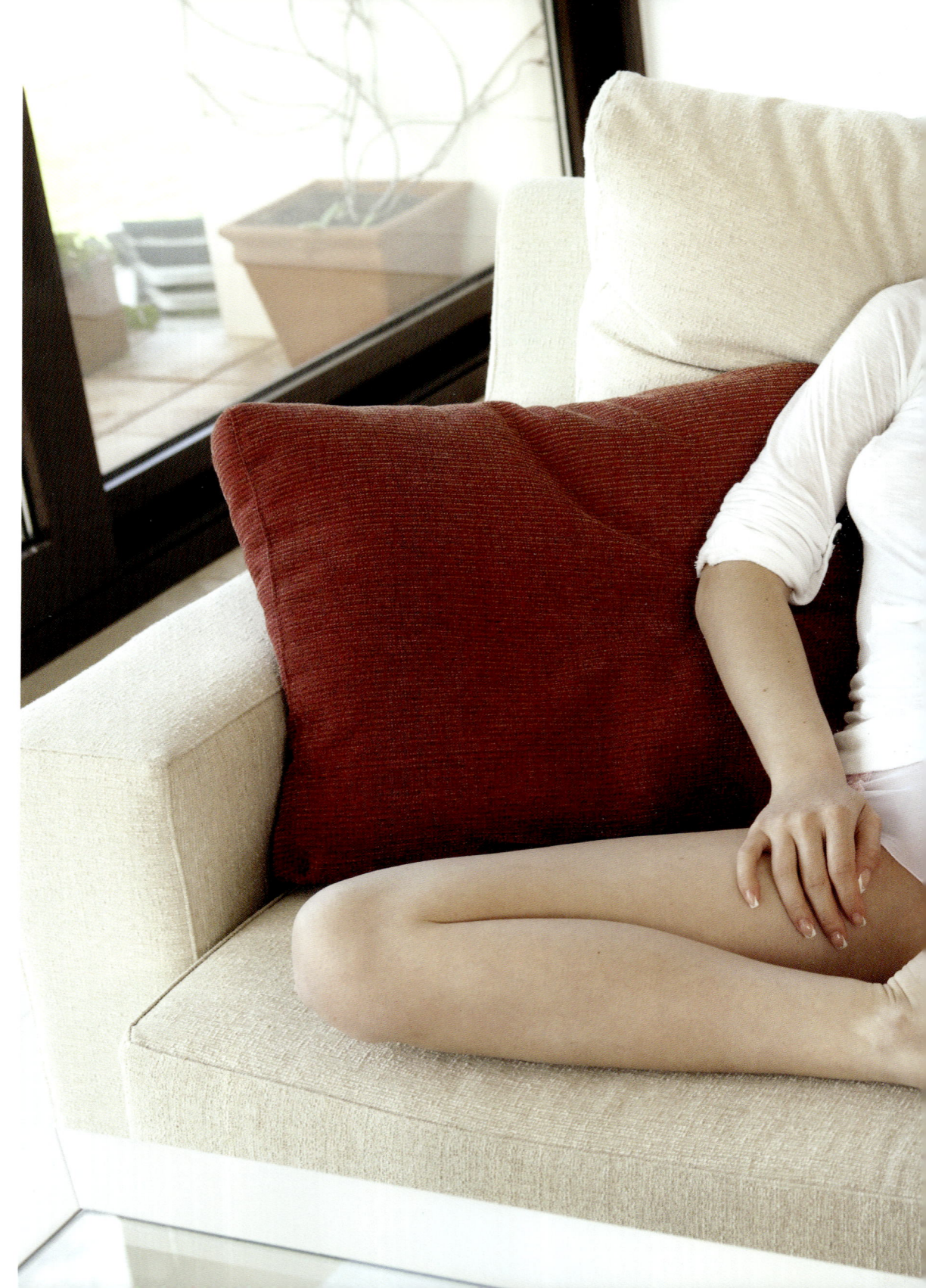

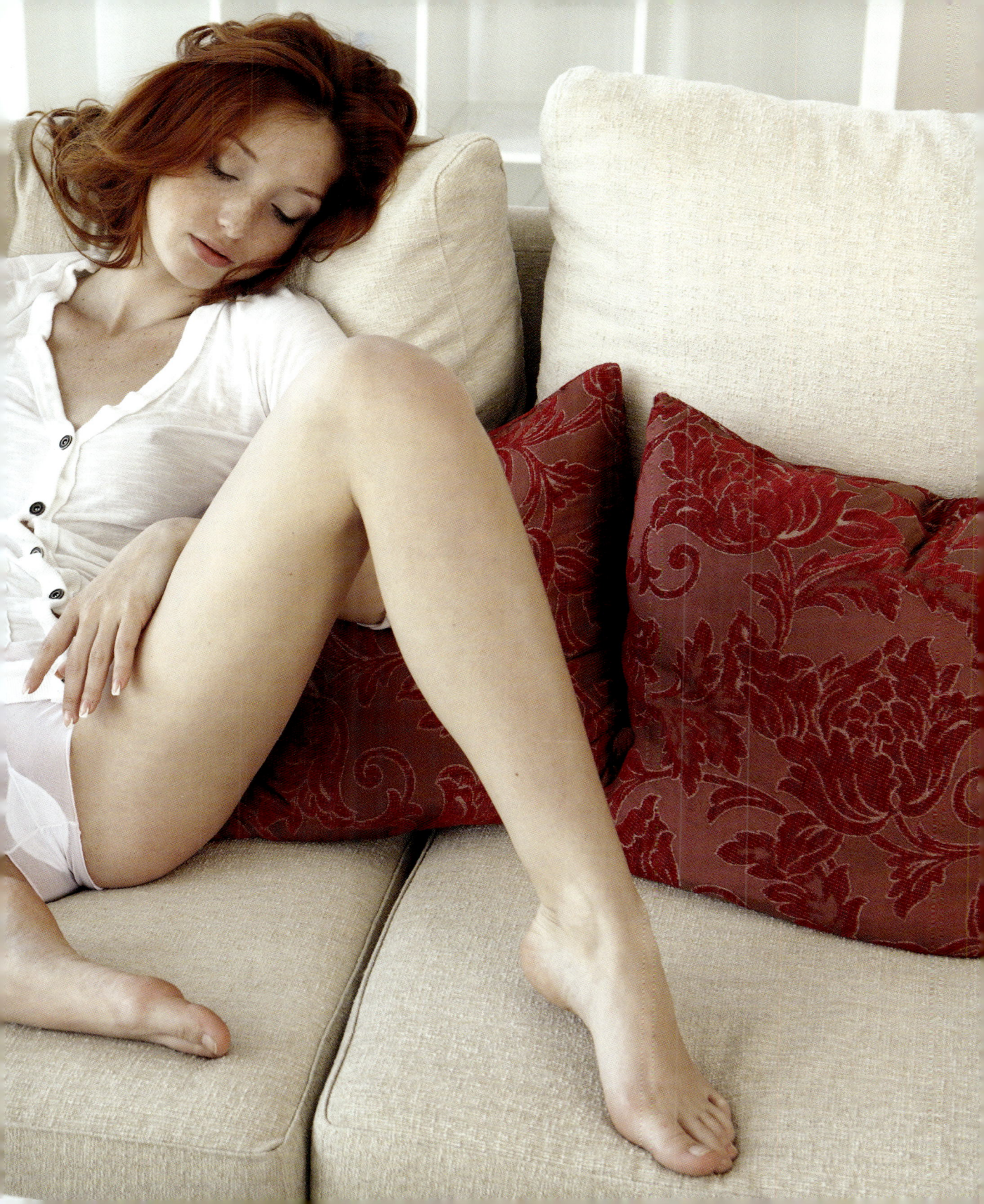

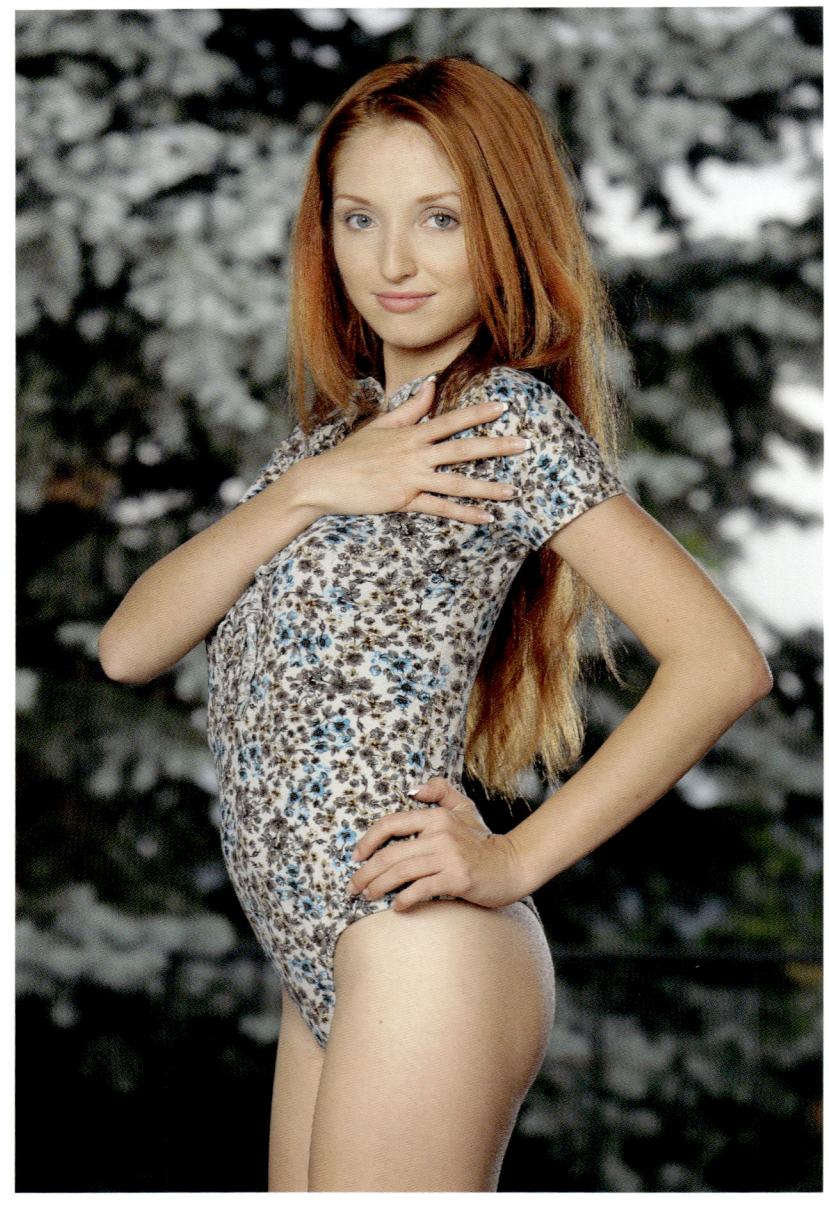

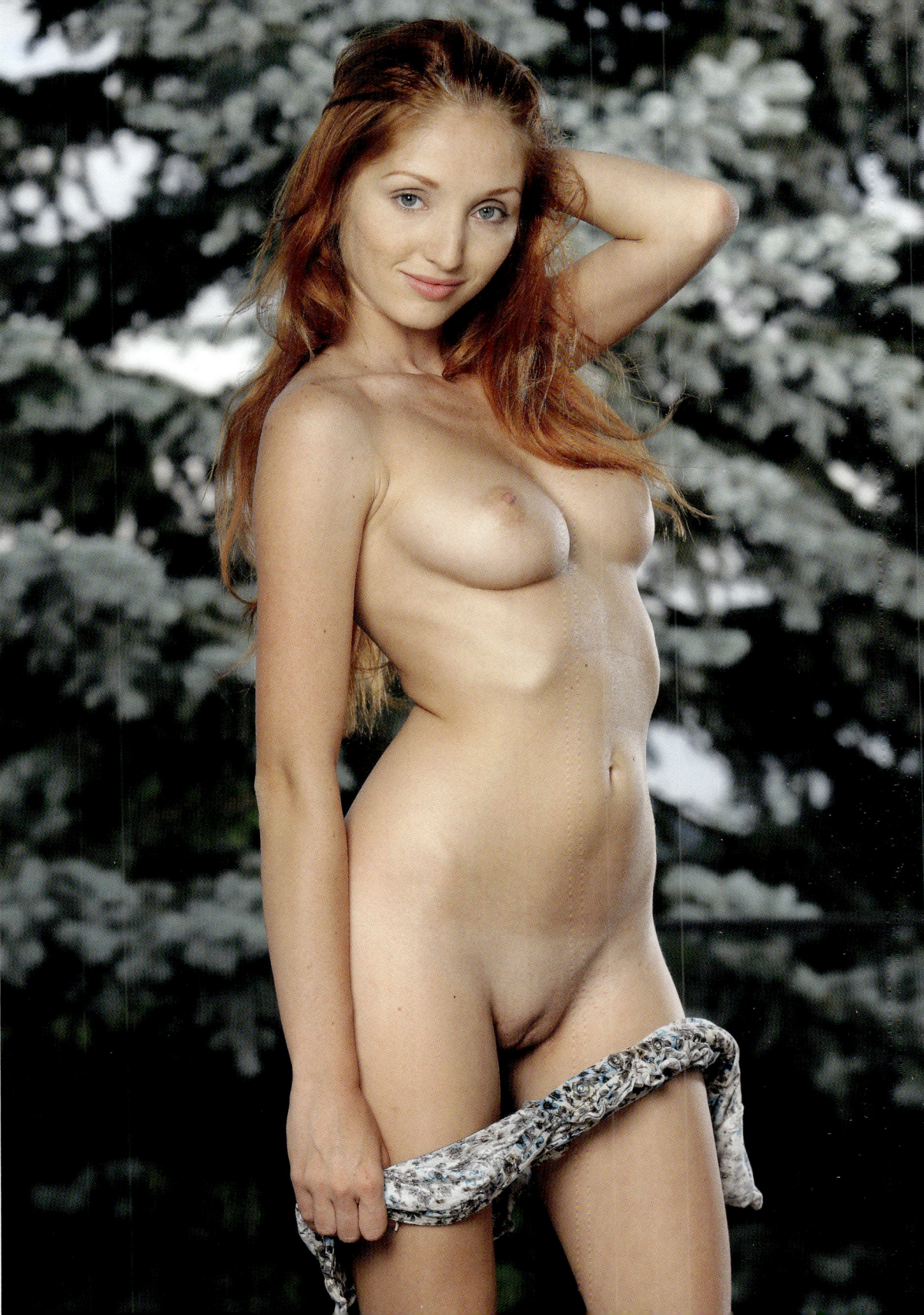

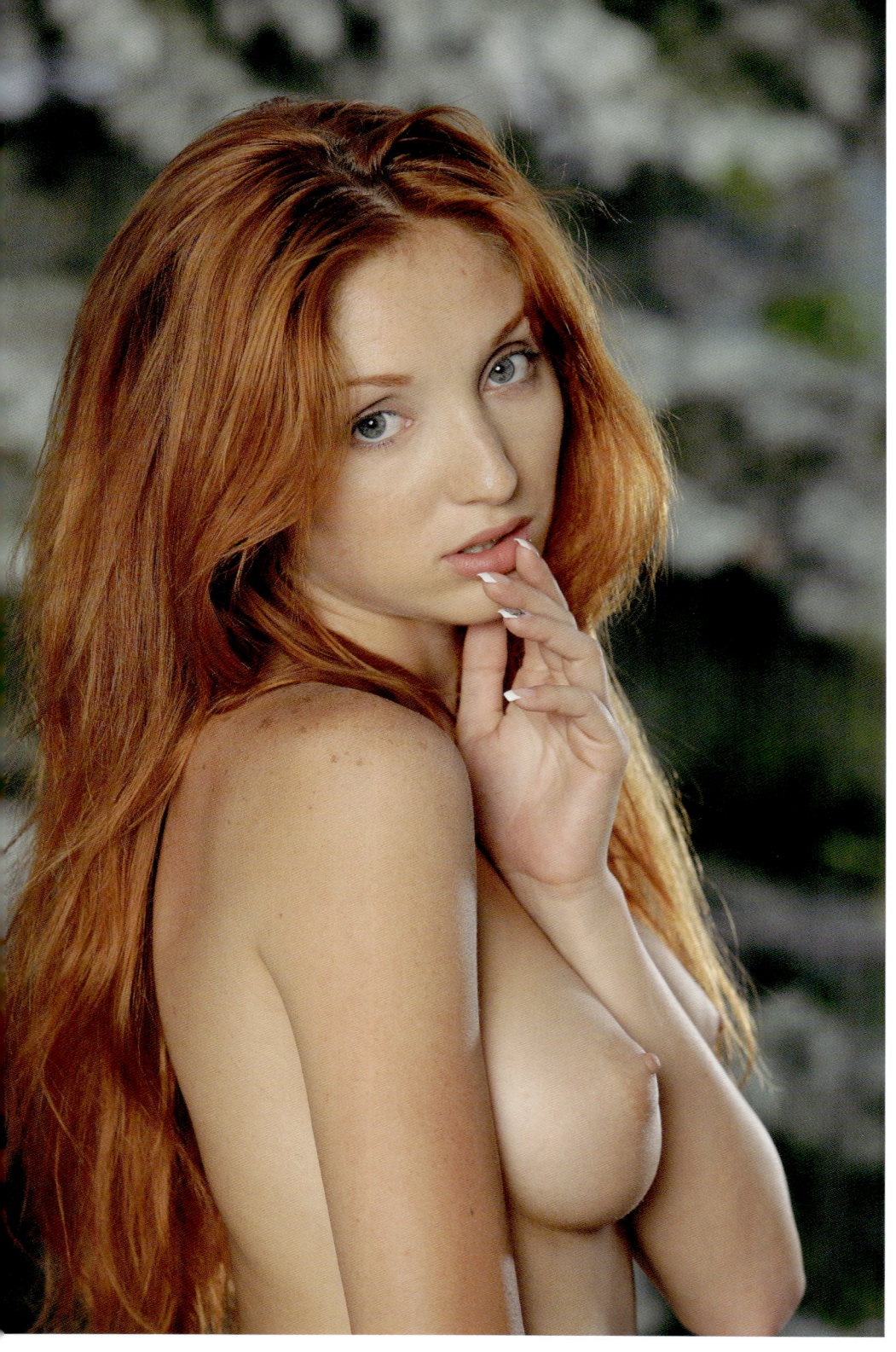

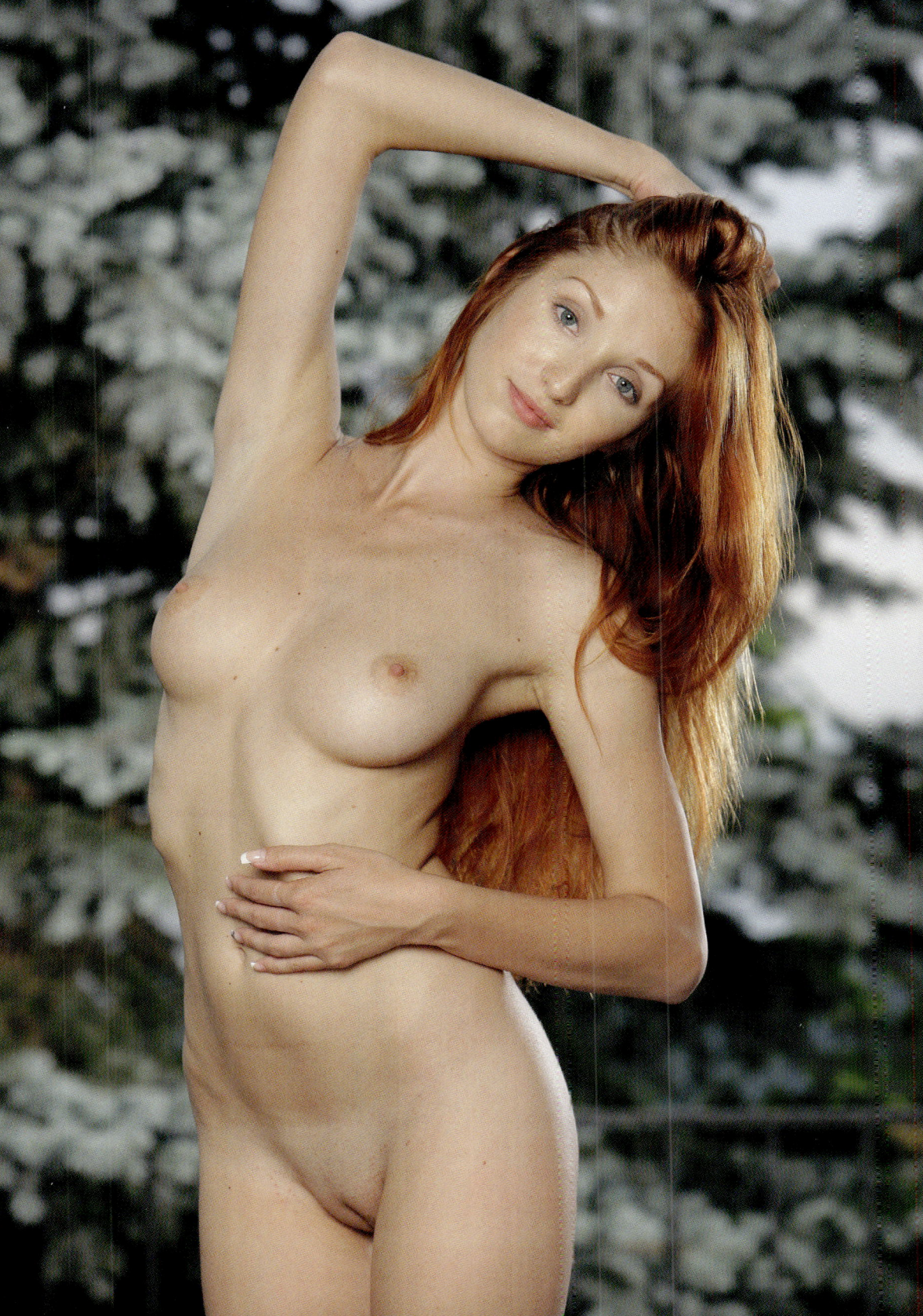

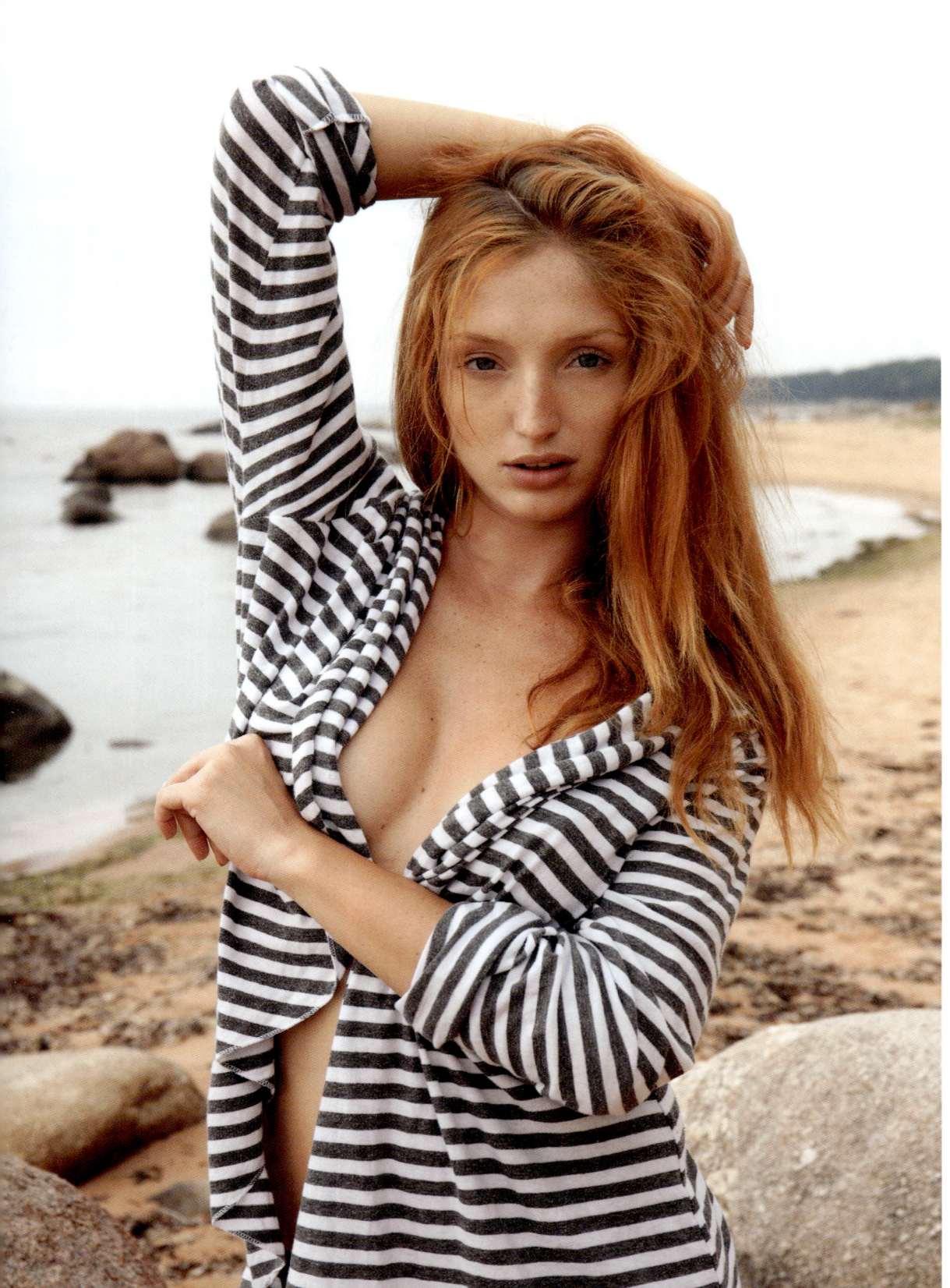

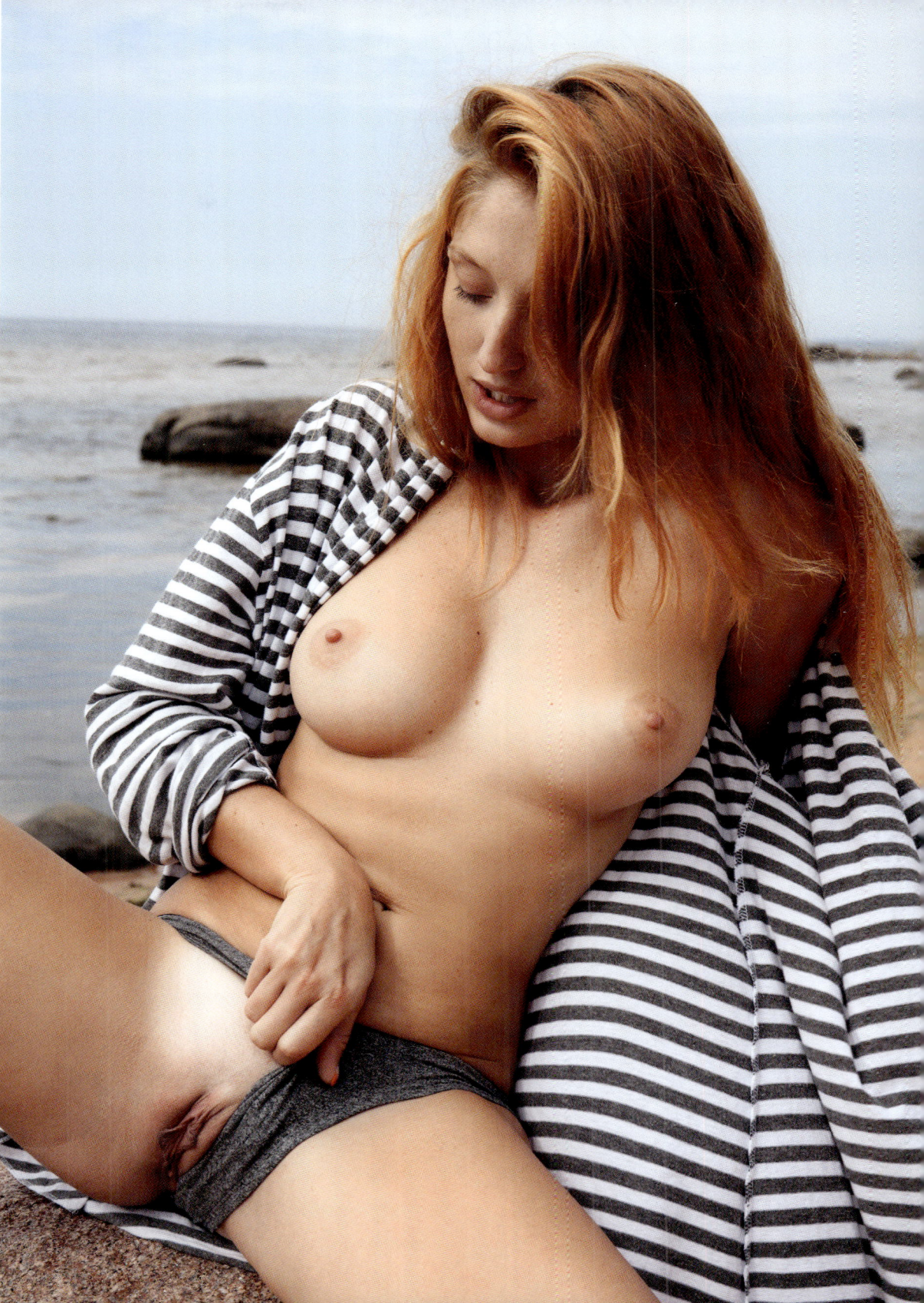

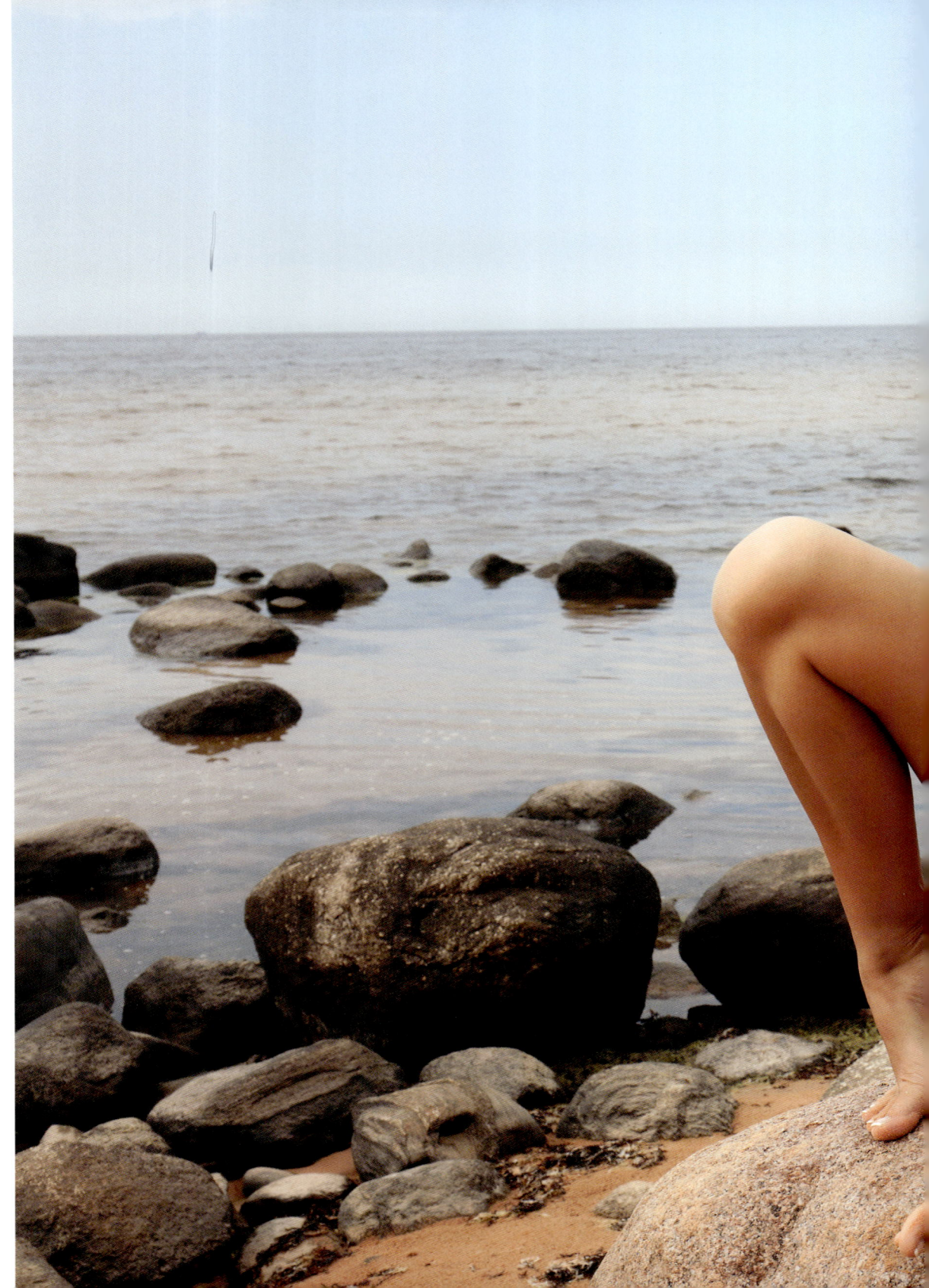

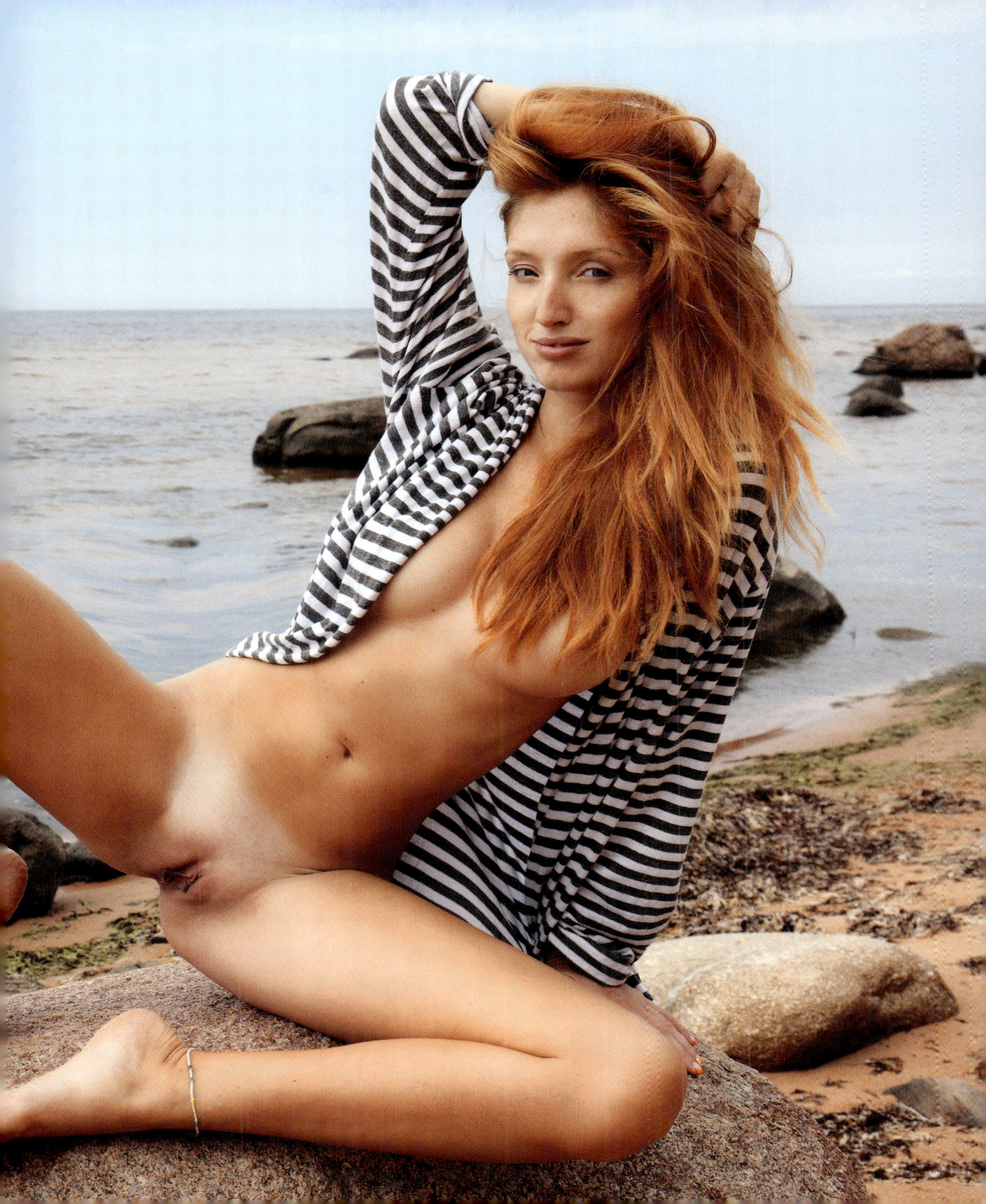

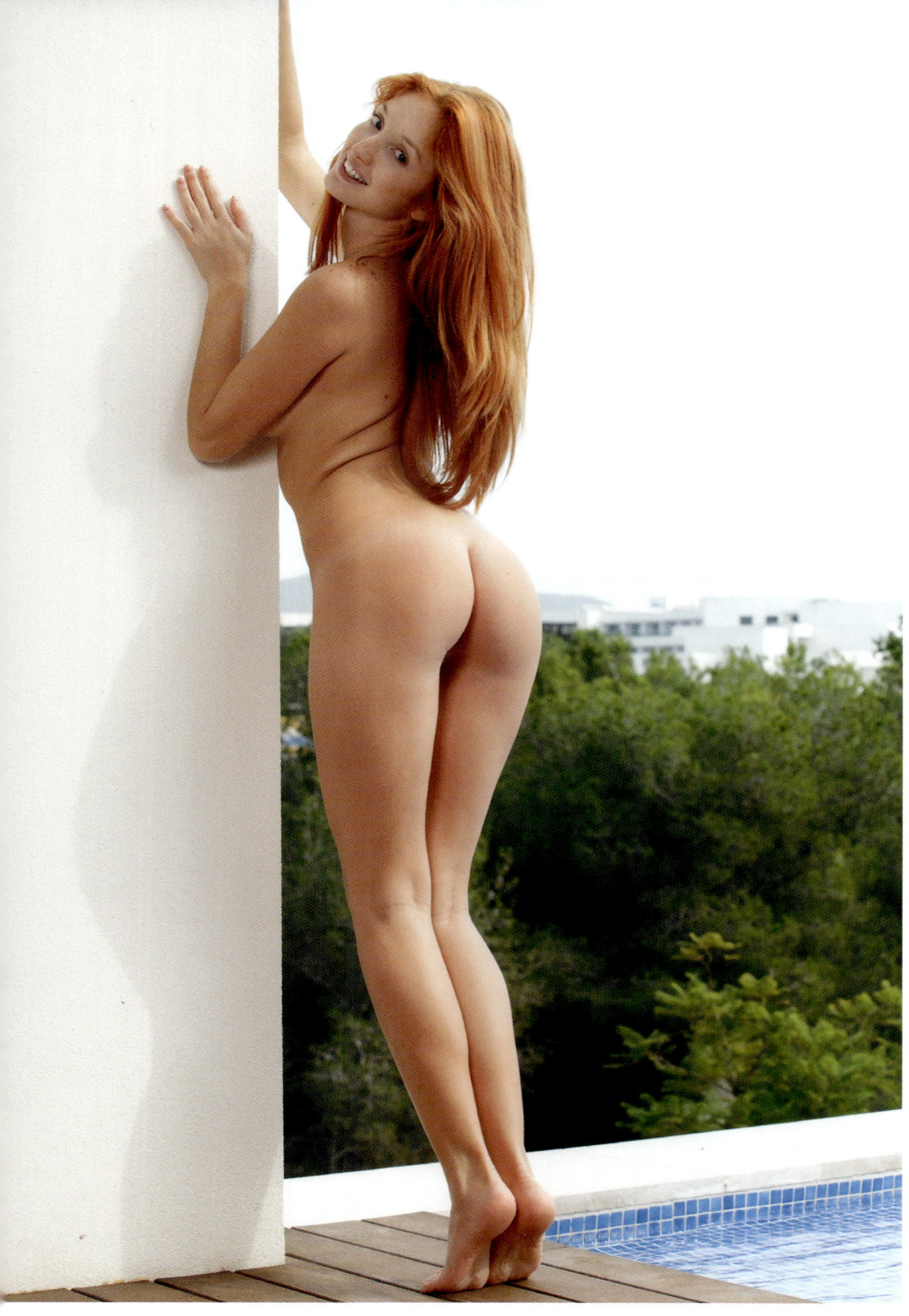

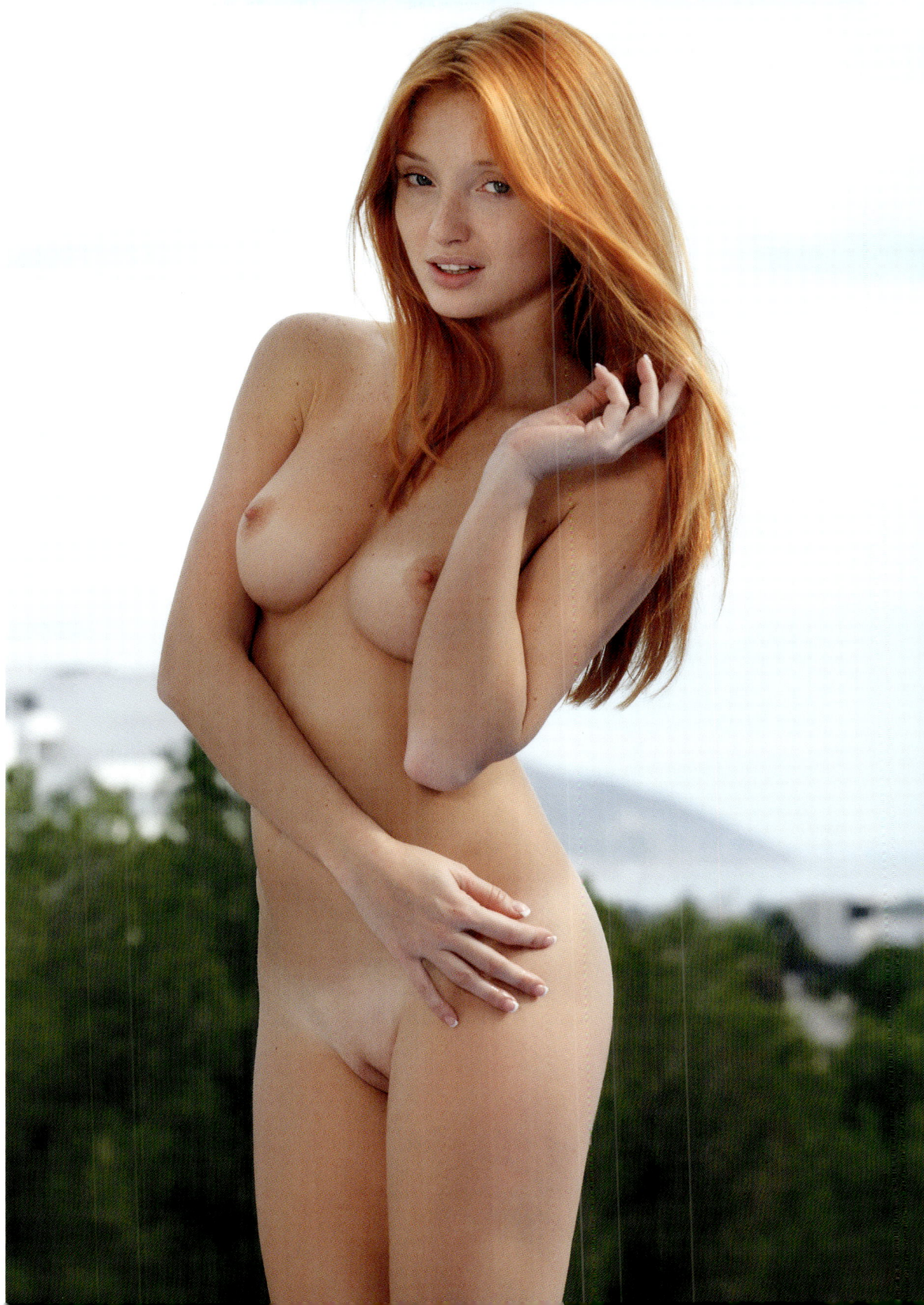

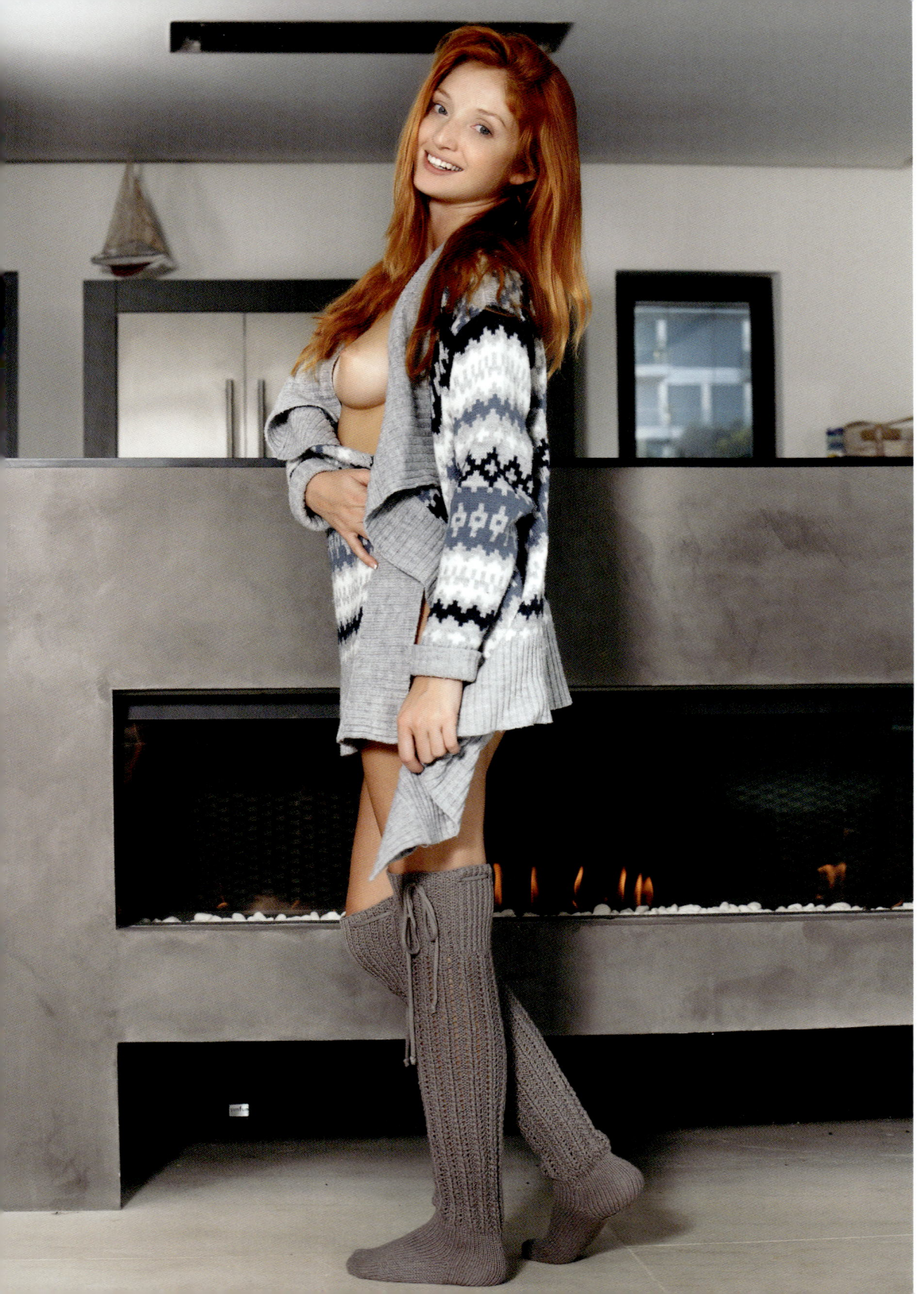

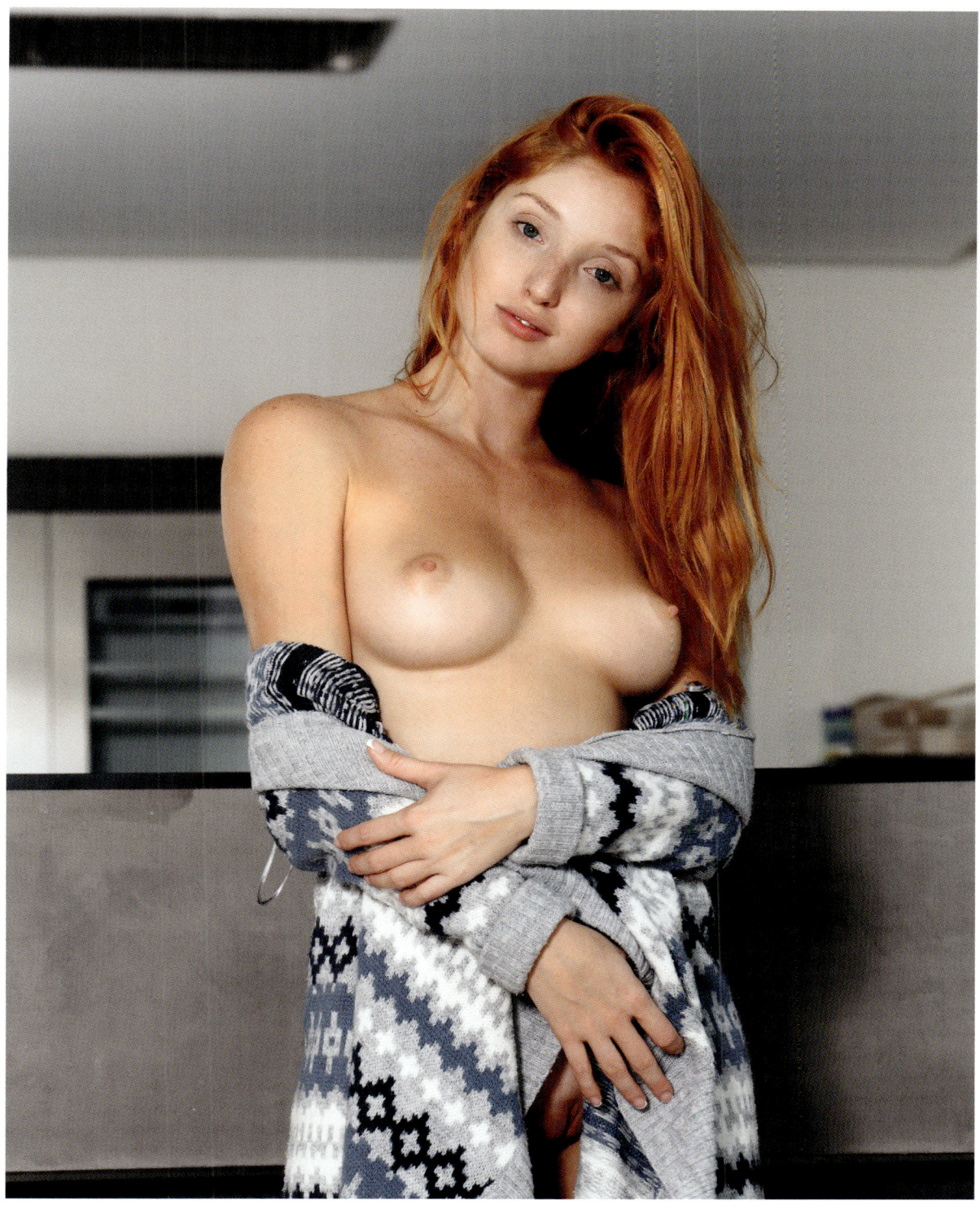

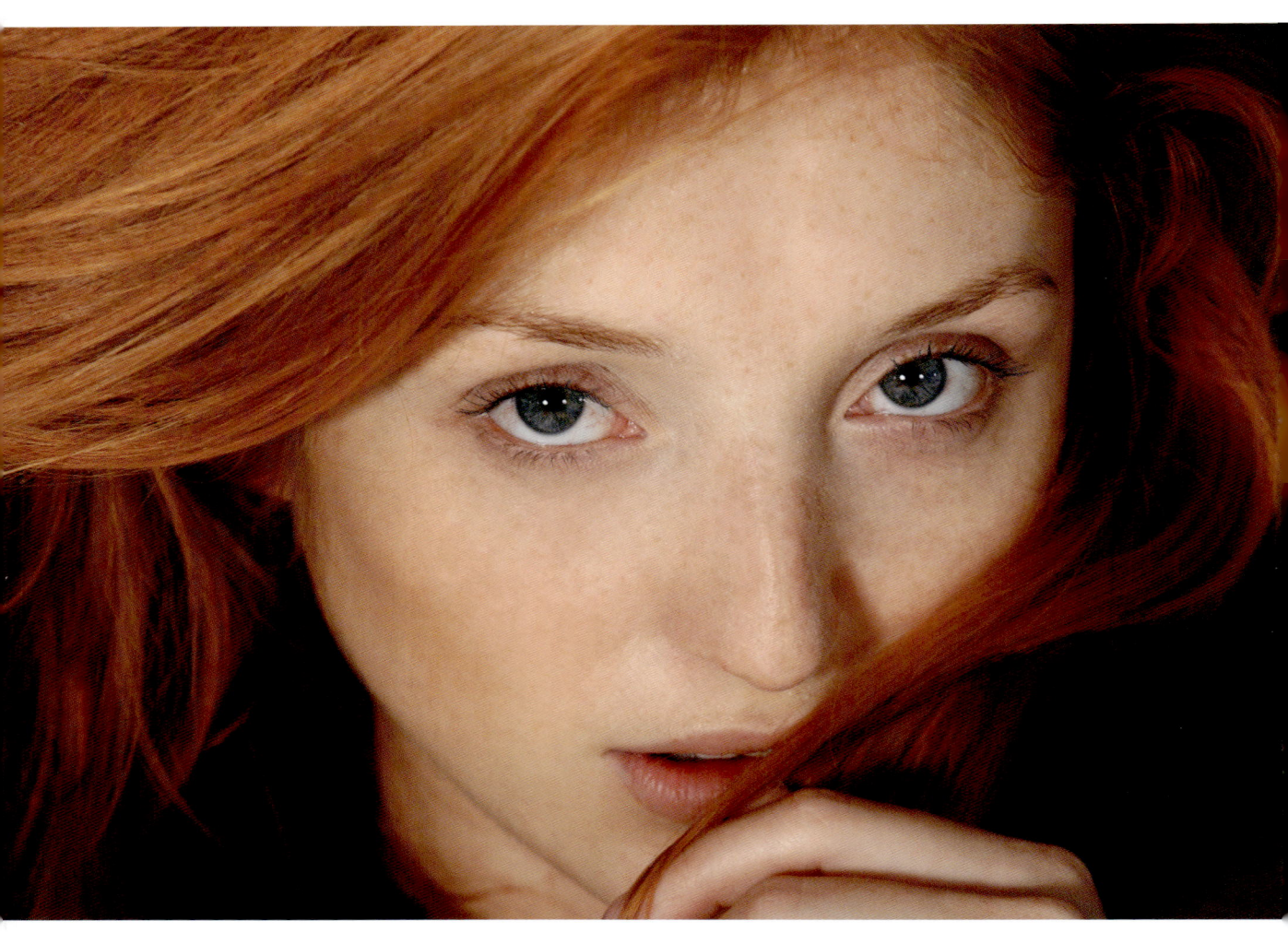

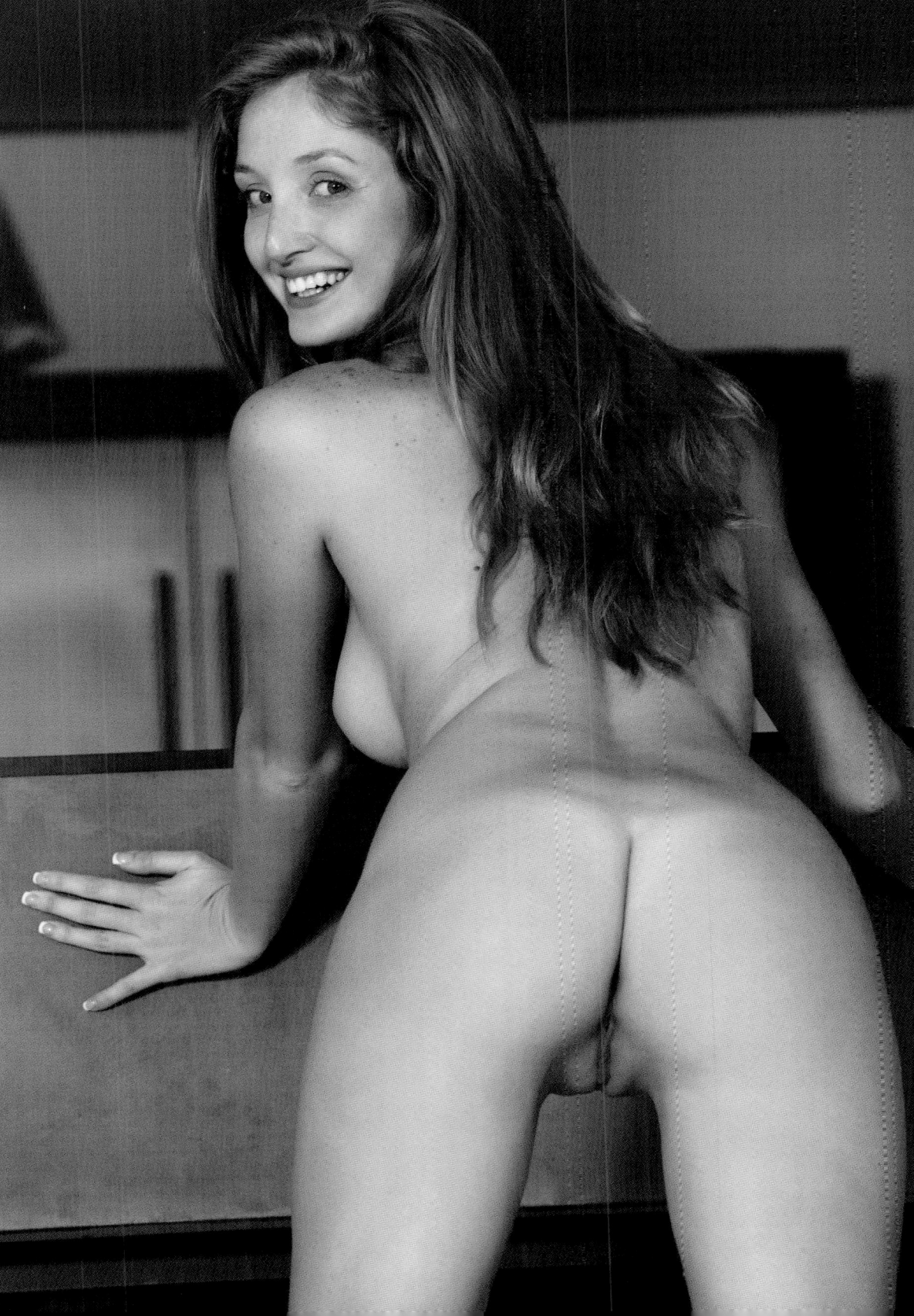

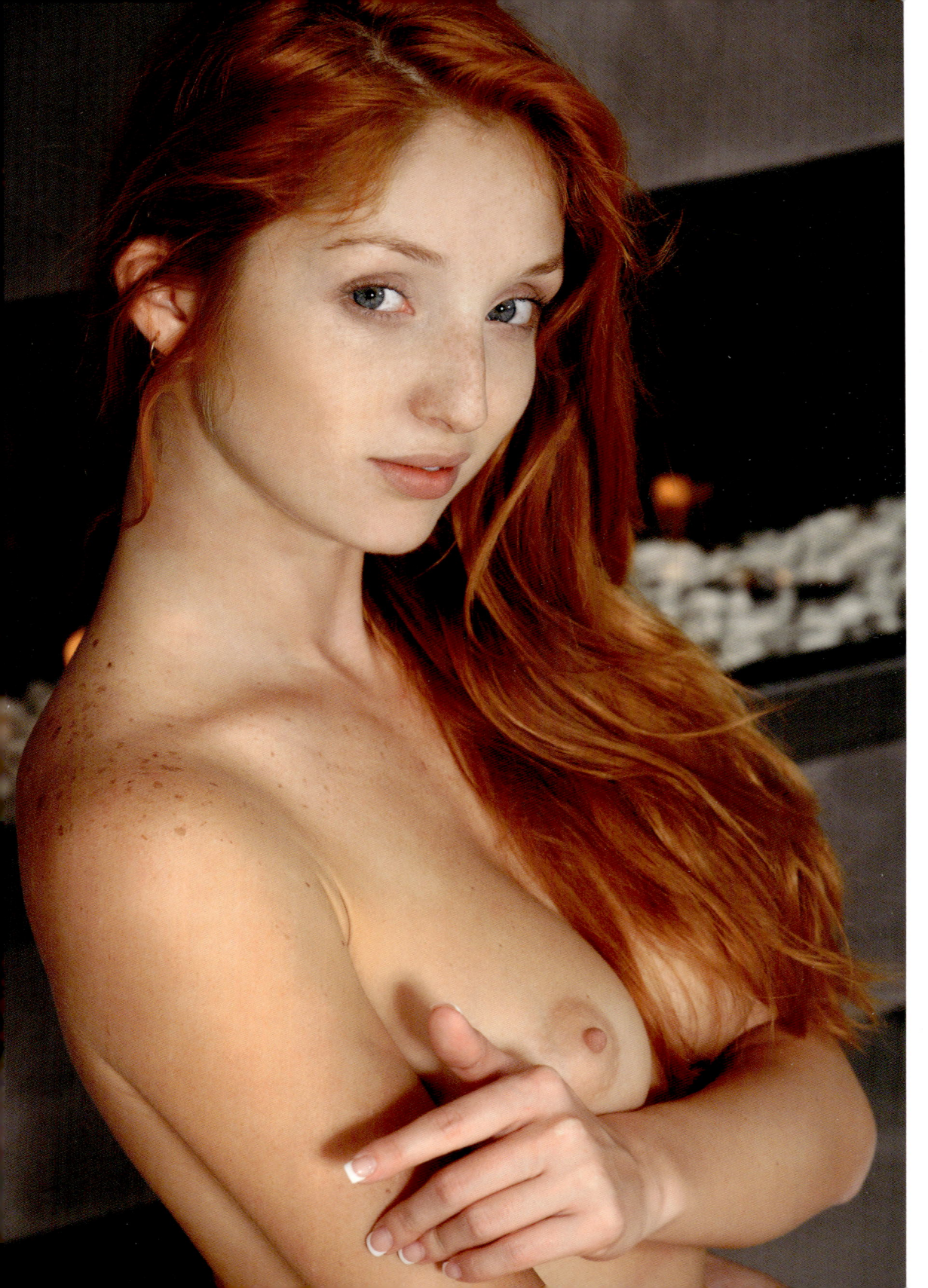

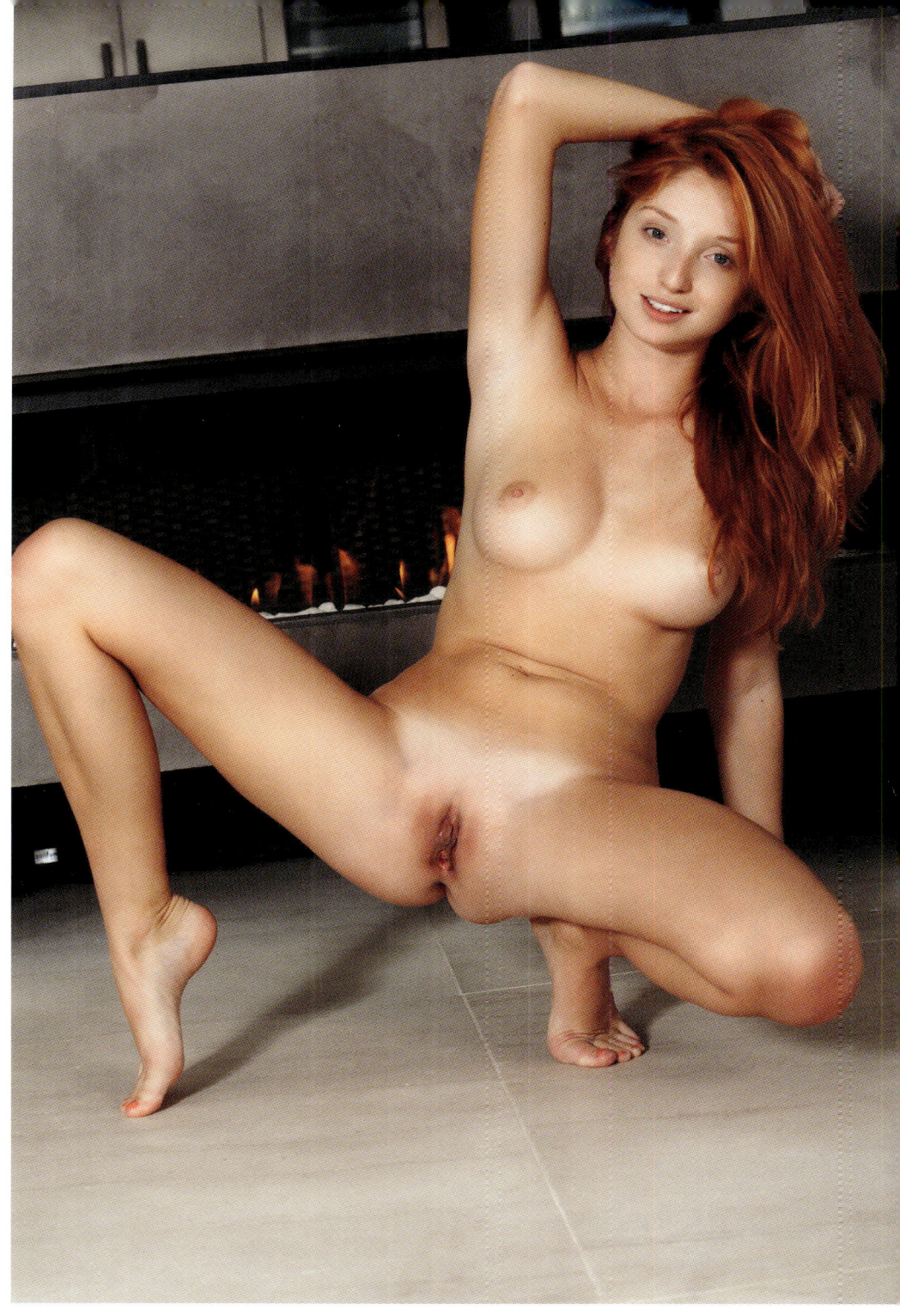

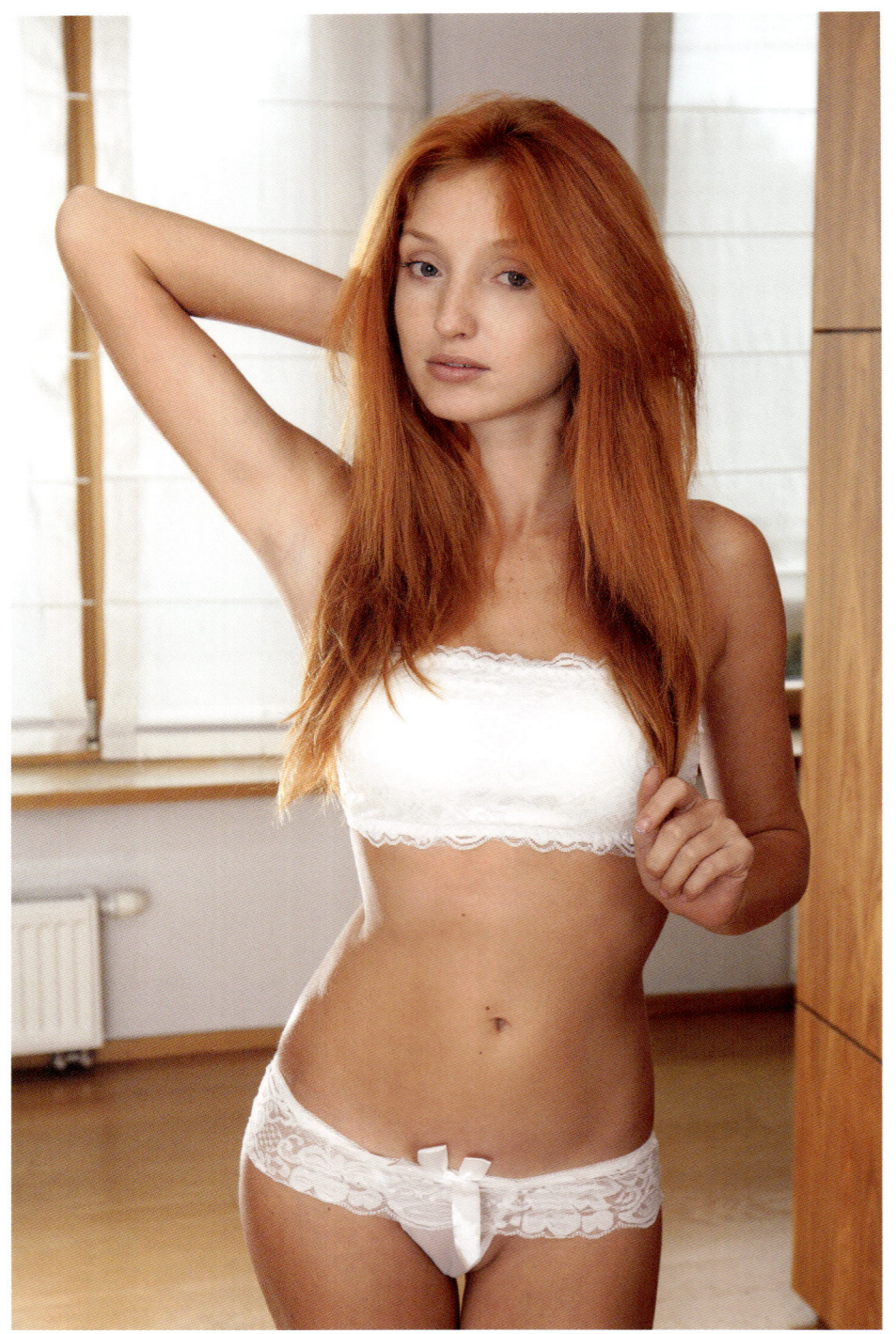

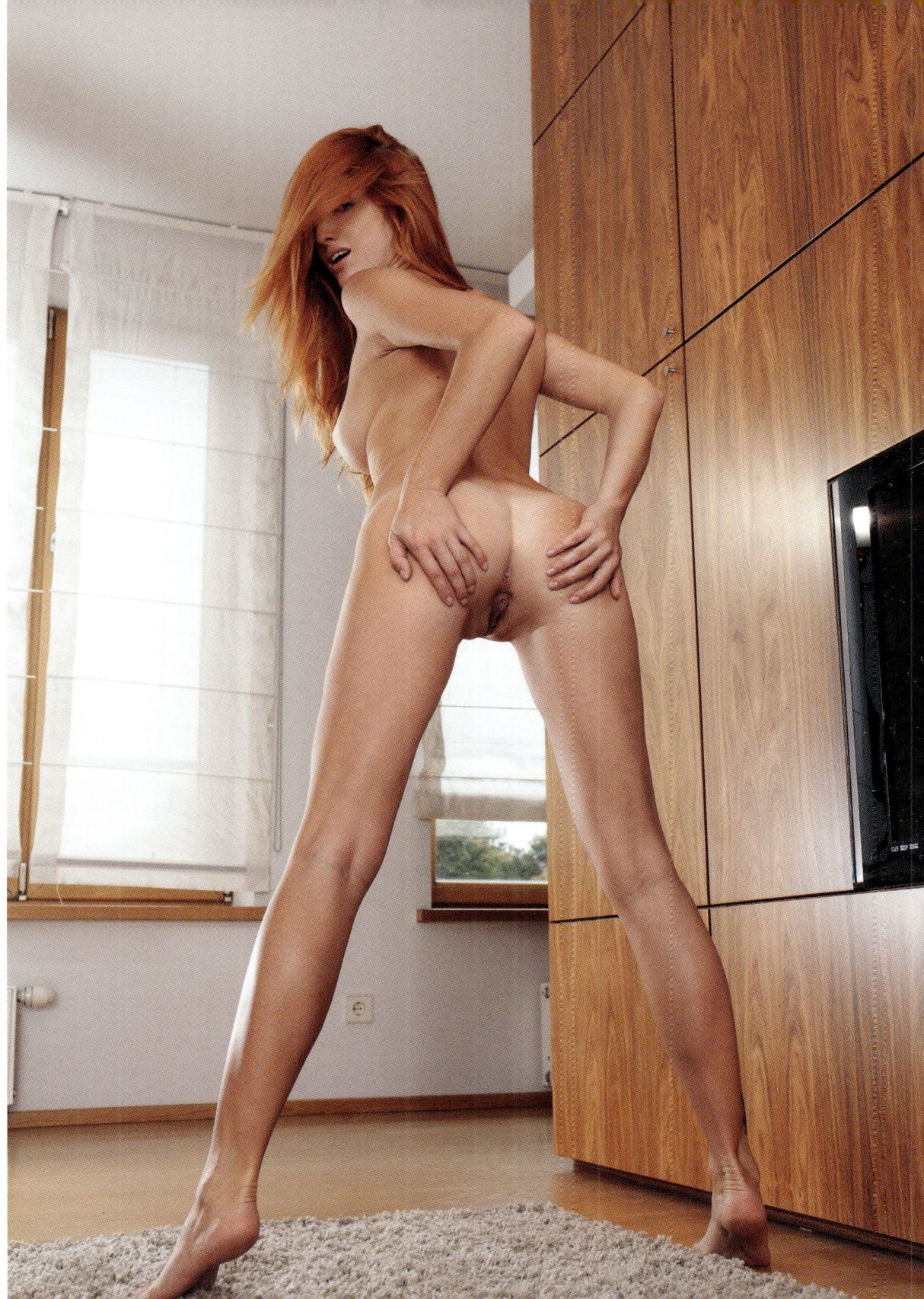

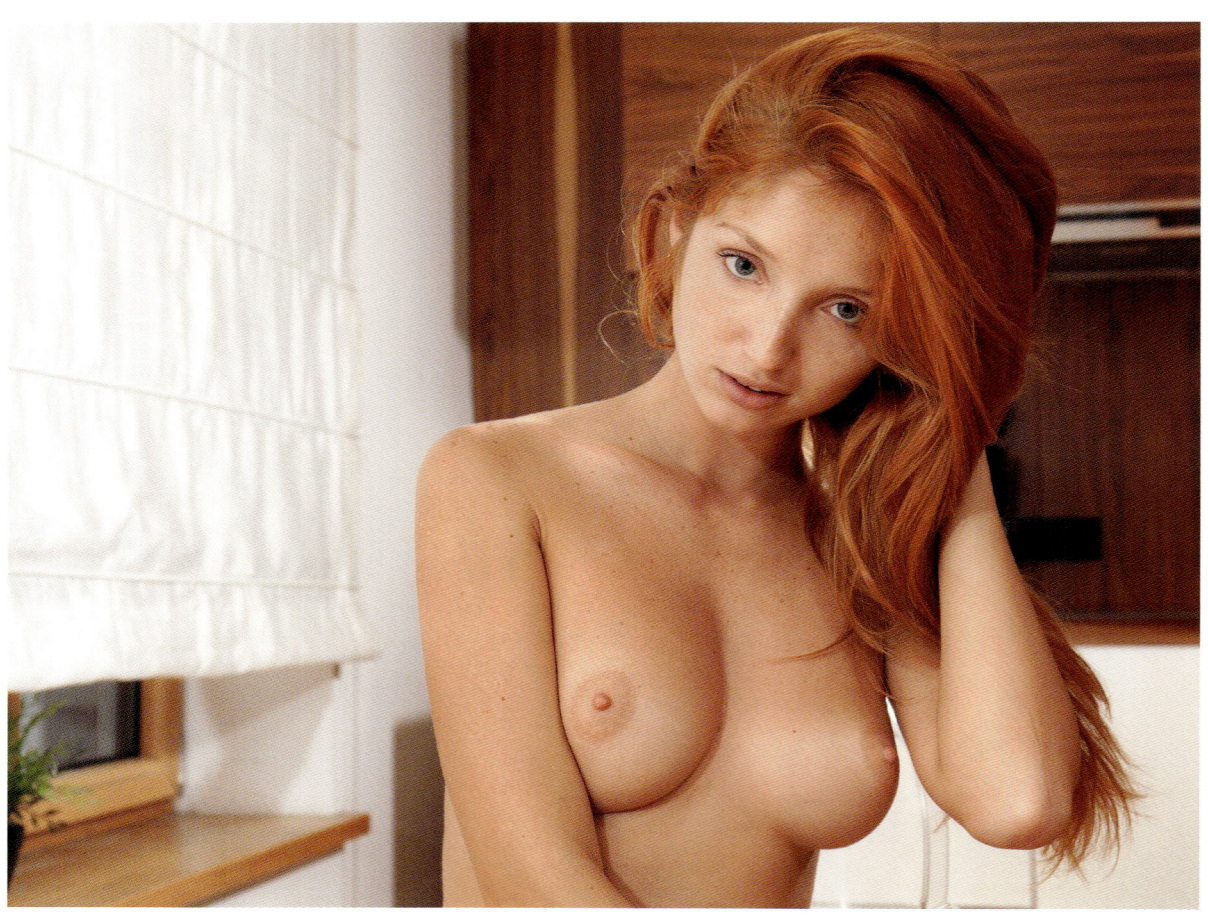

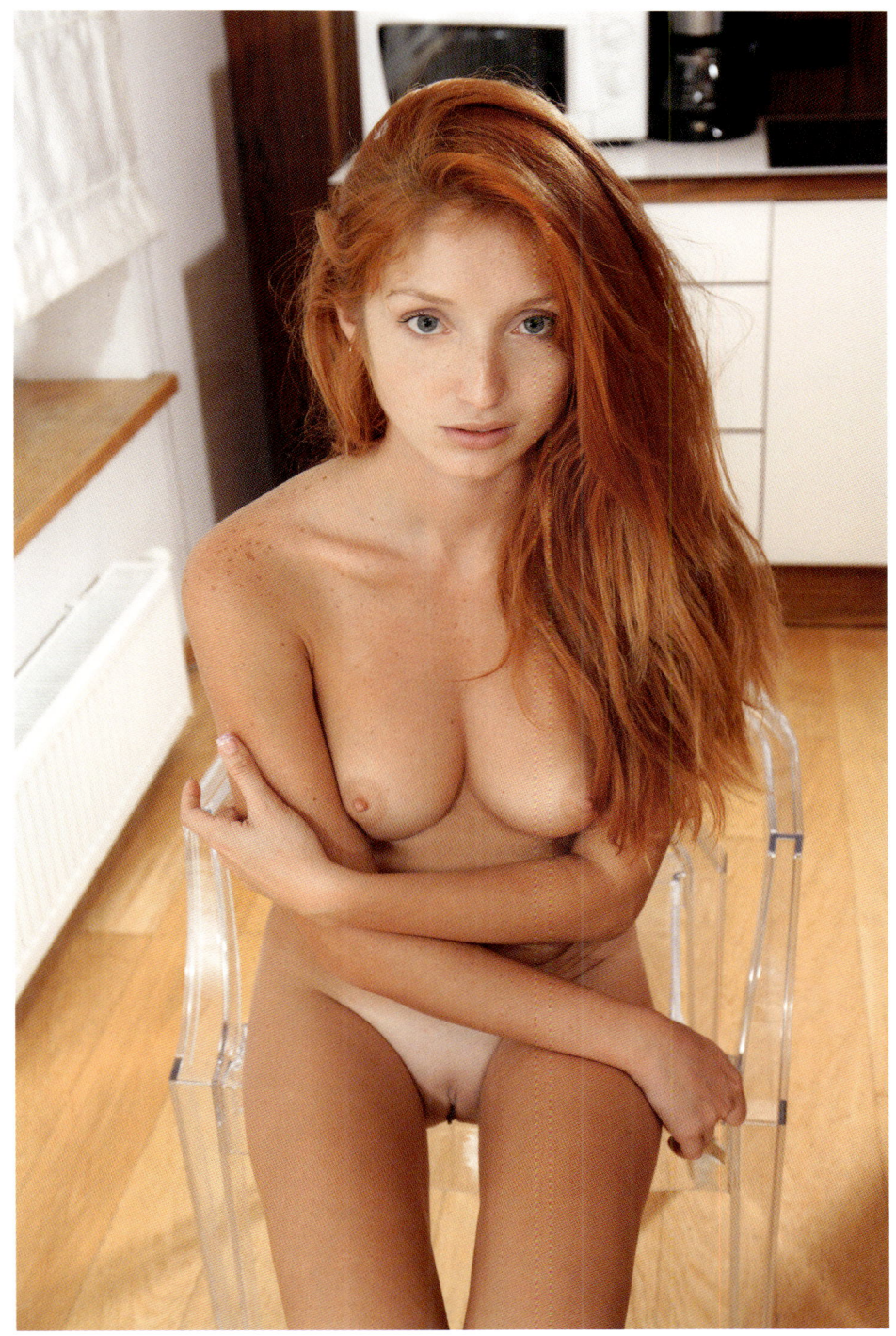

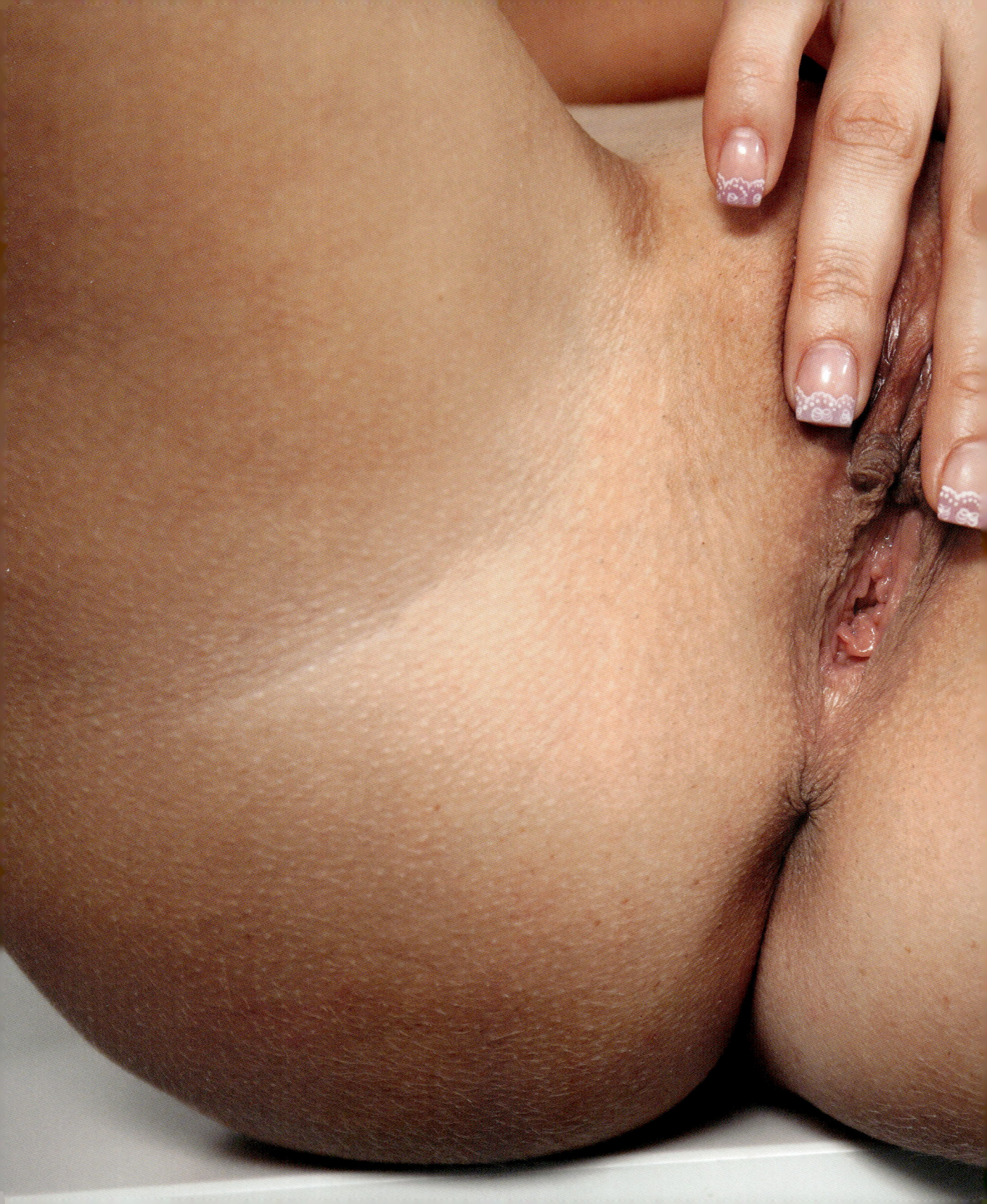

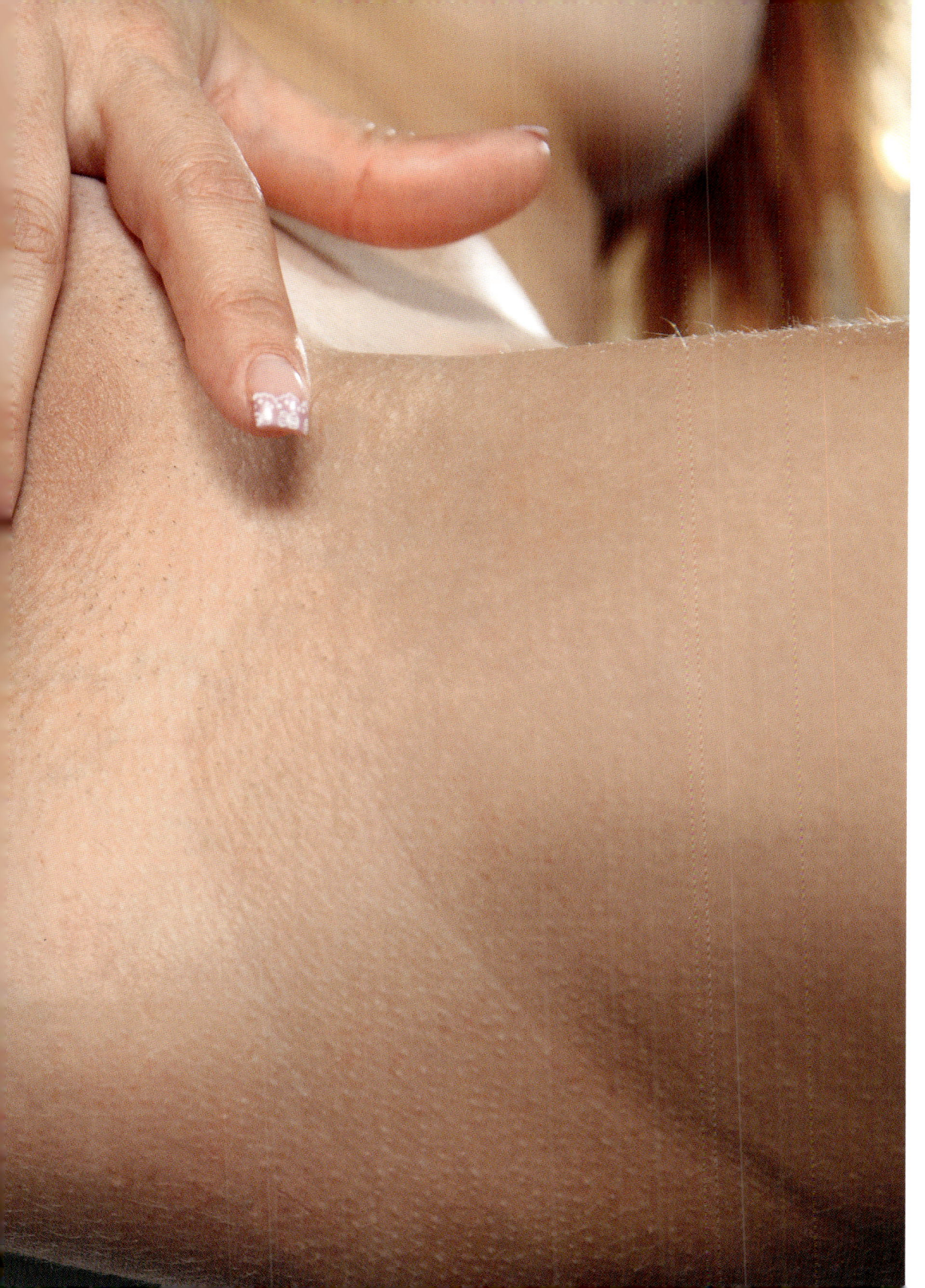

31

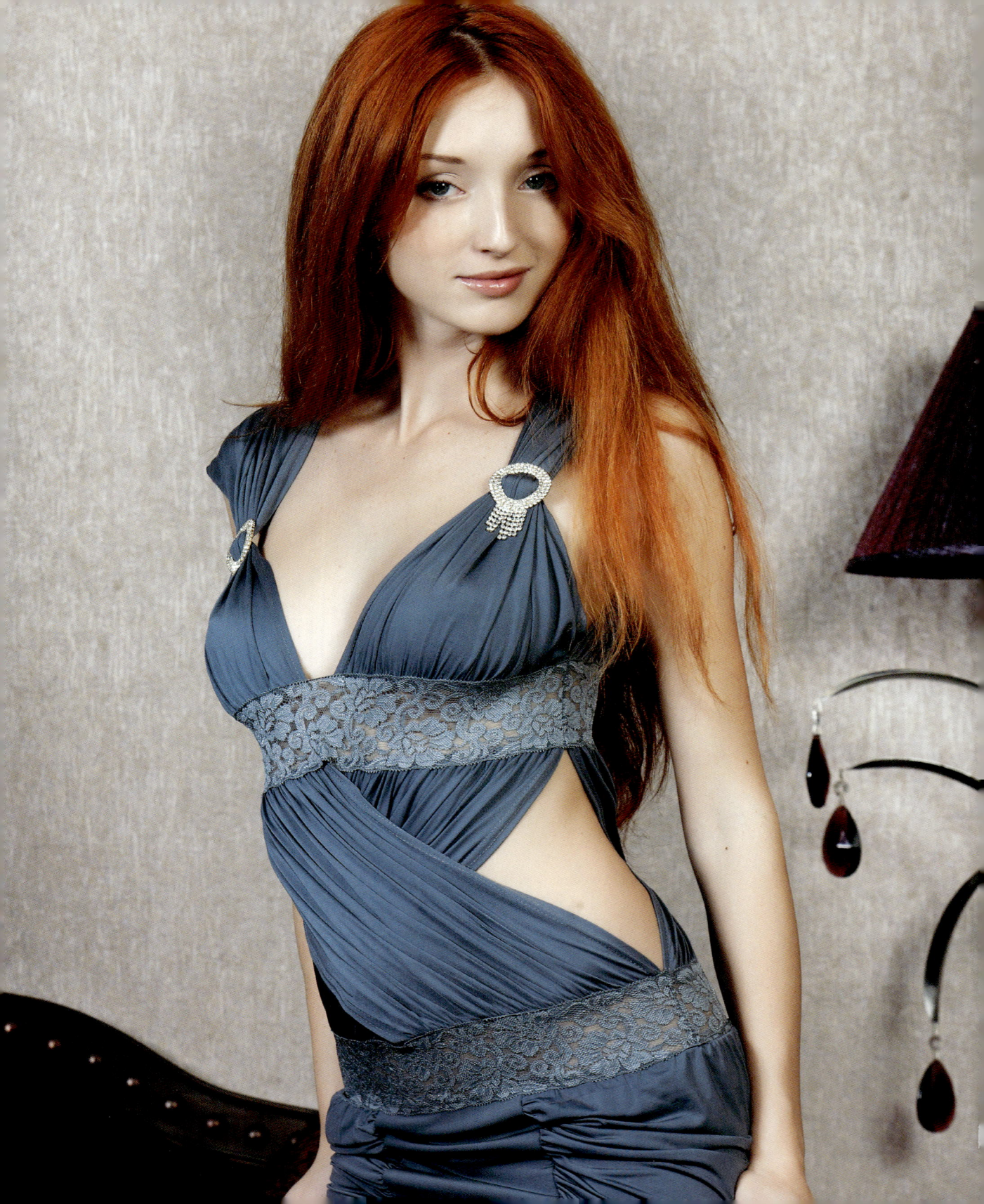

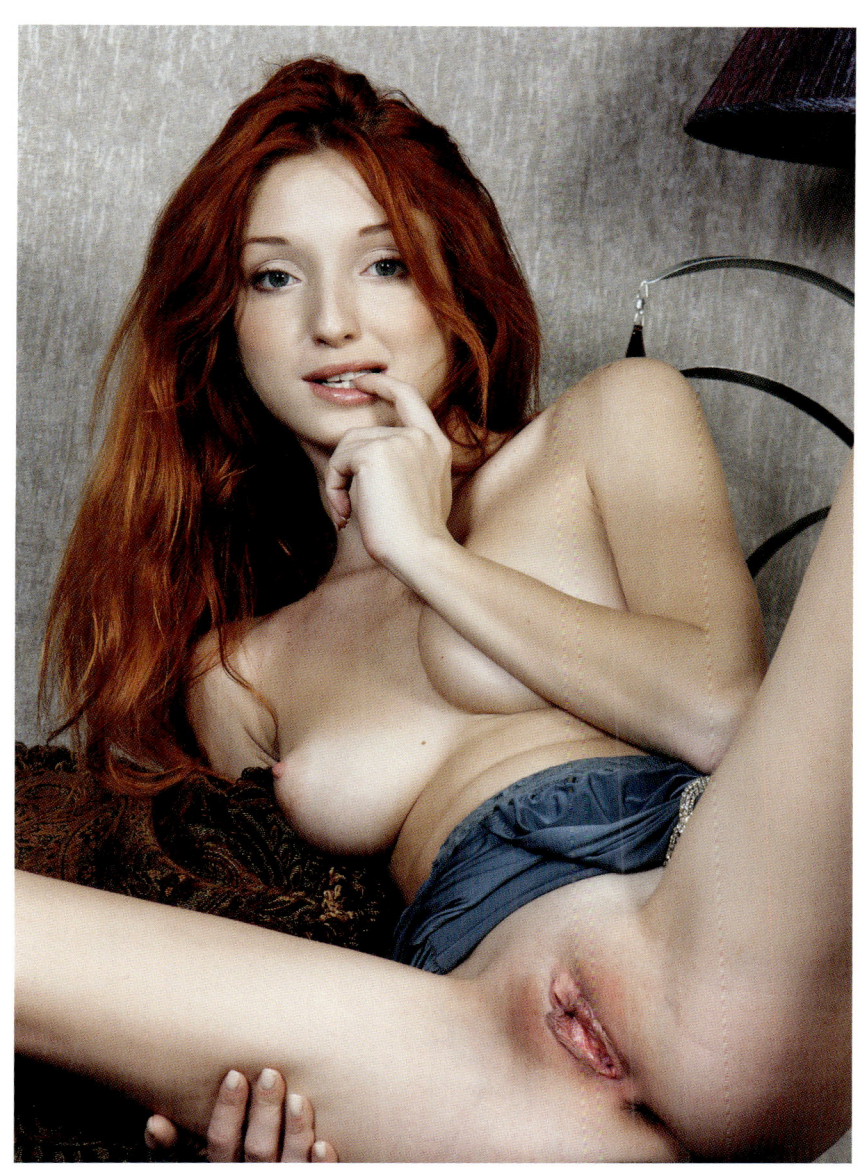

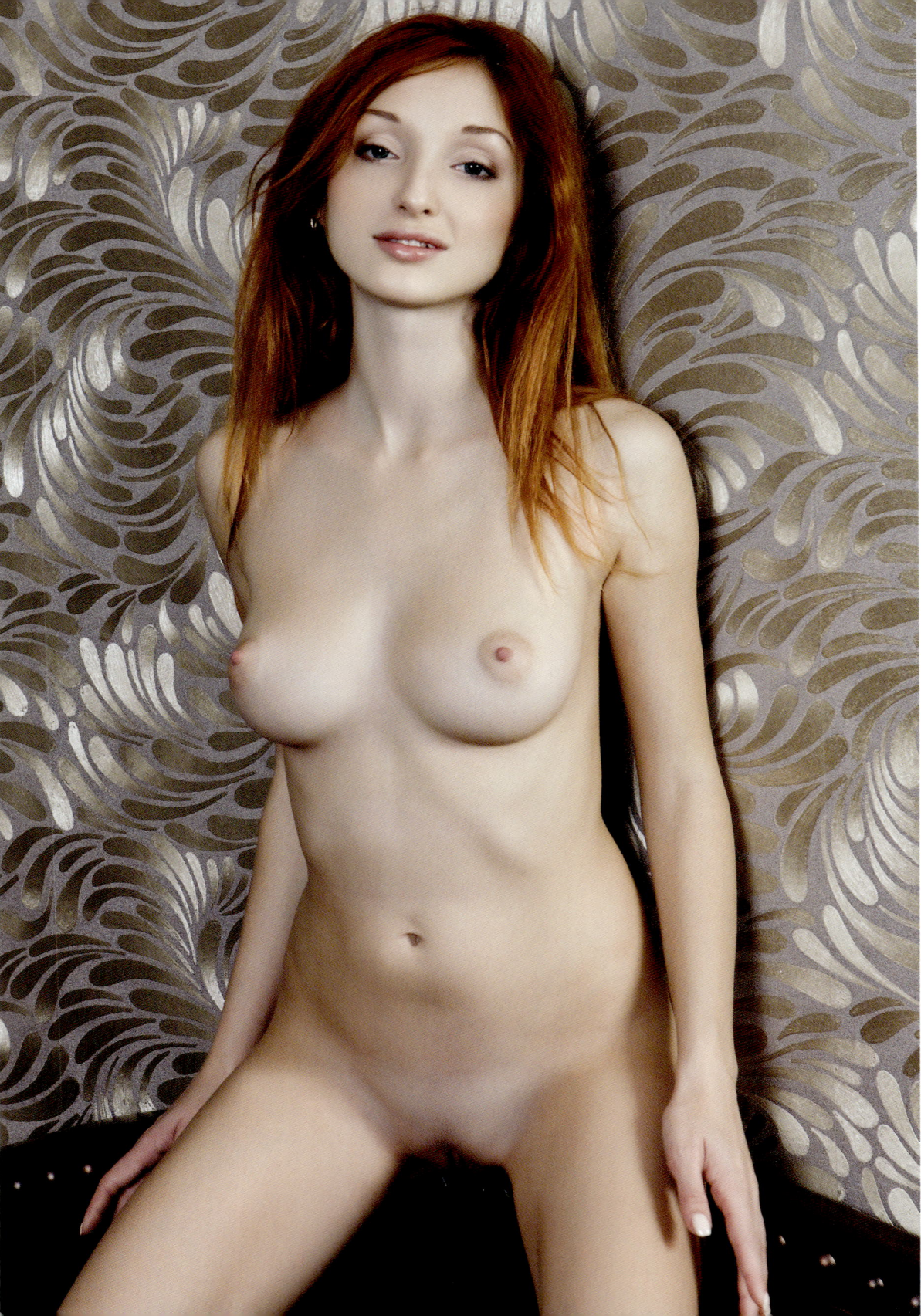

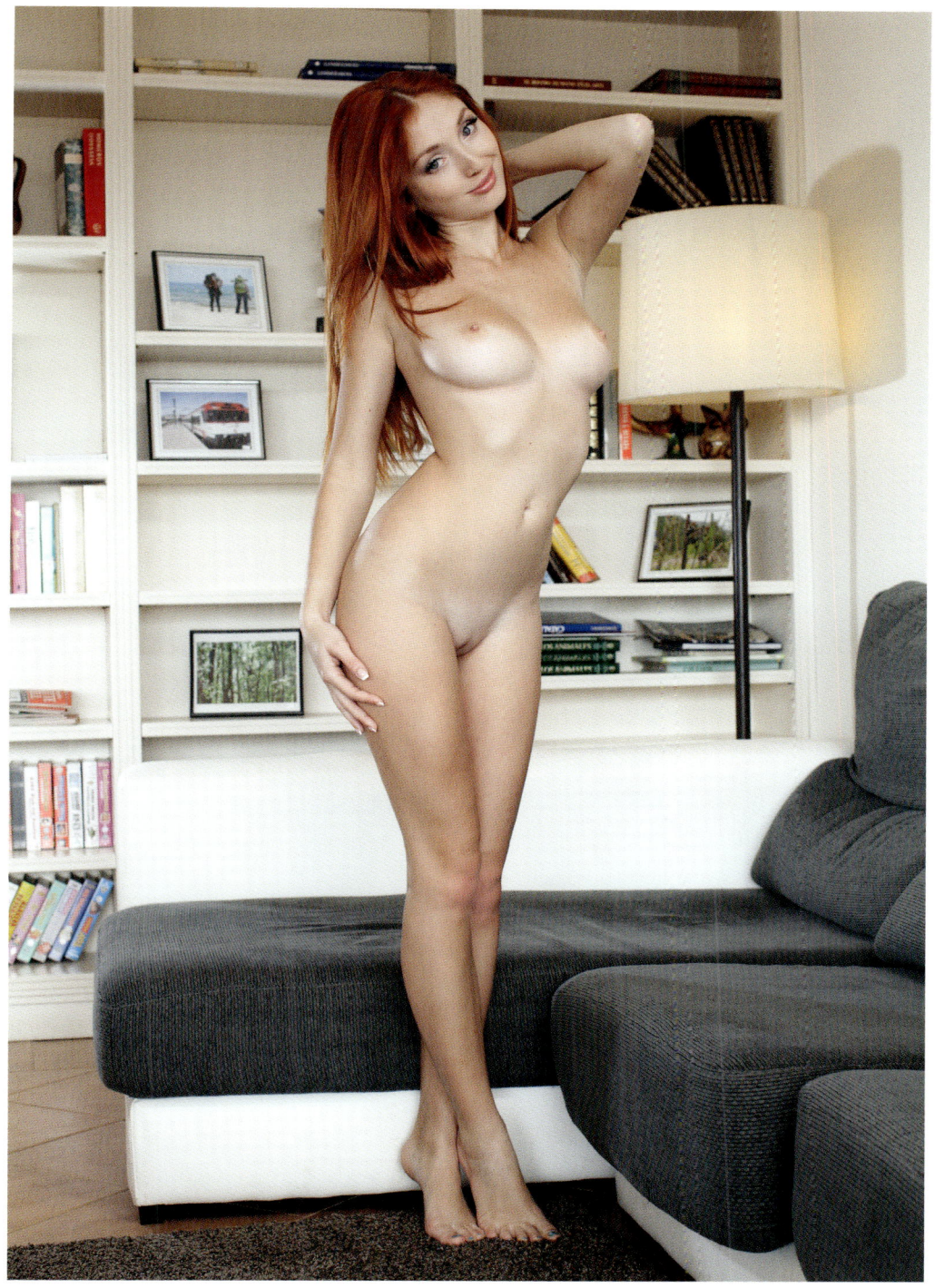

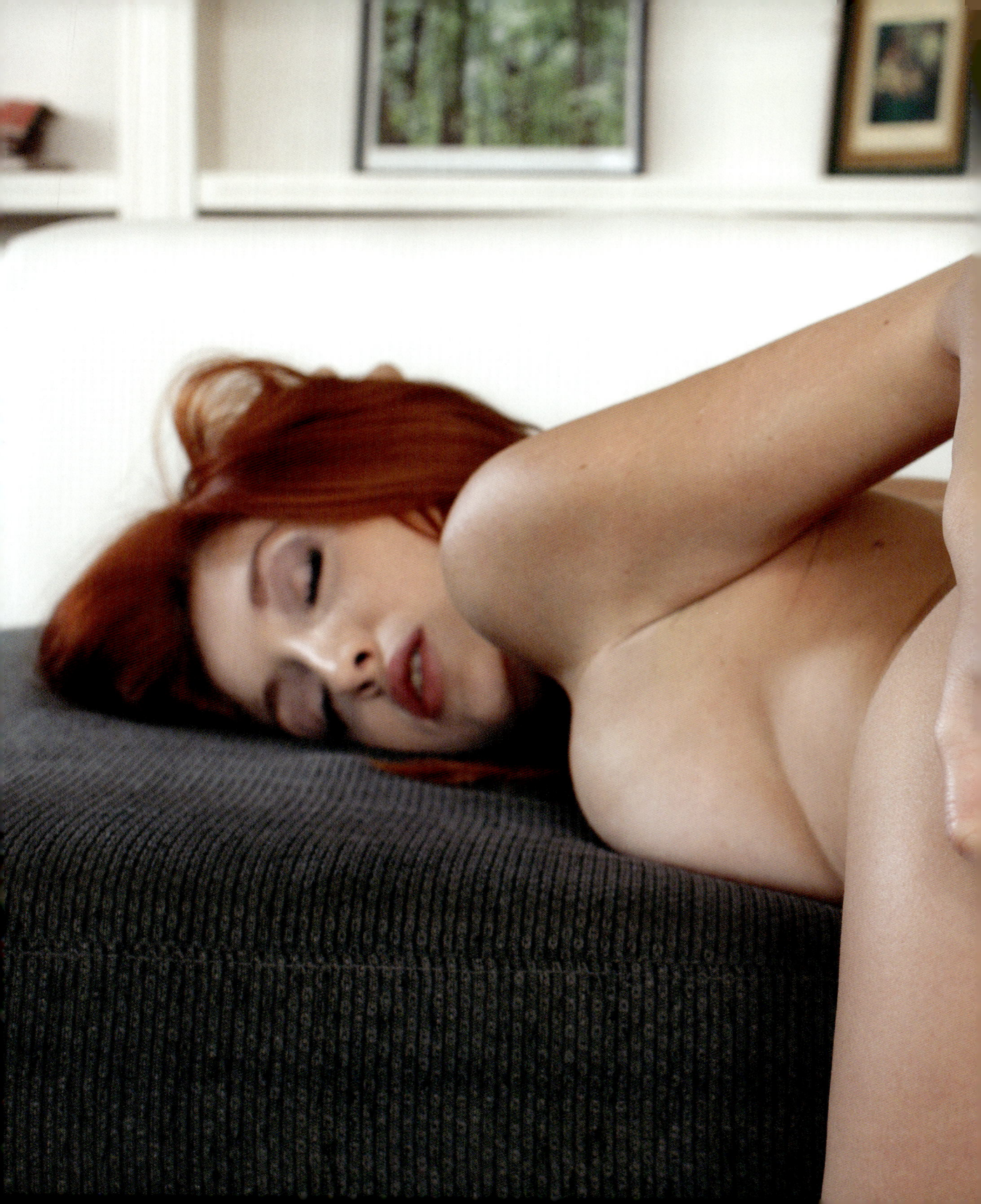

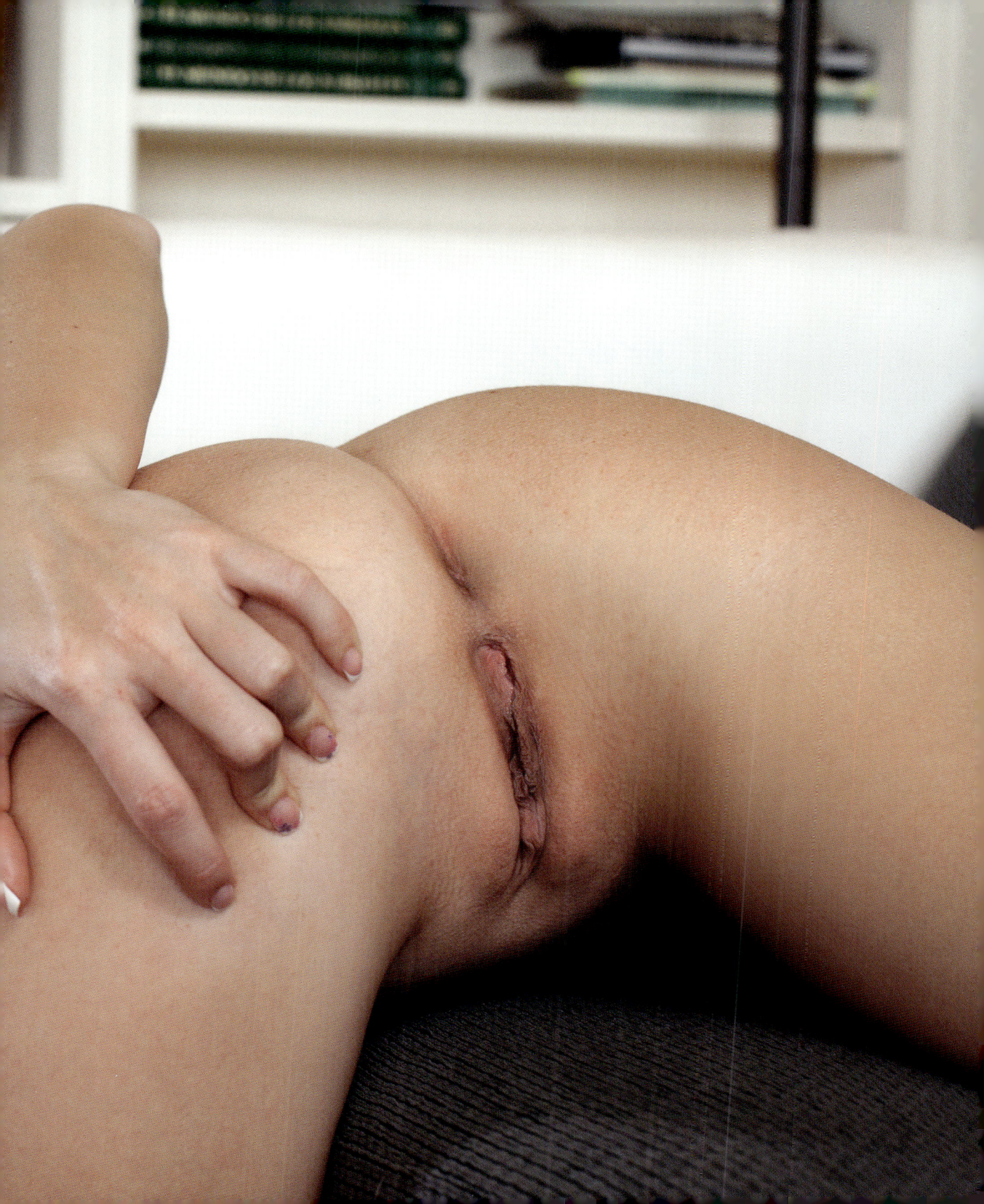

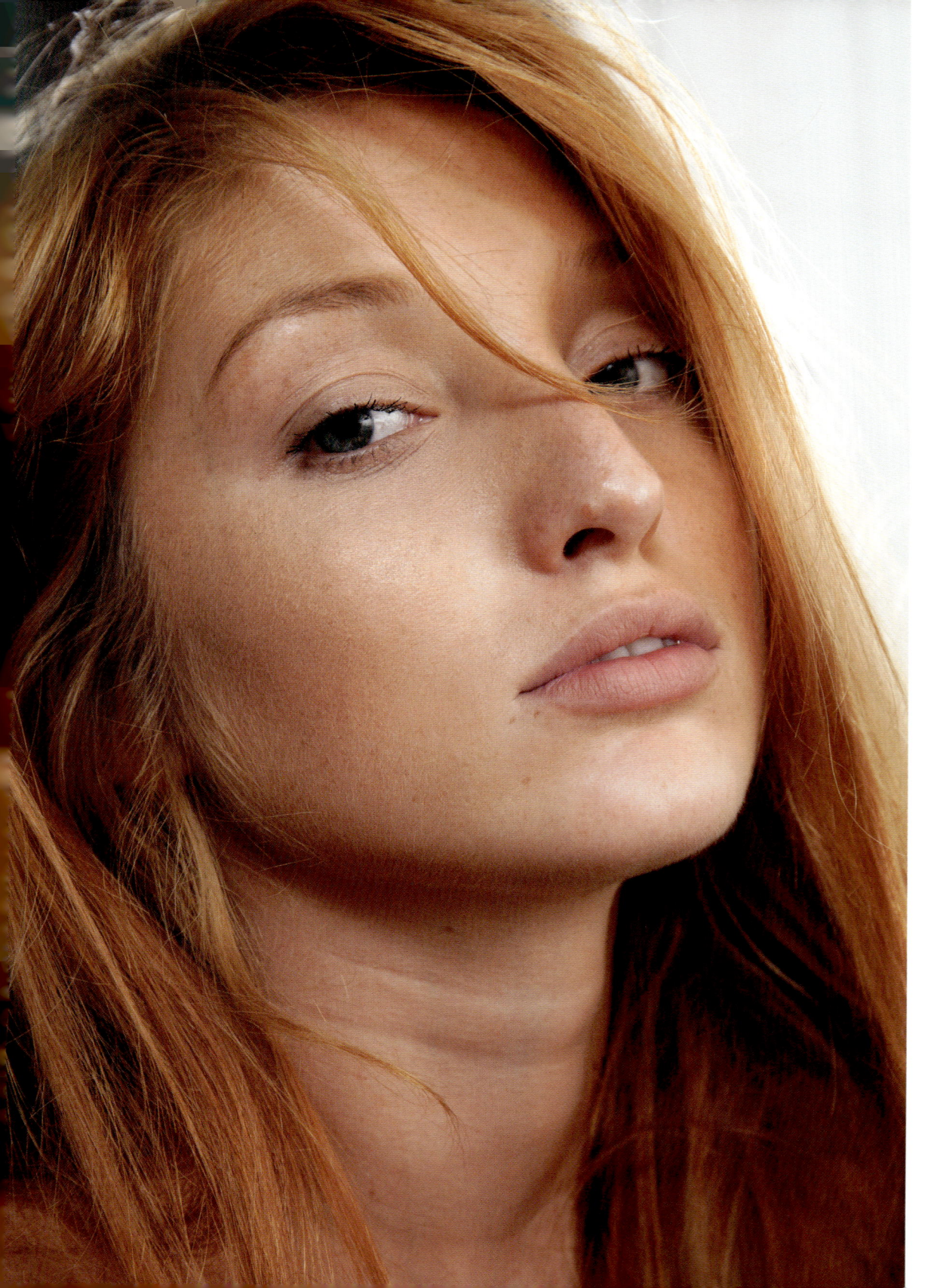

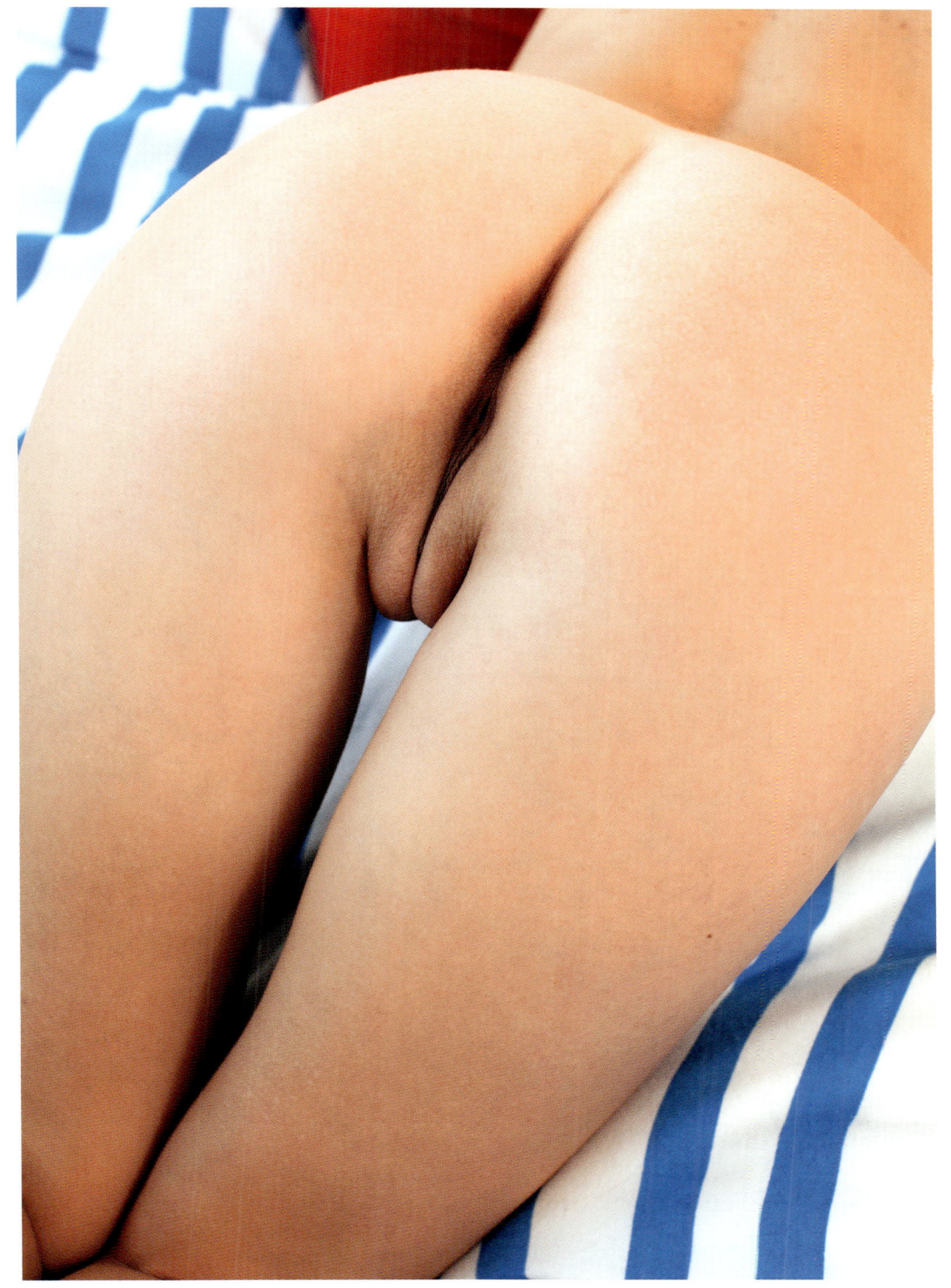

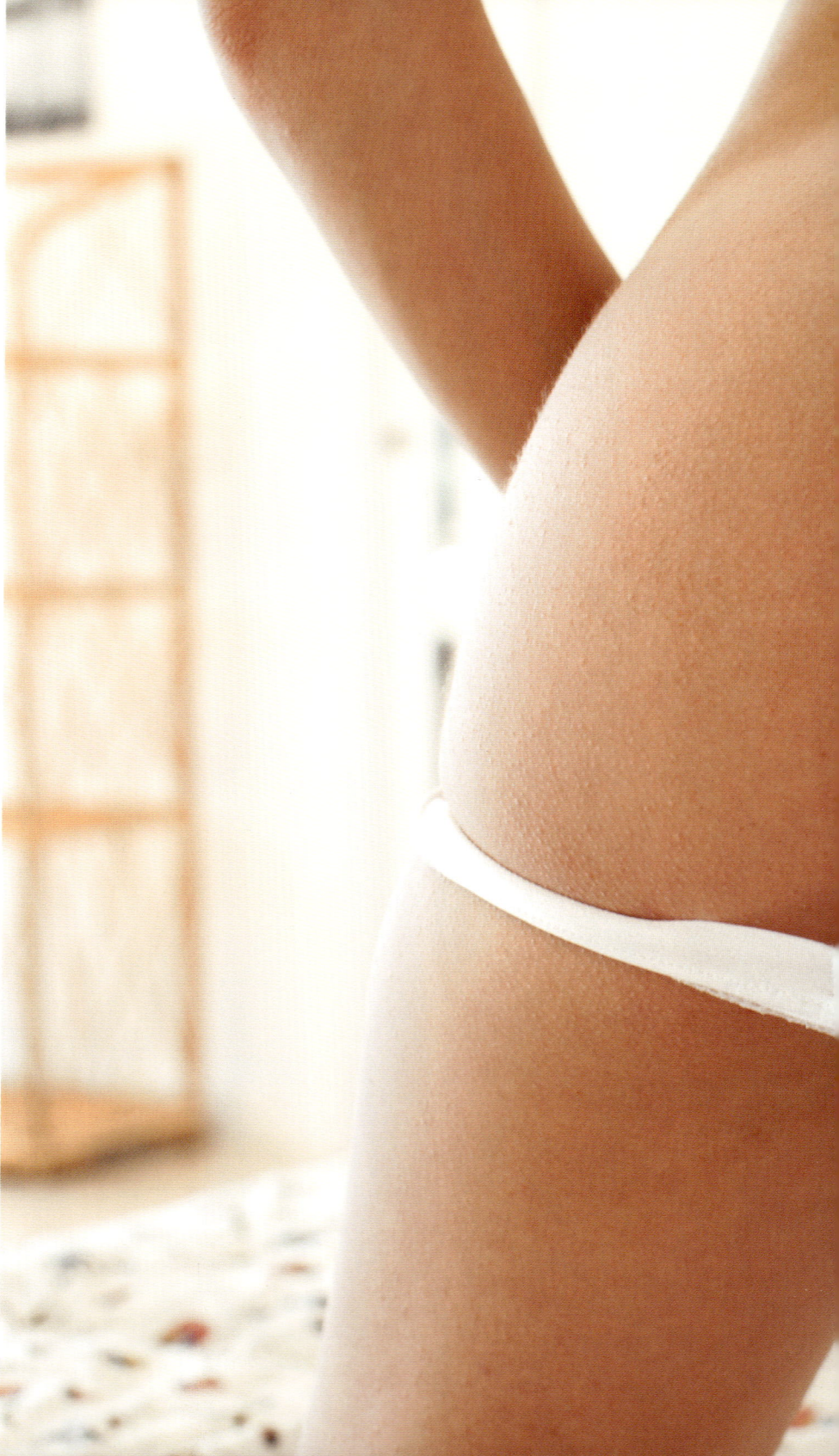

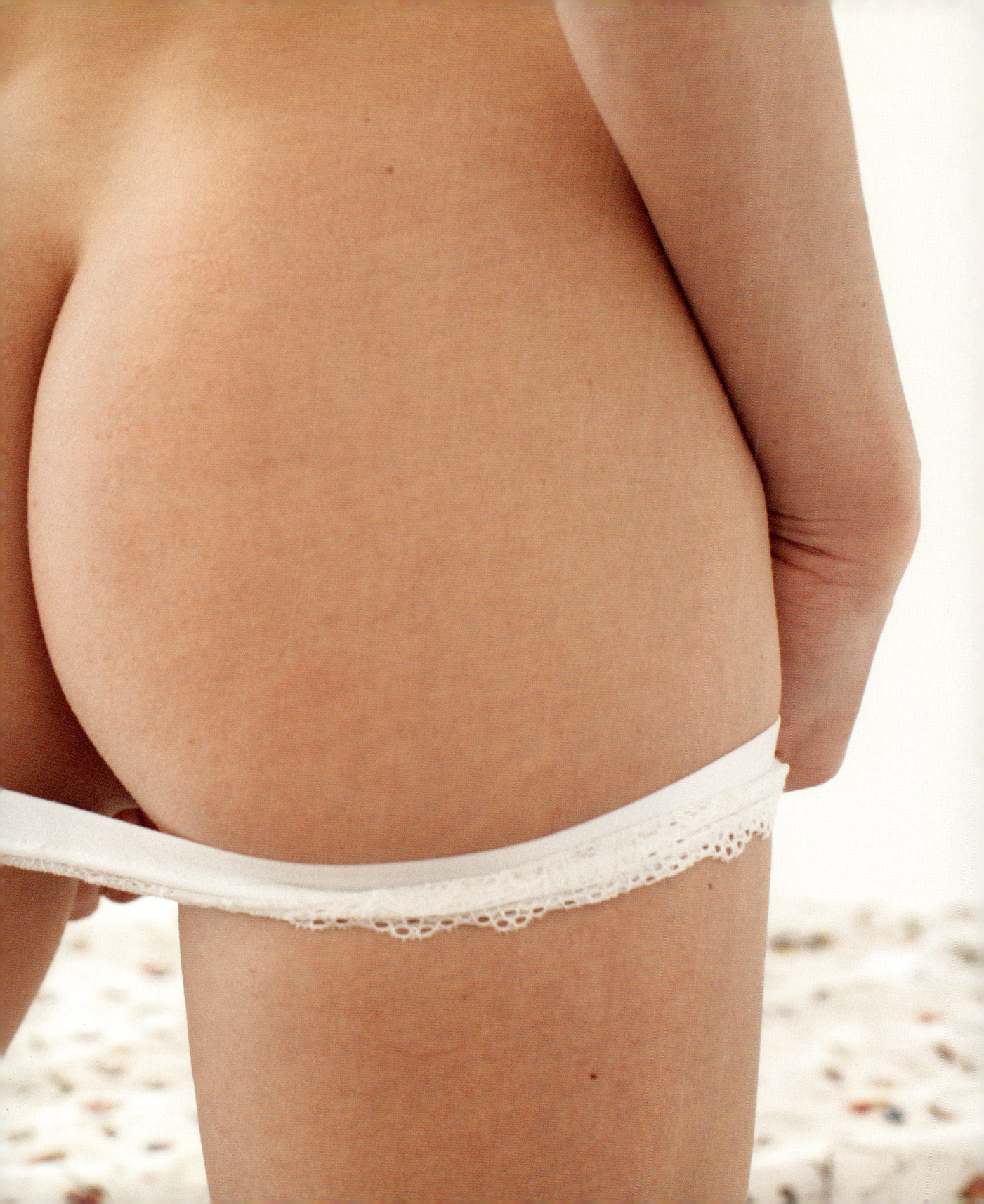

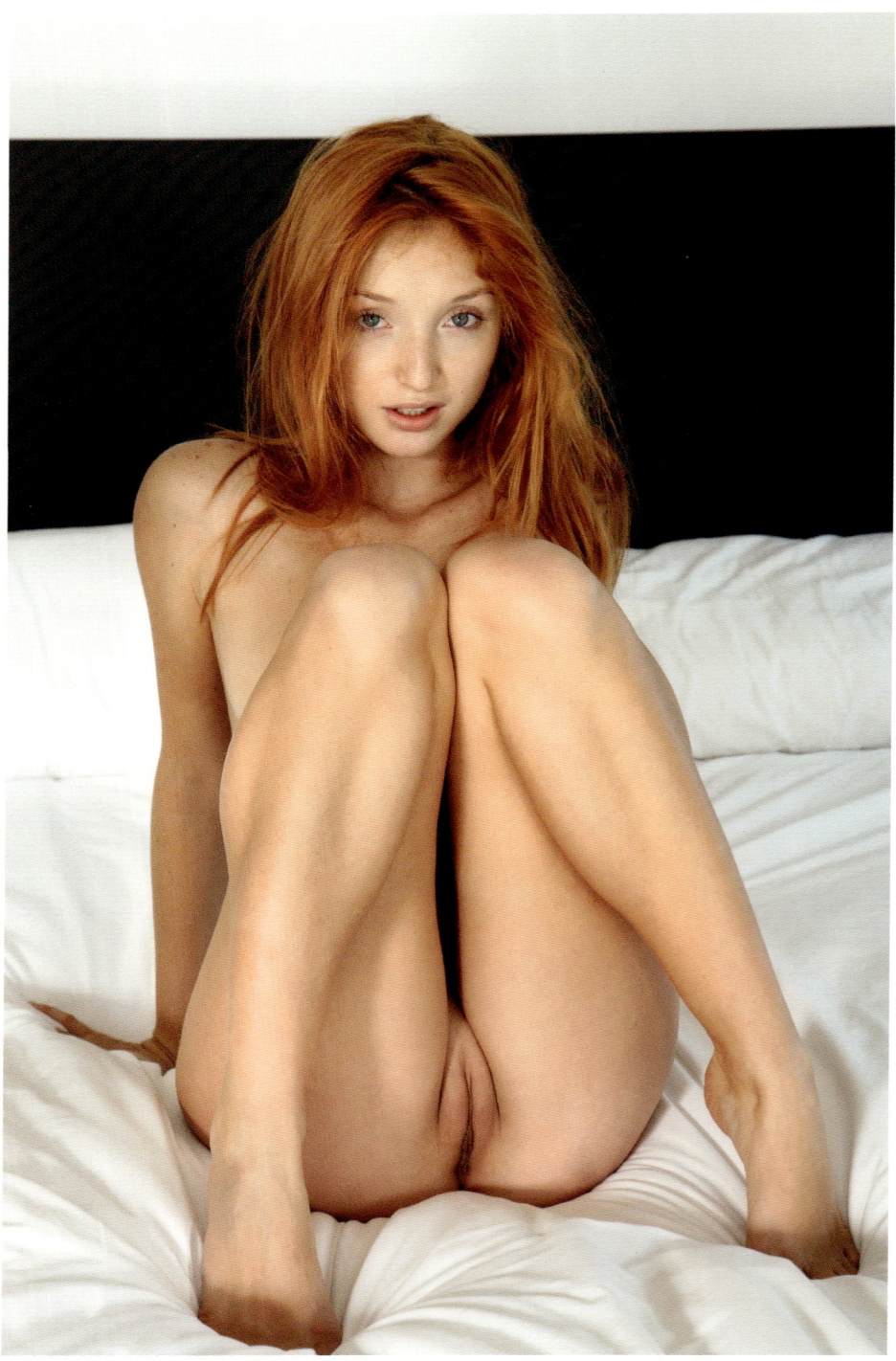

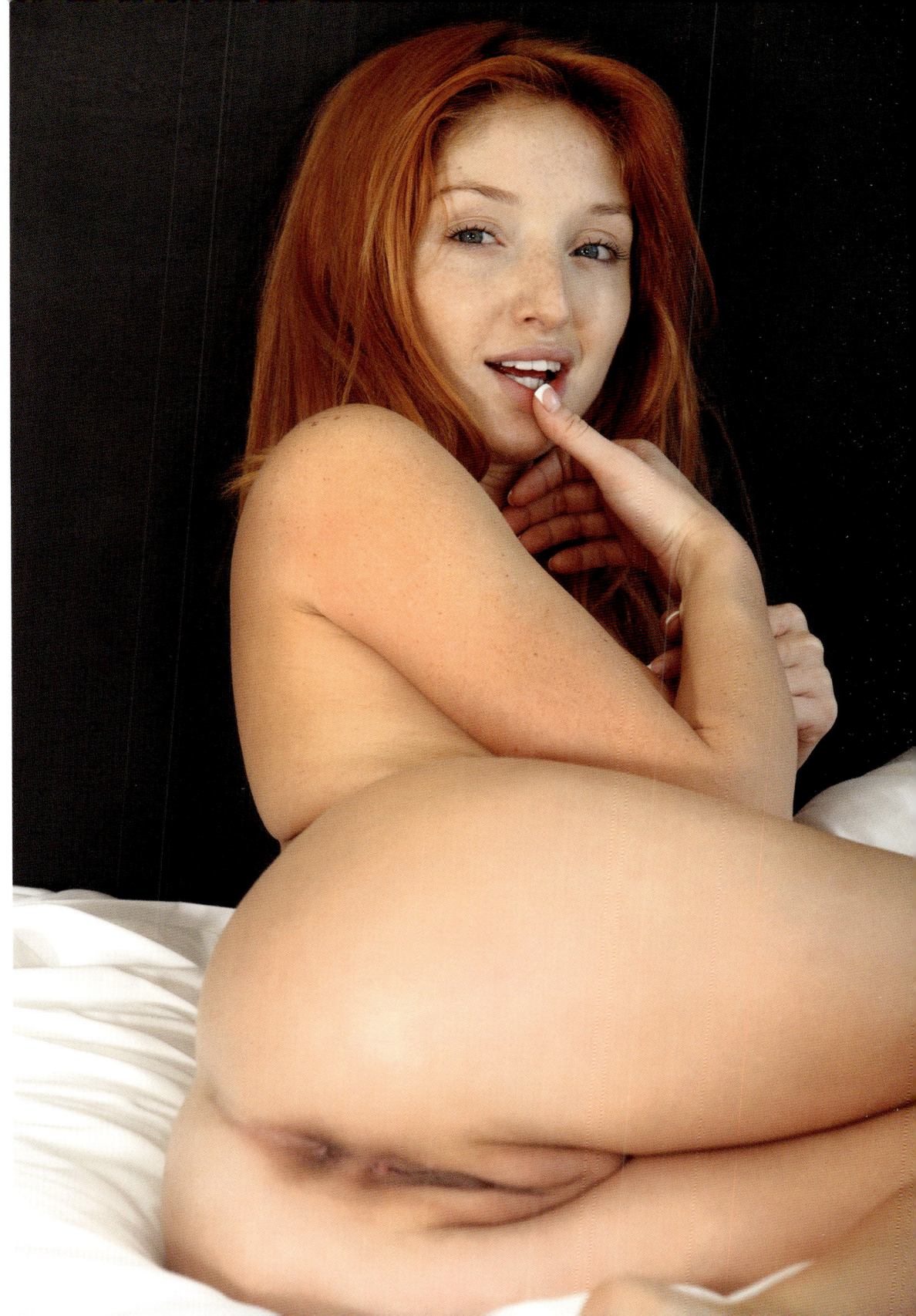

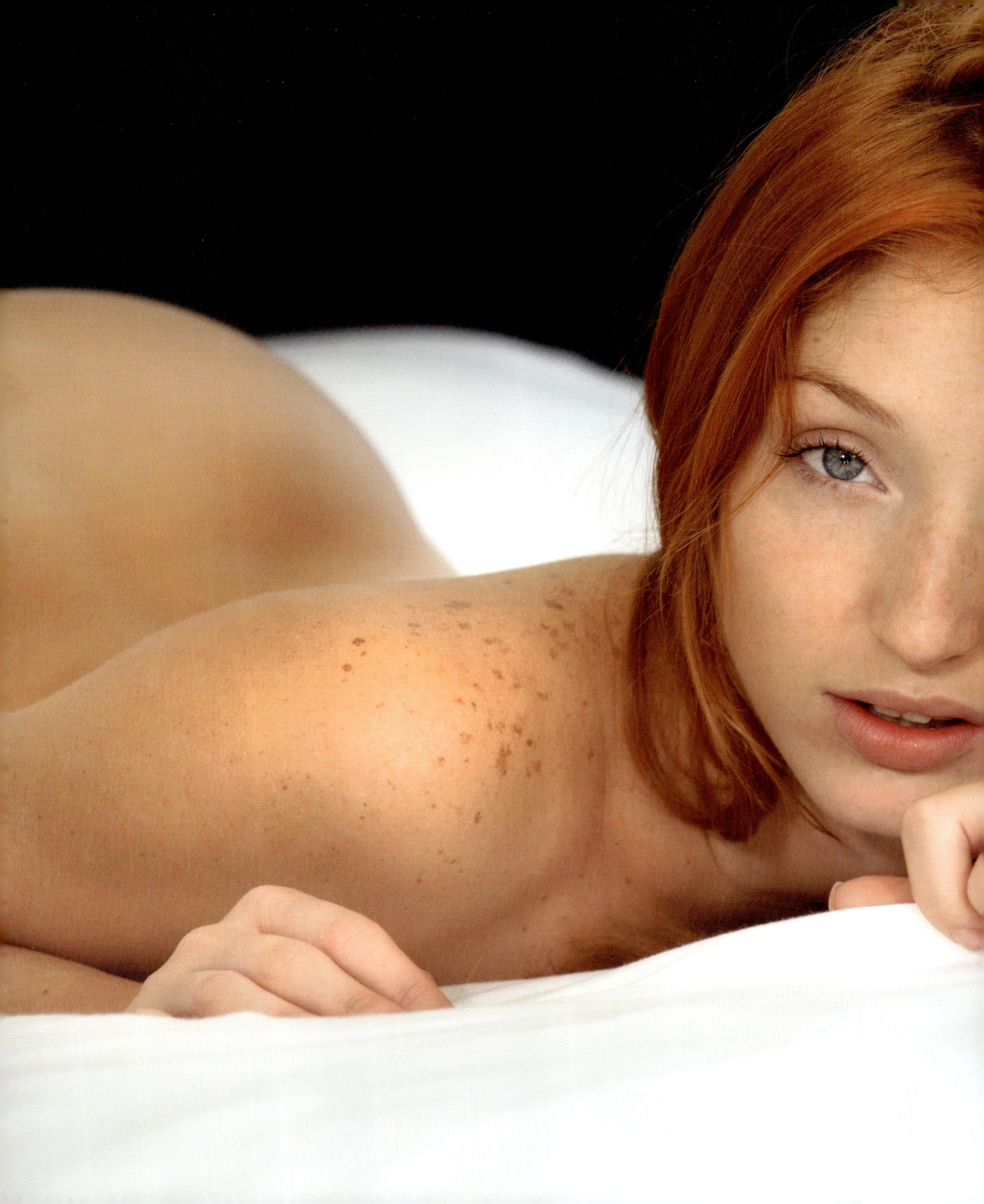

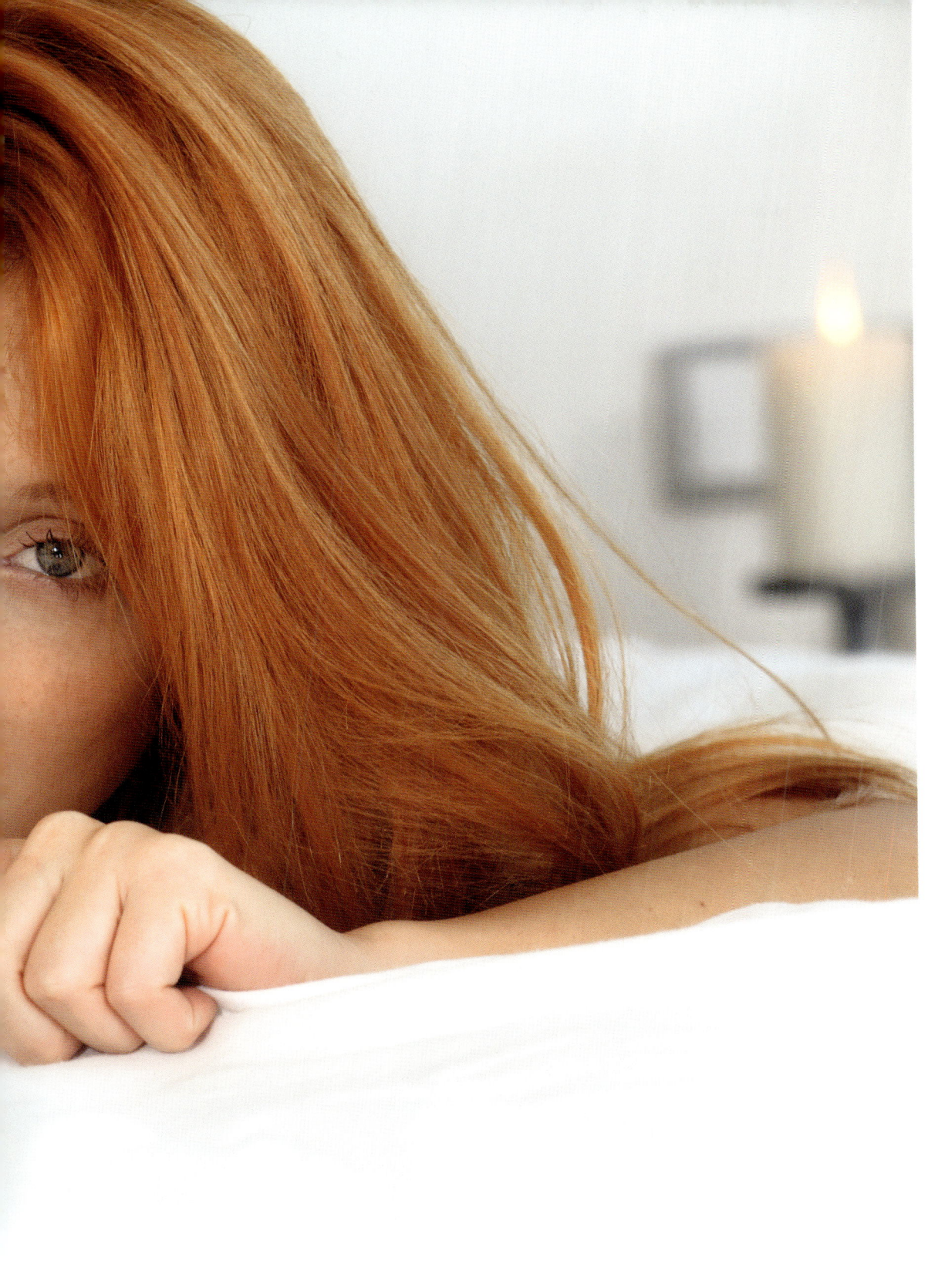

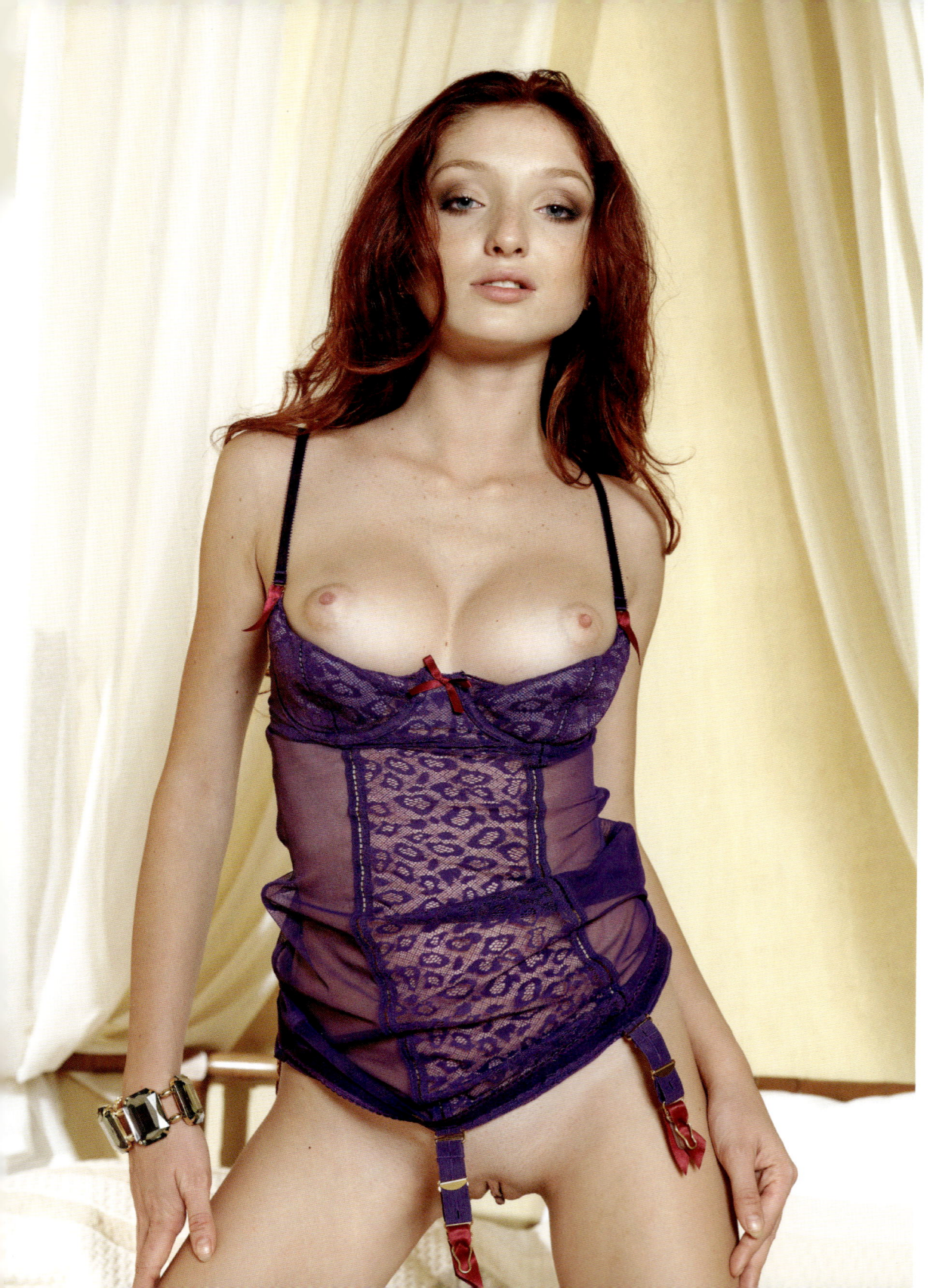

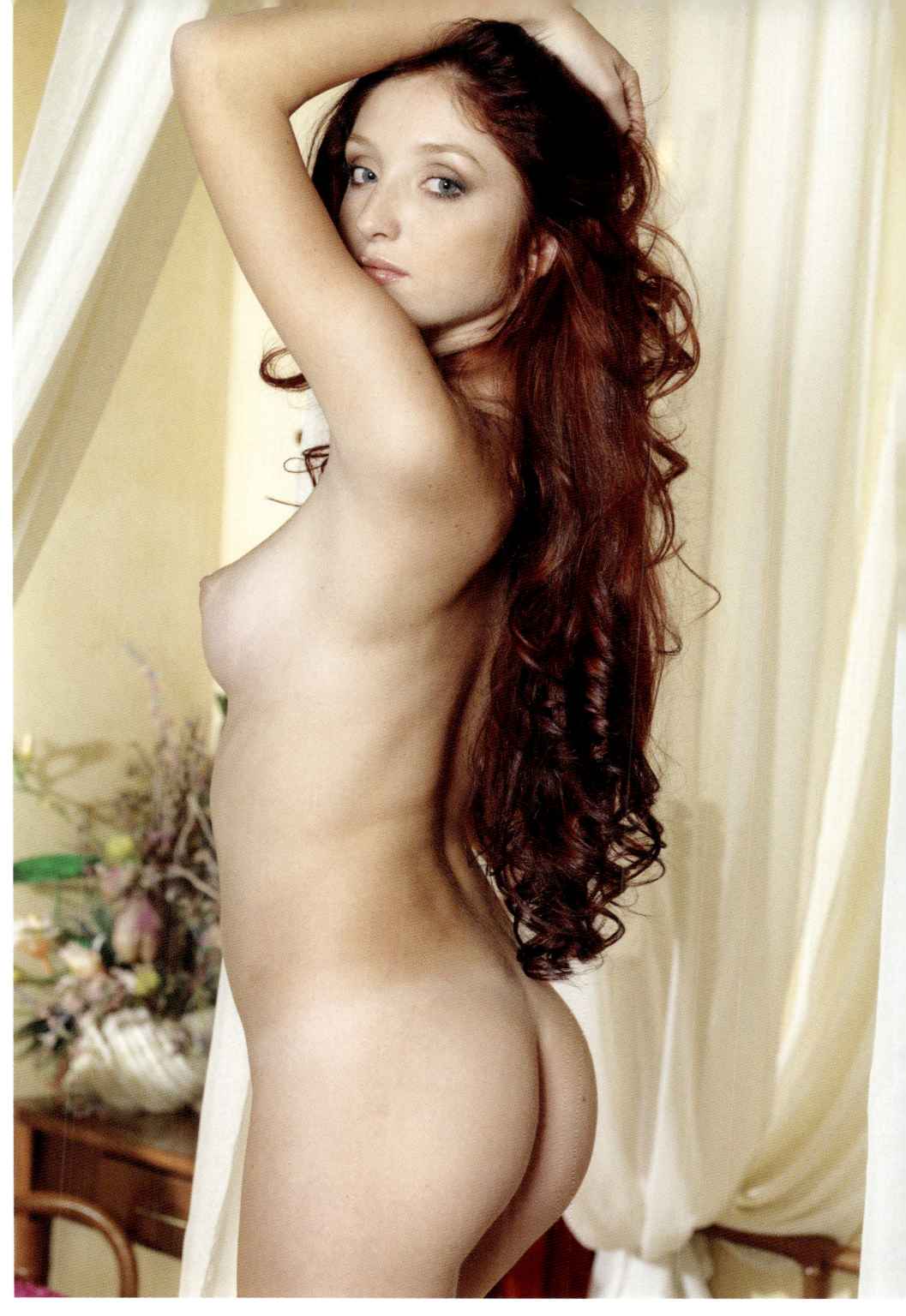

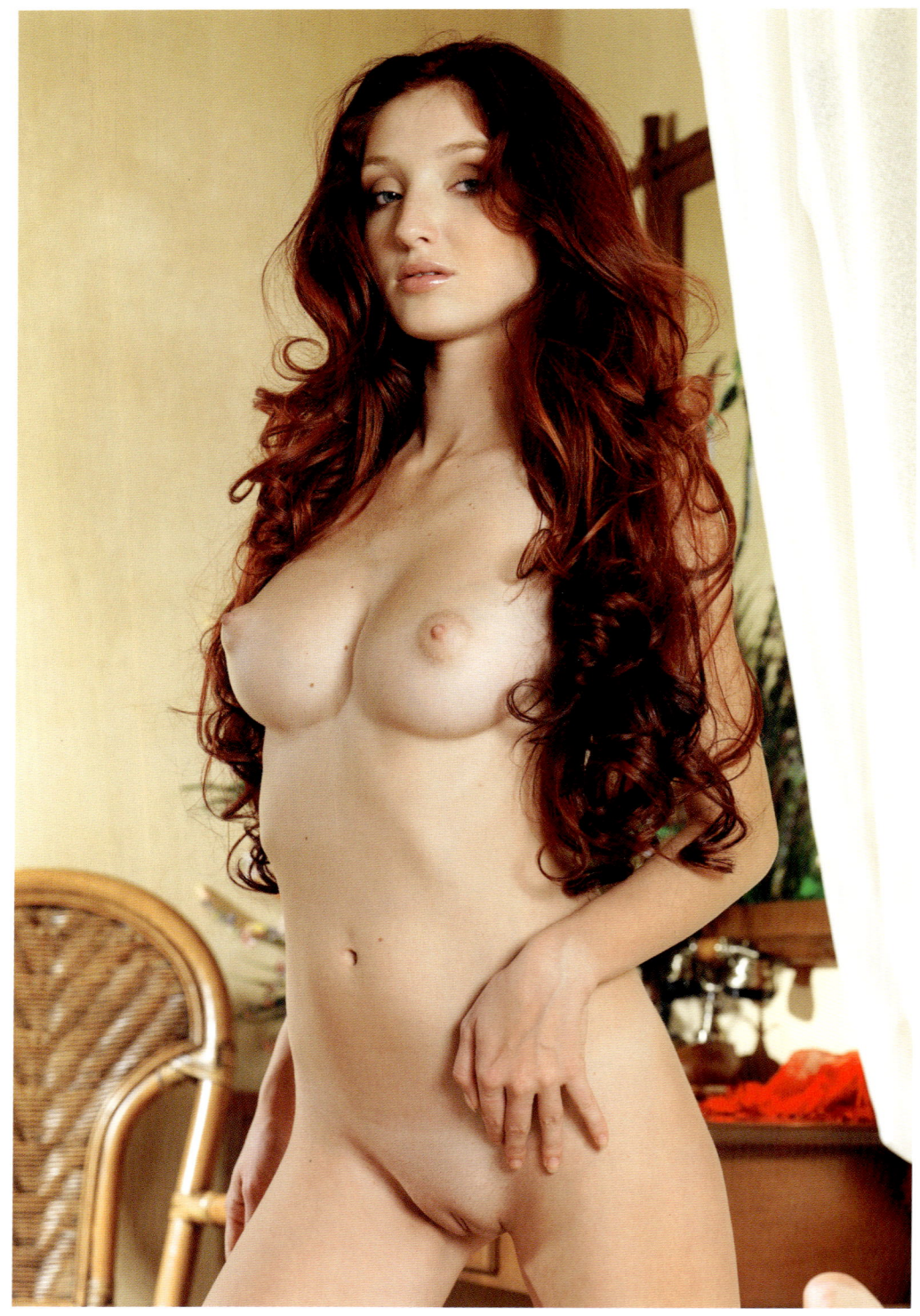

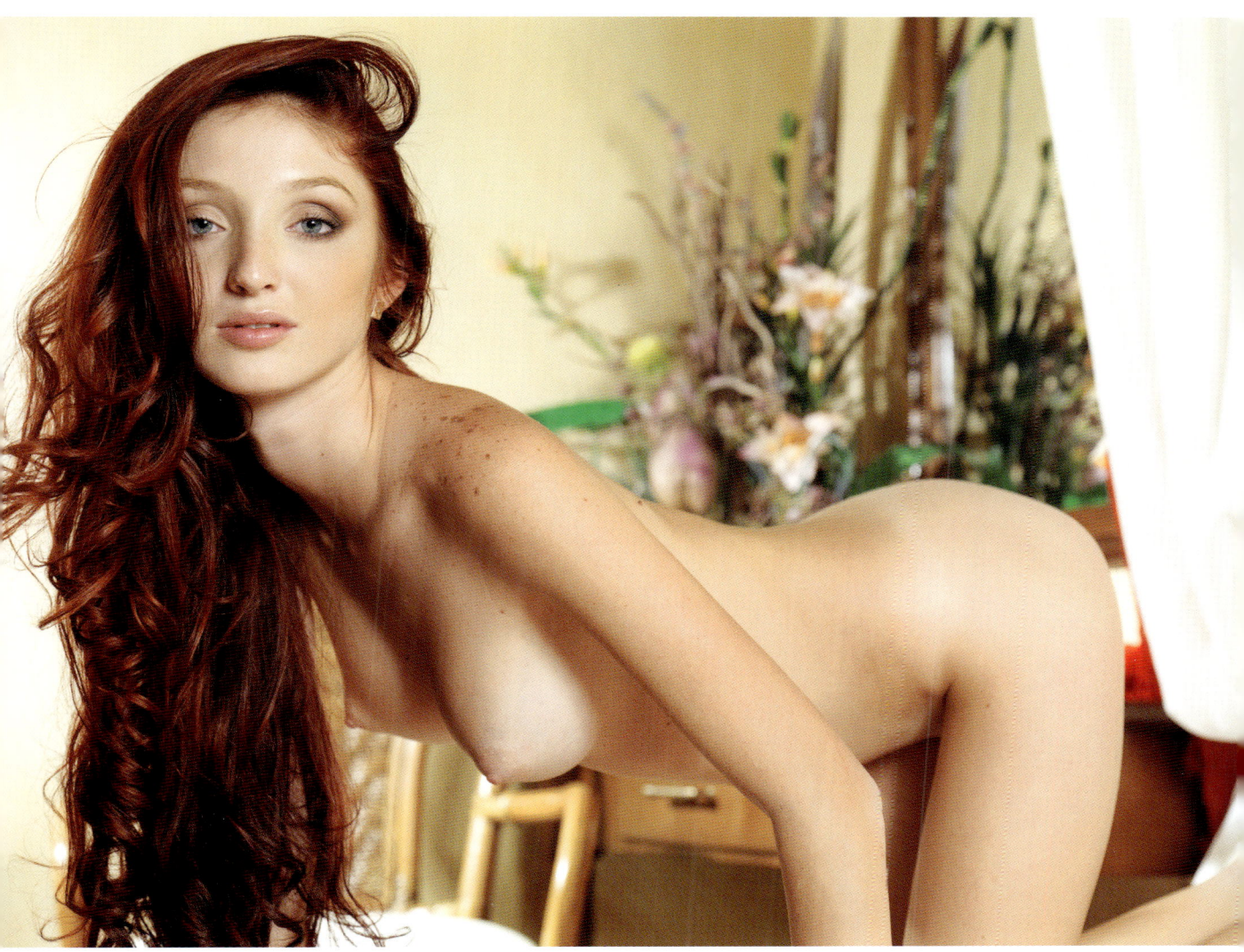

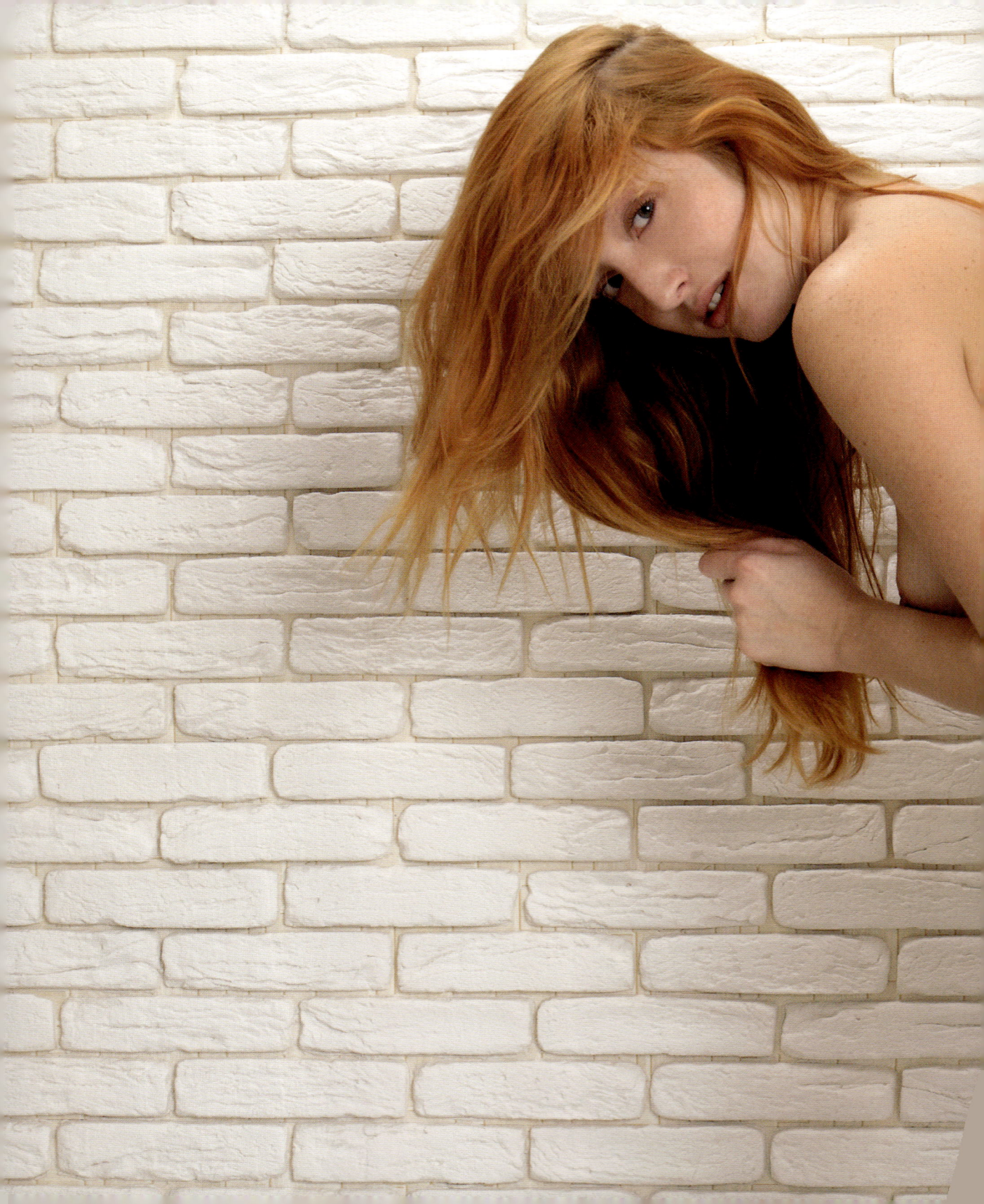

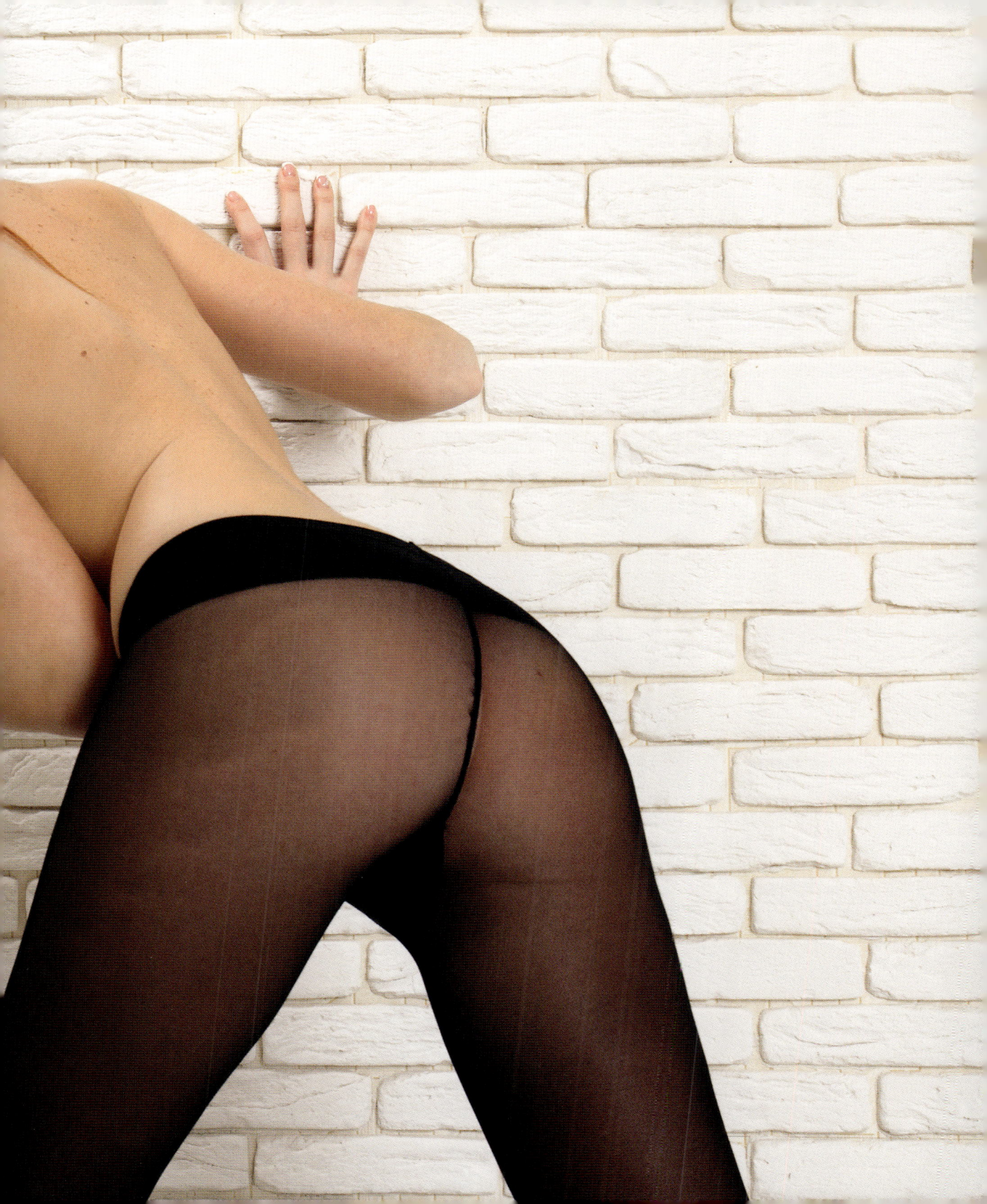

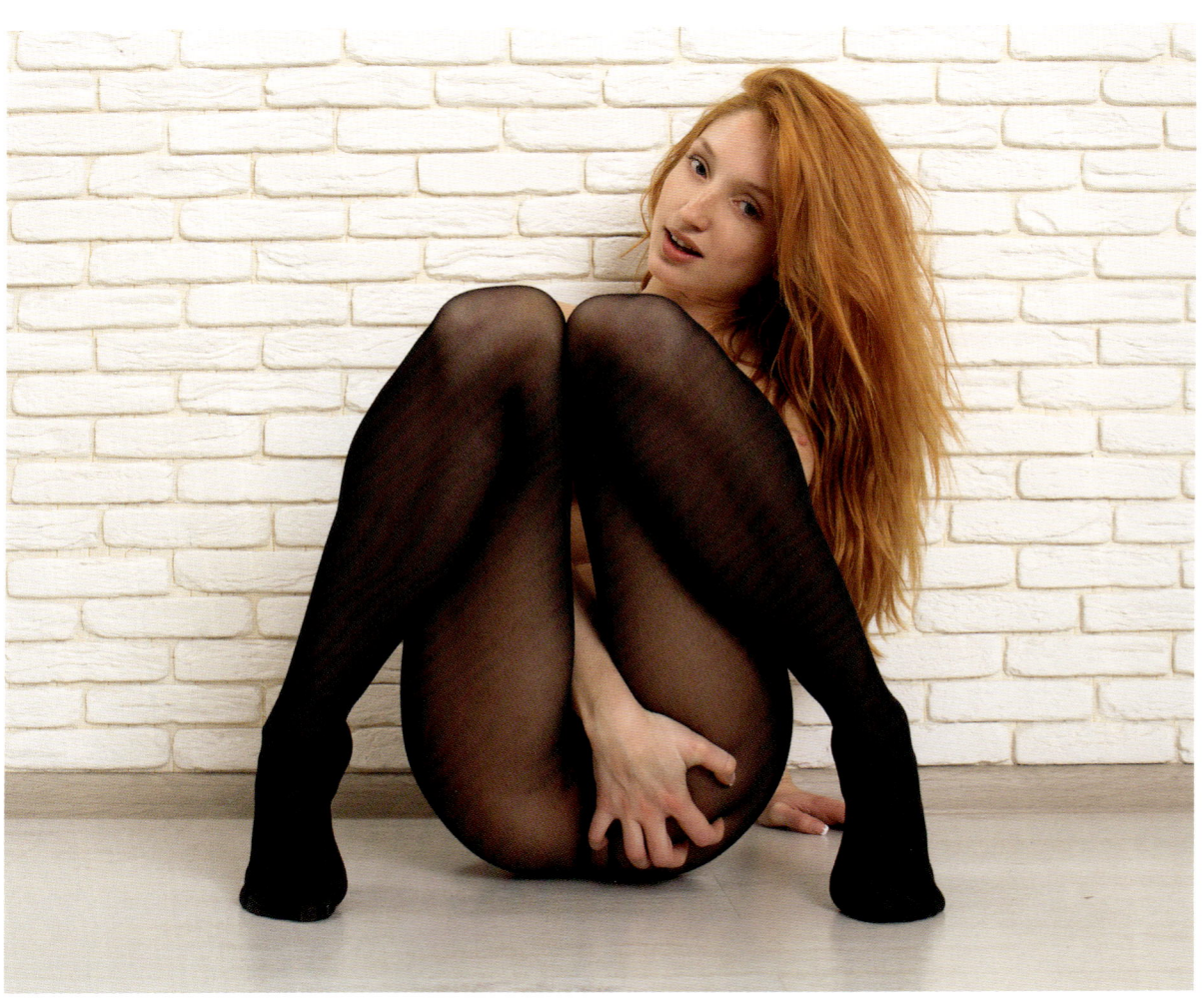

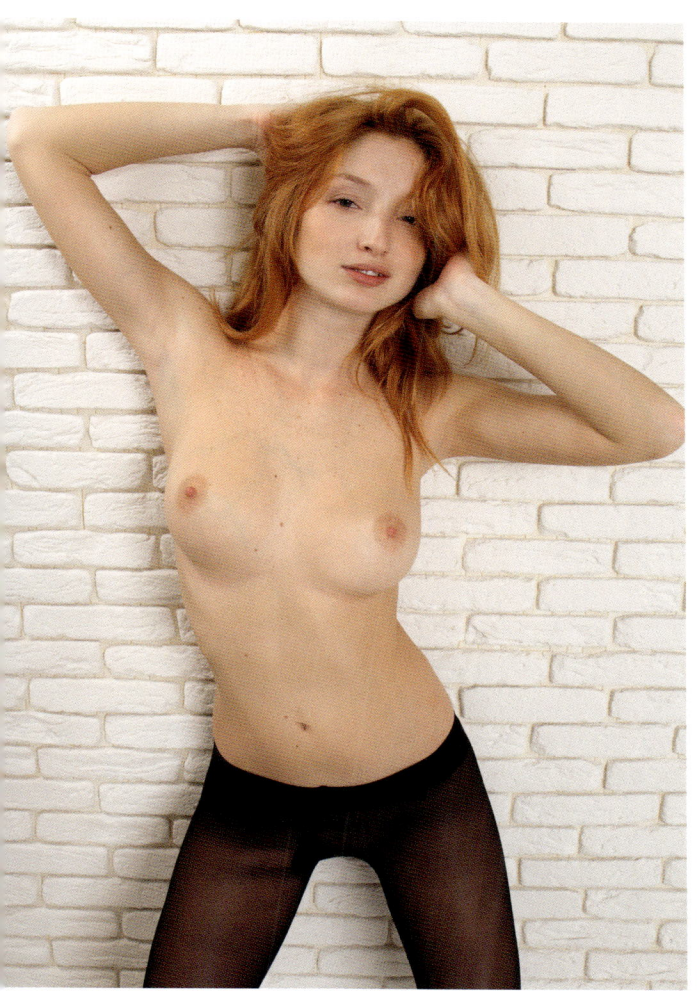
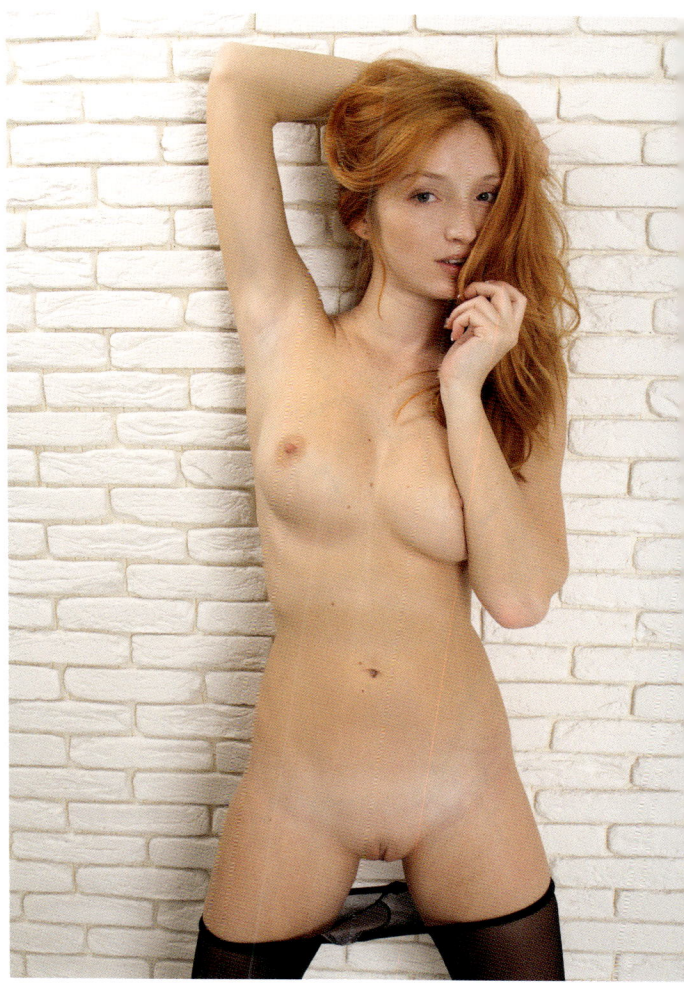

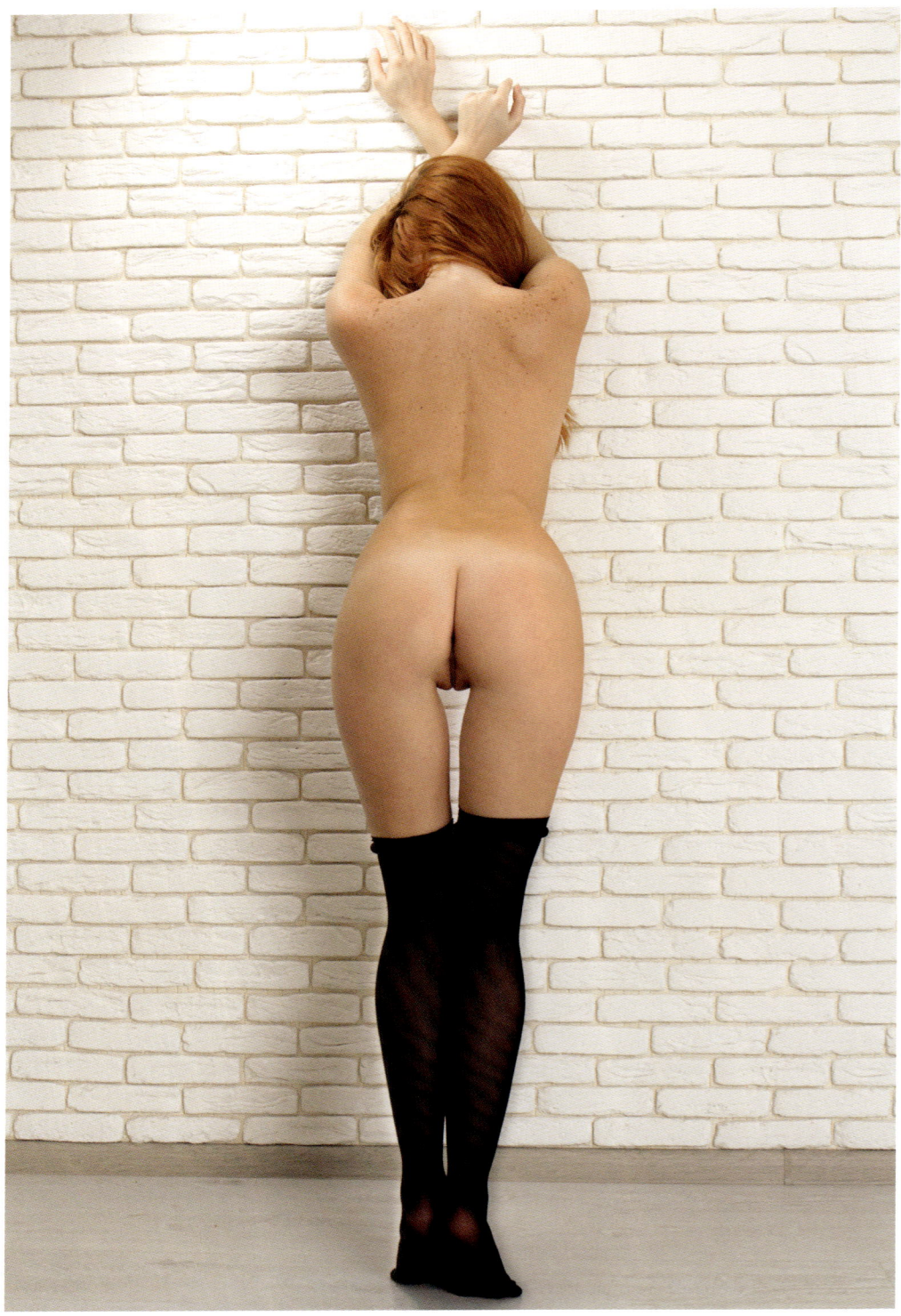

54

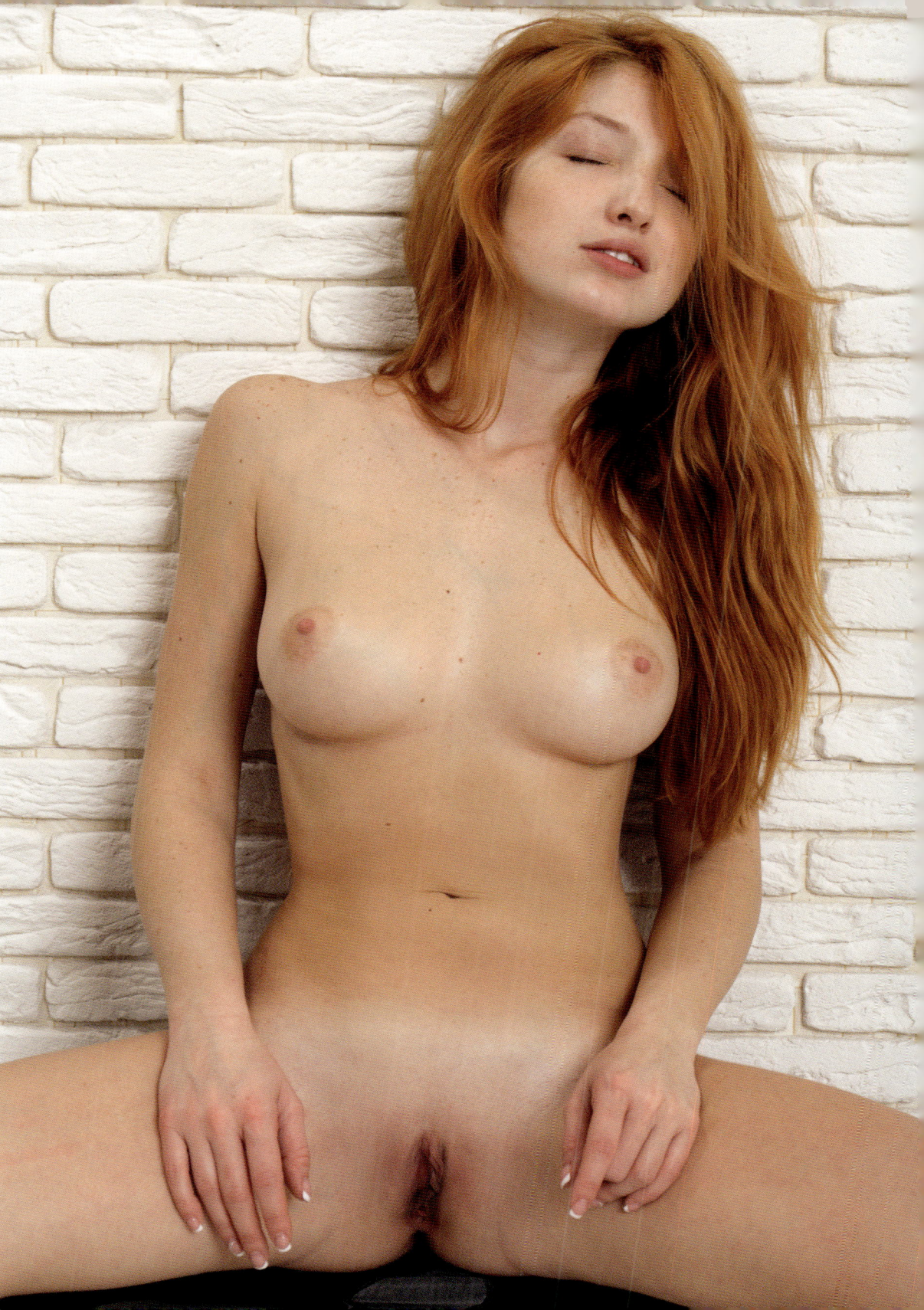

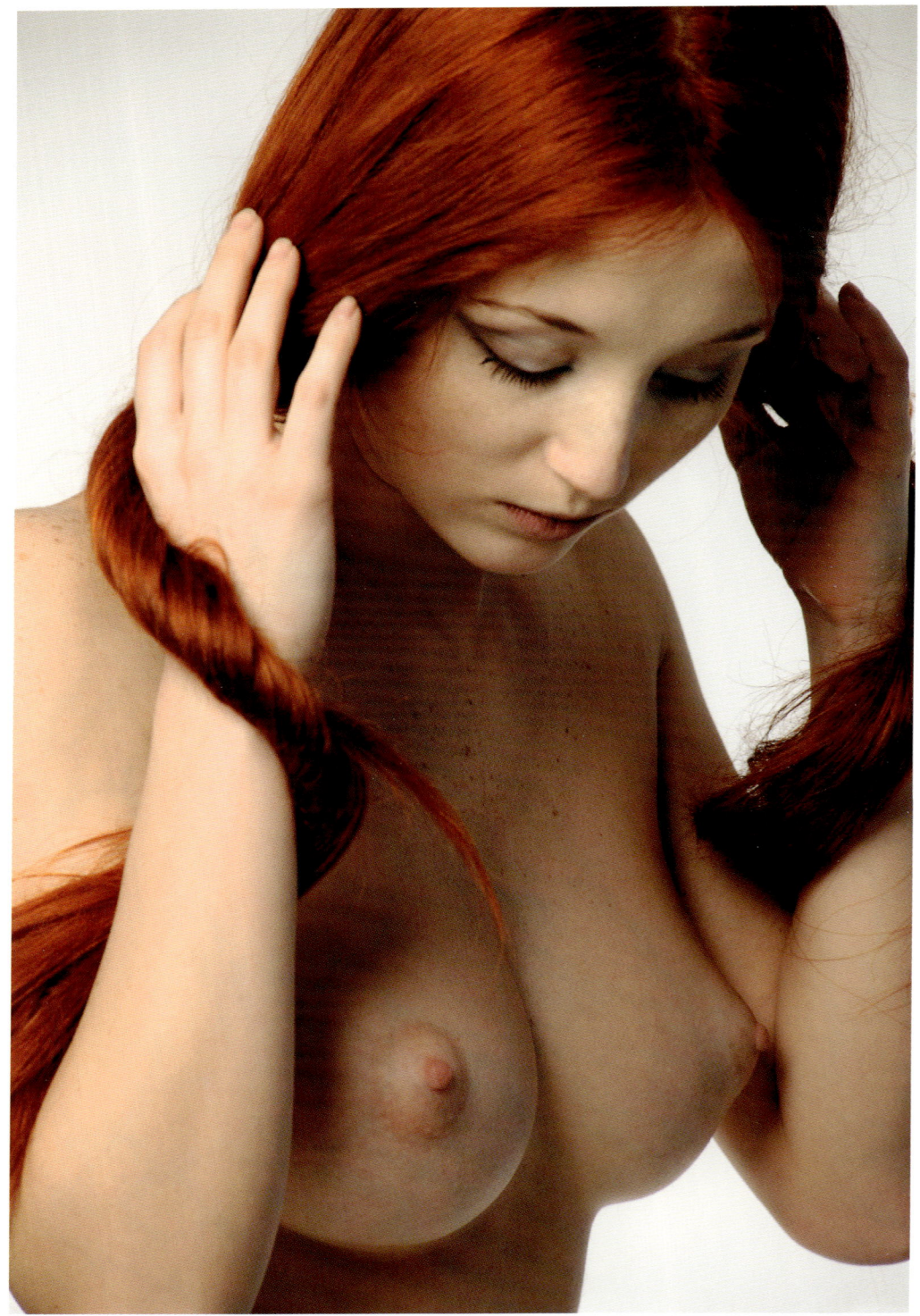

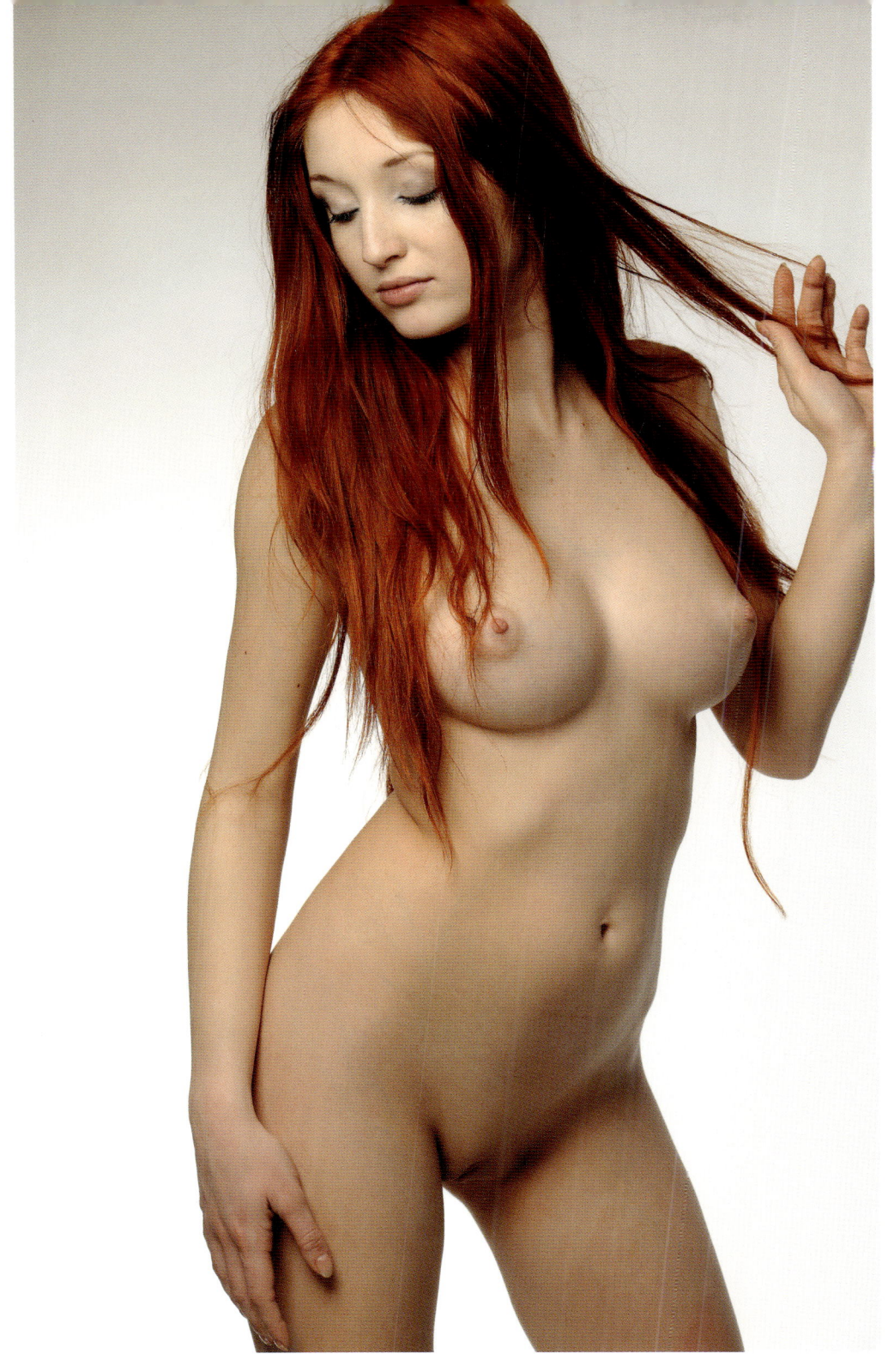

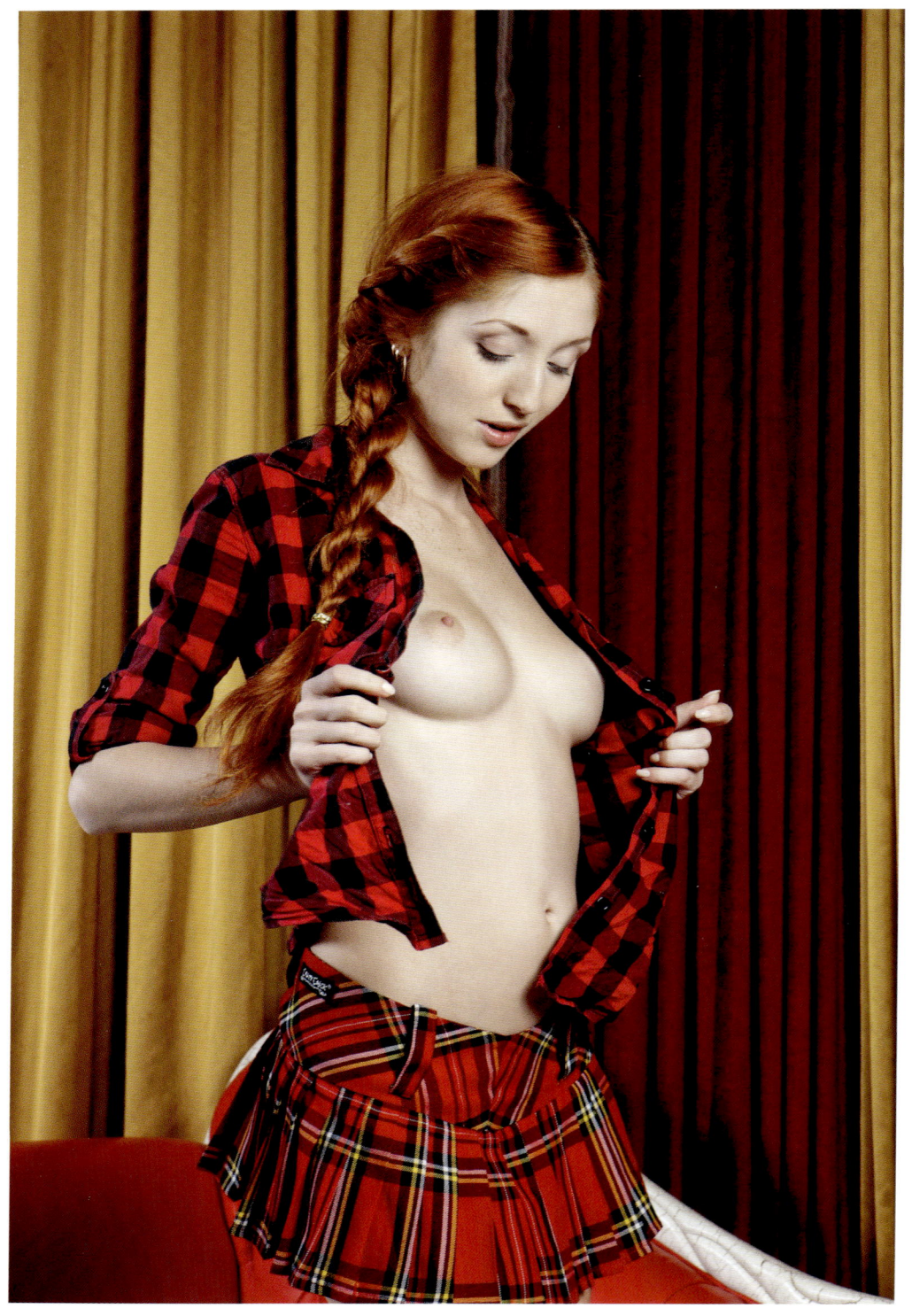

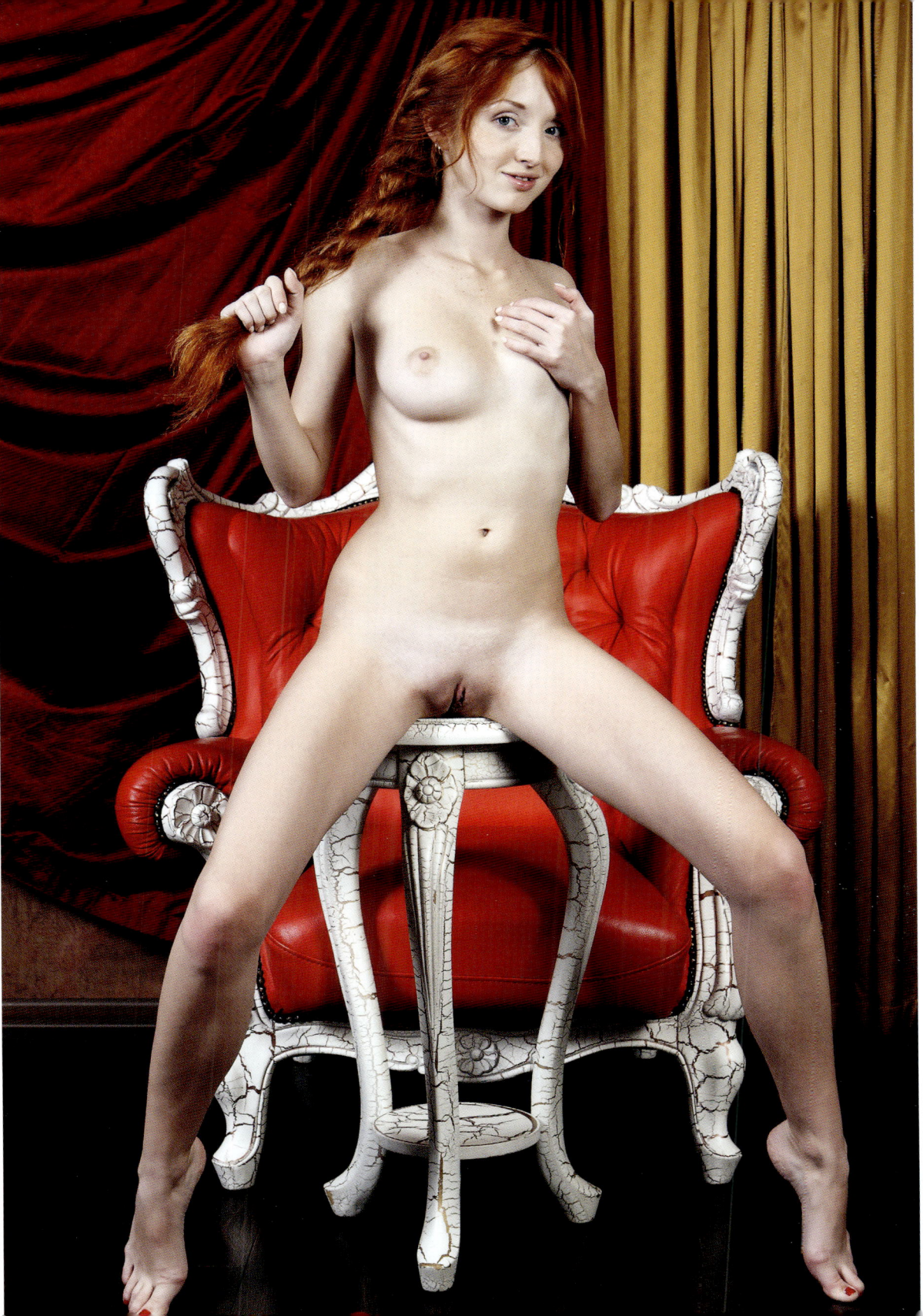

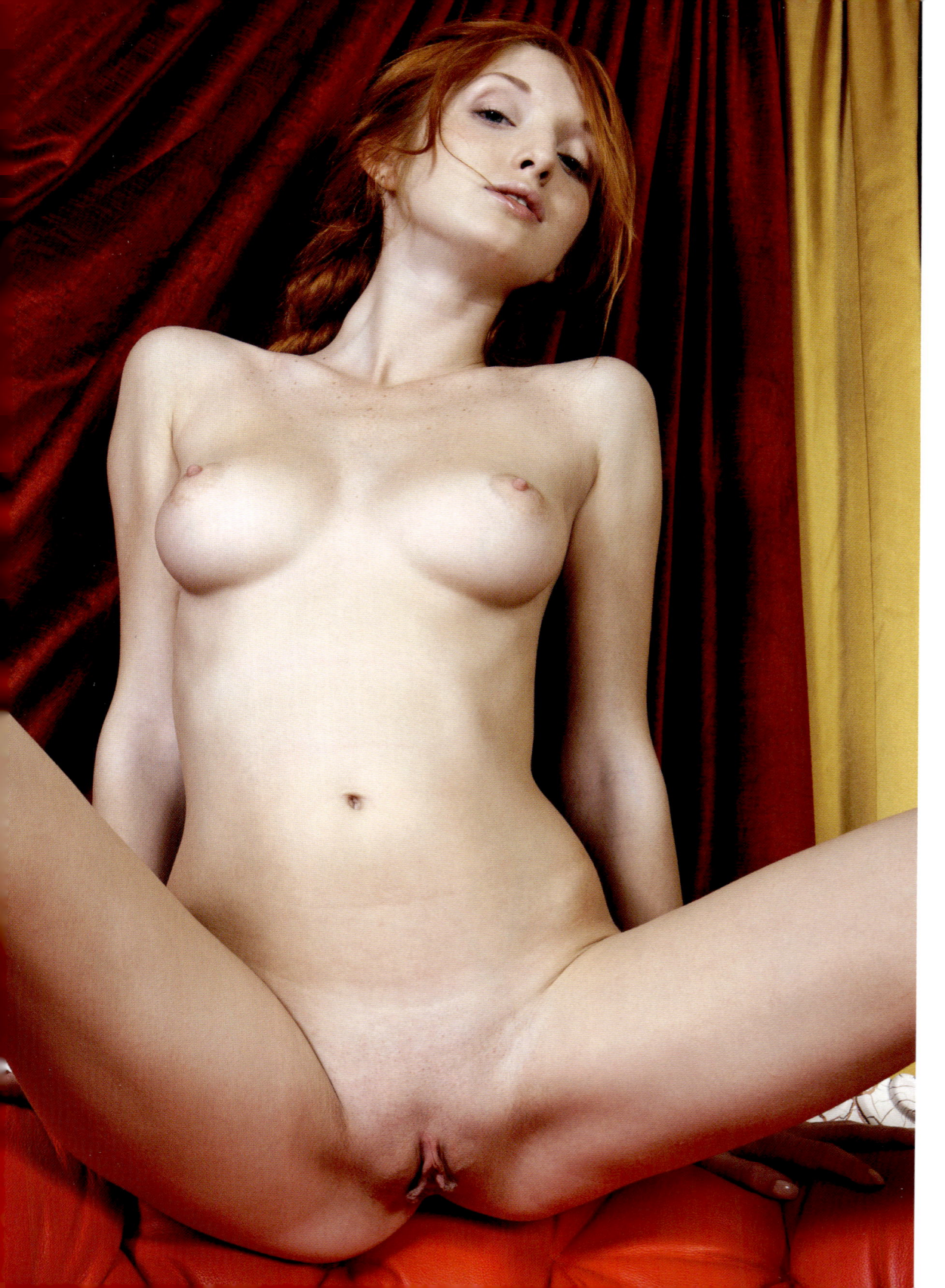

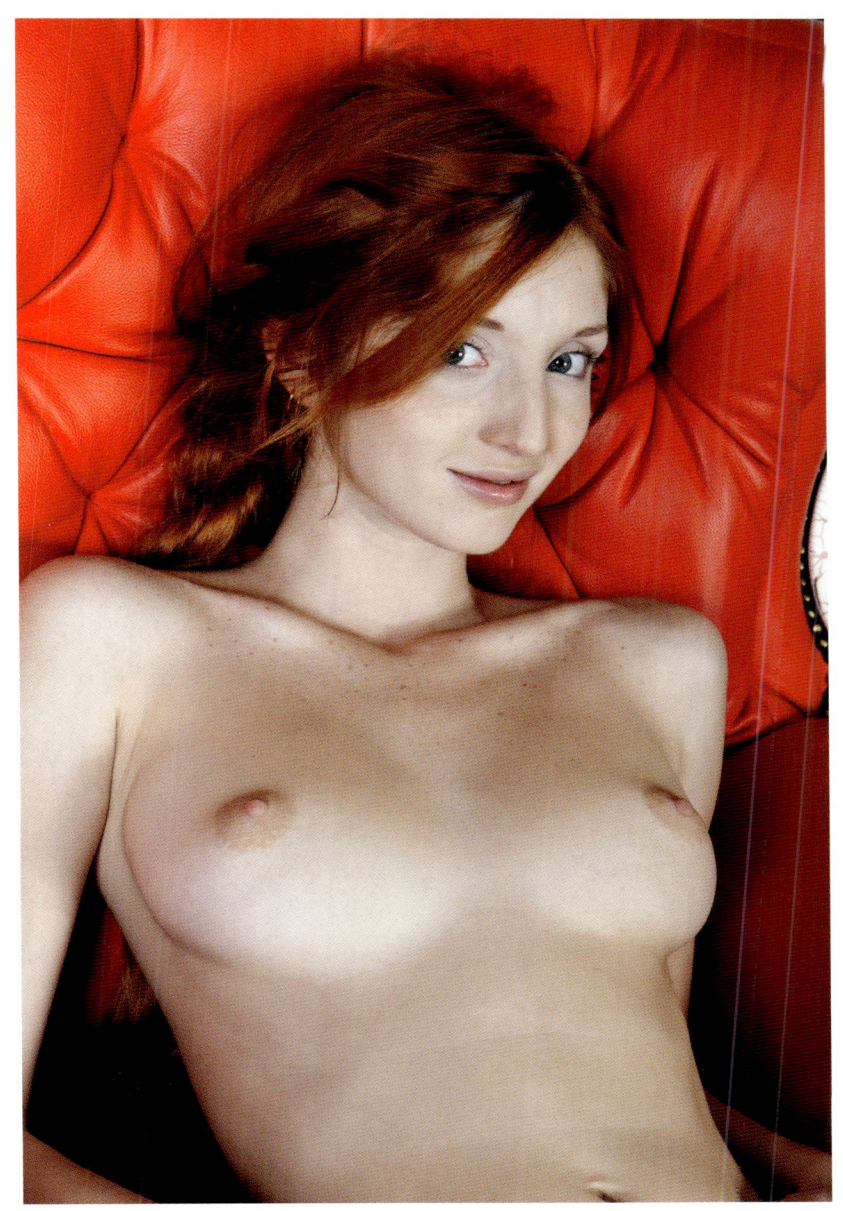

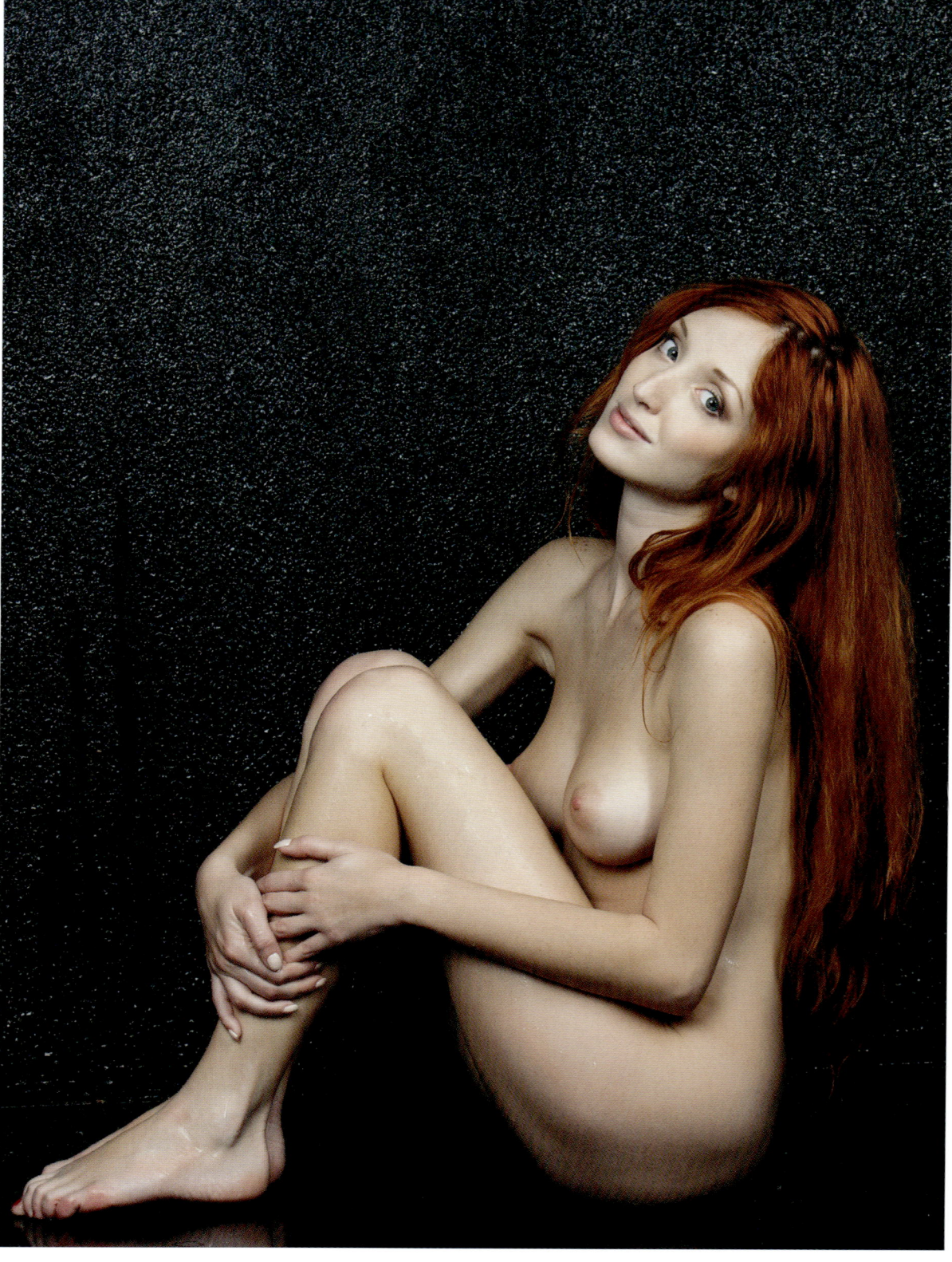

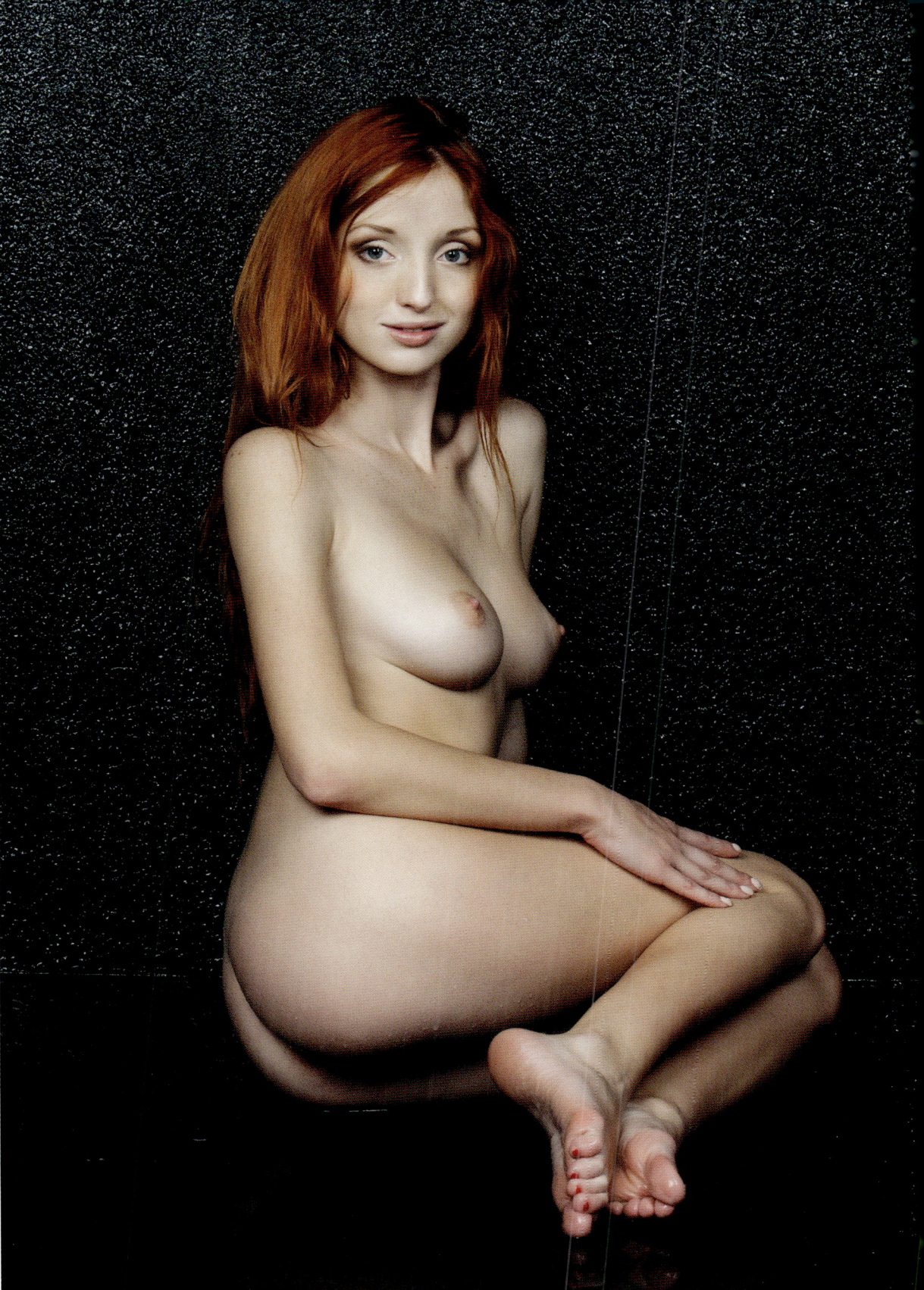

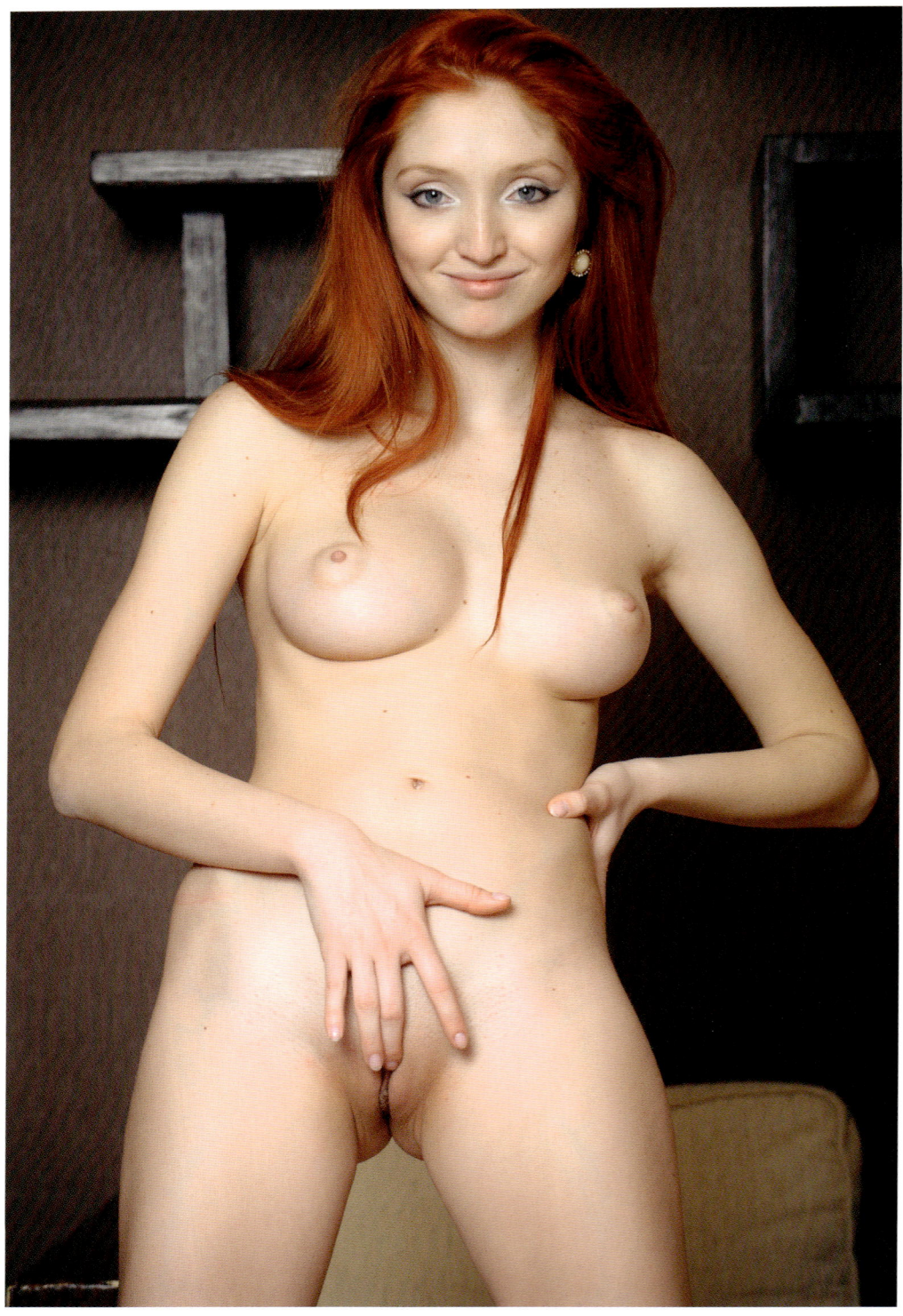

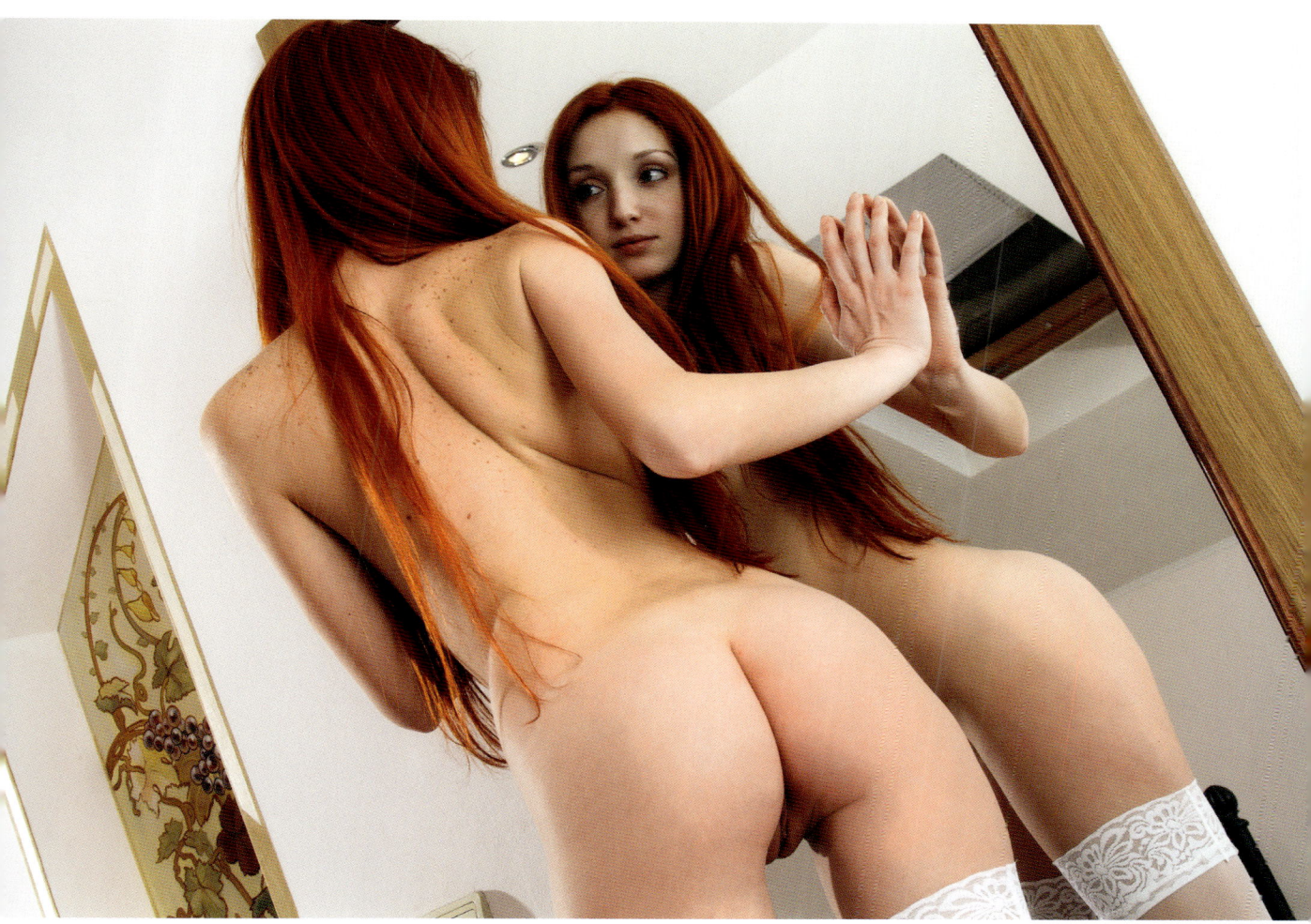

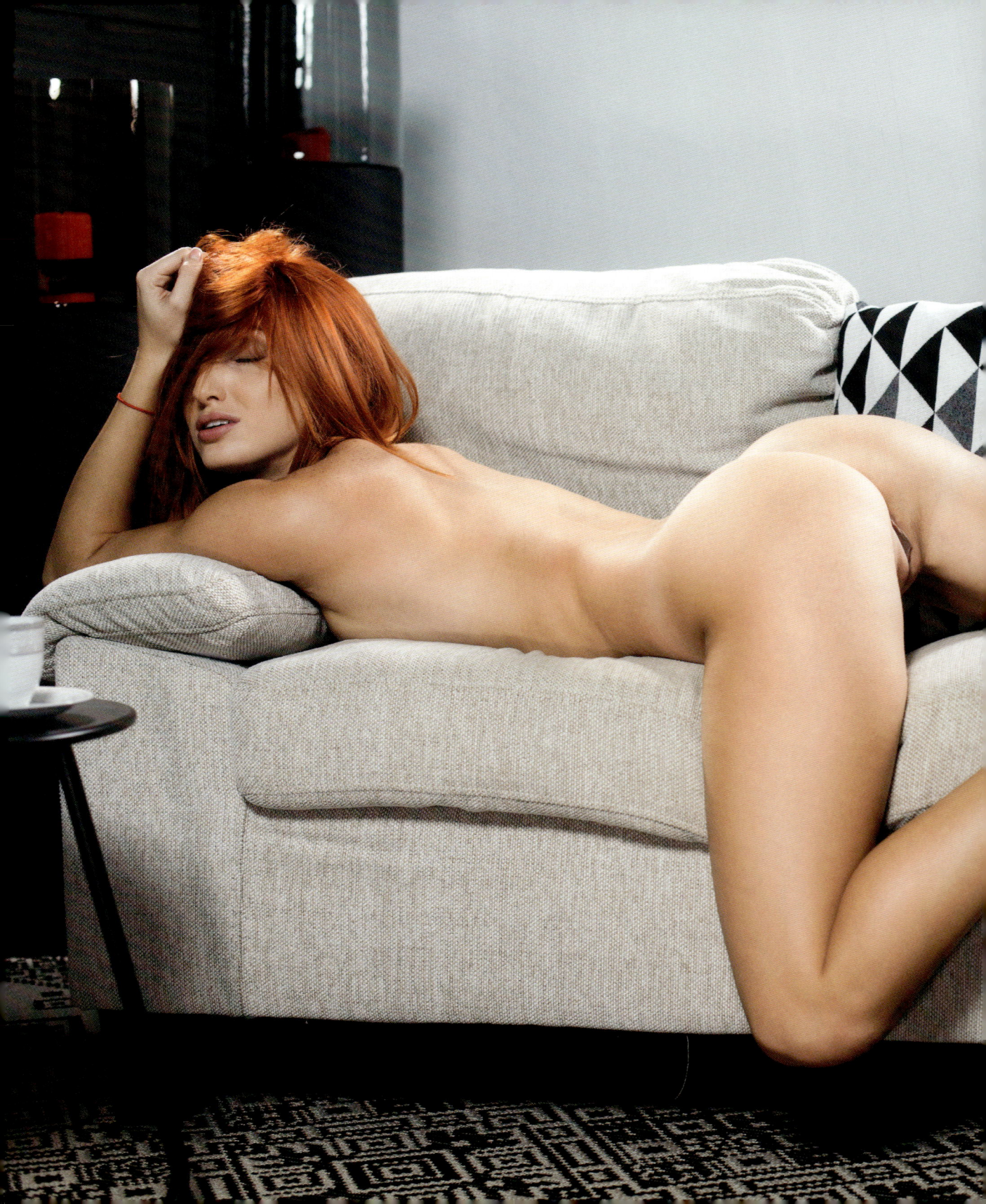

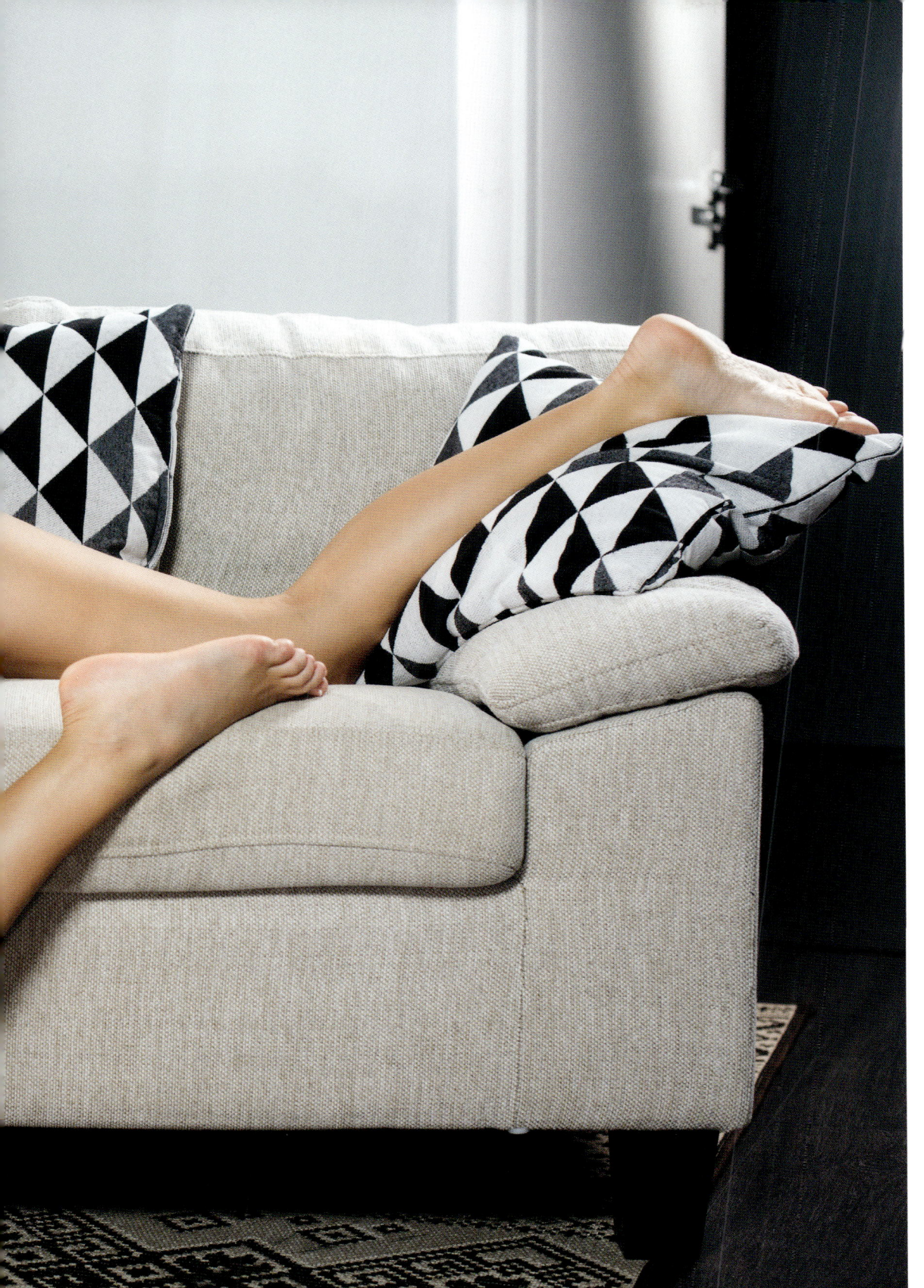

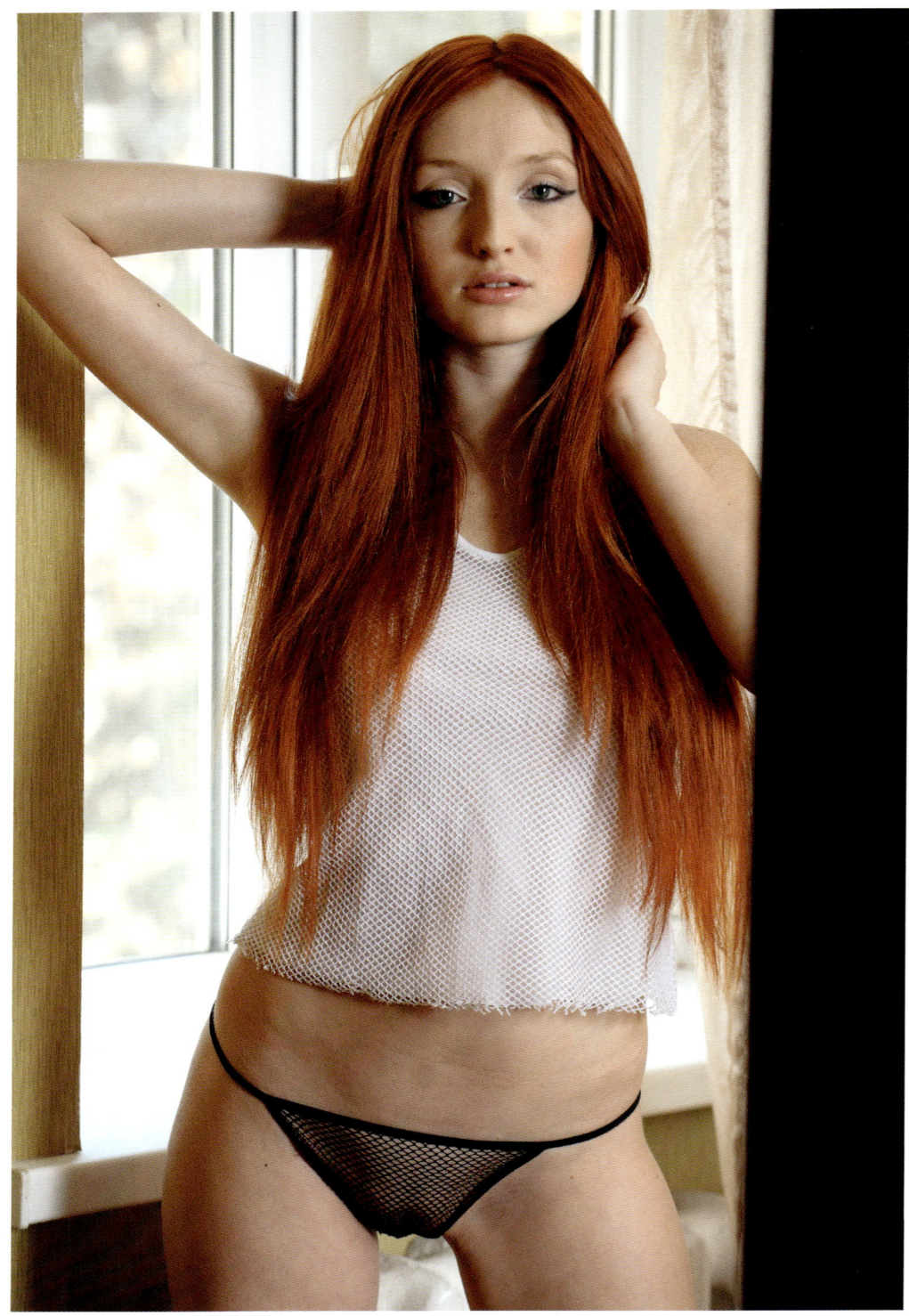

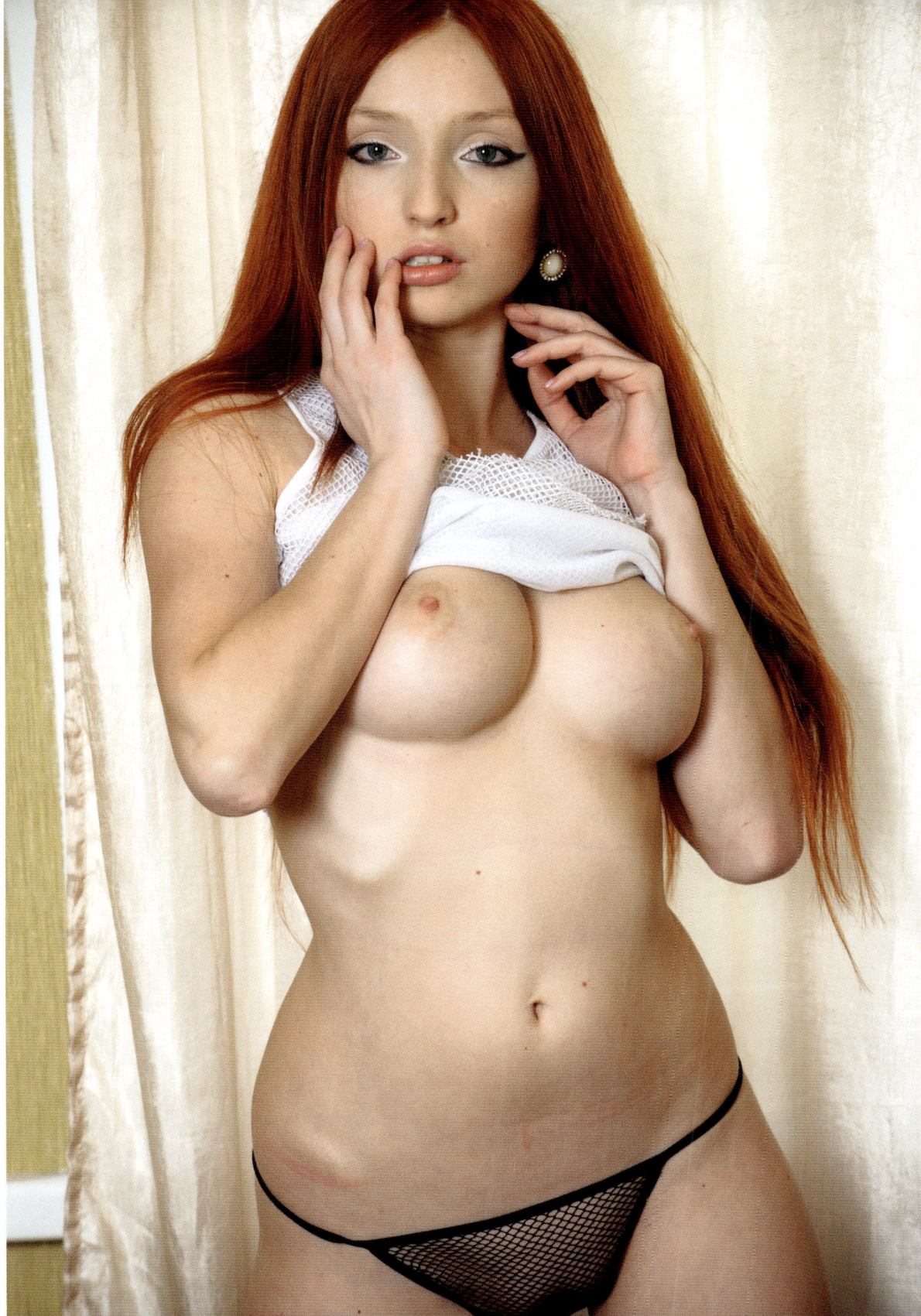

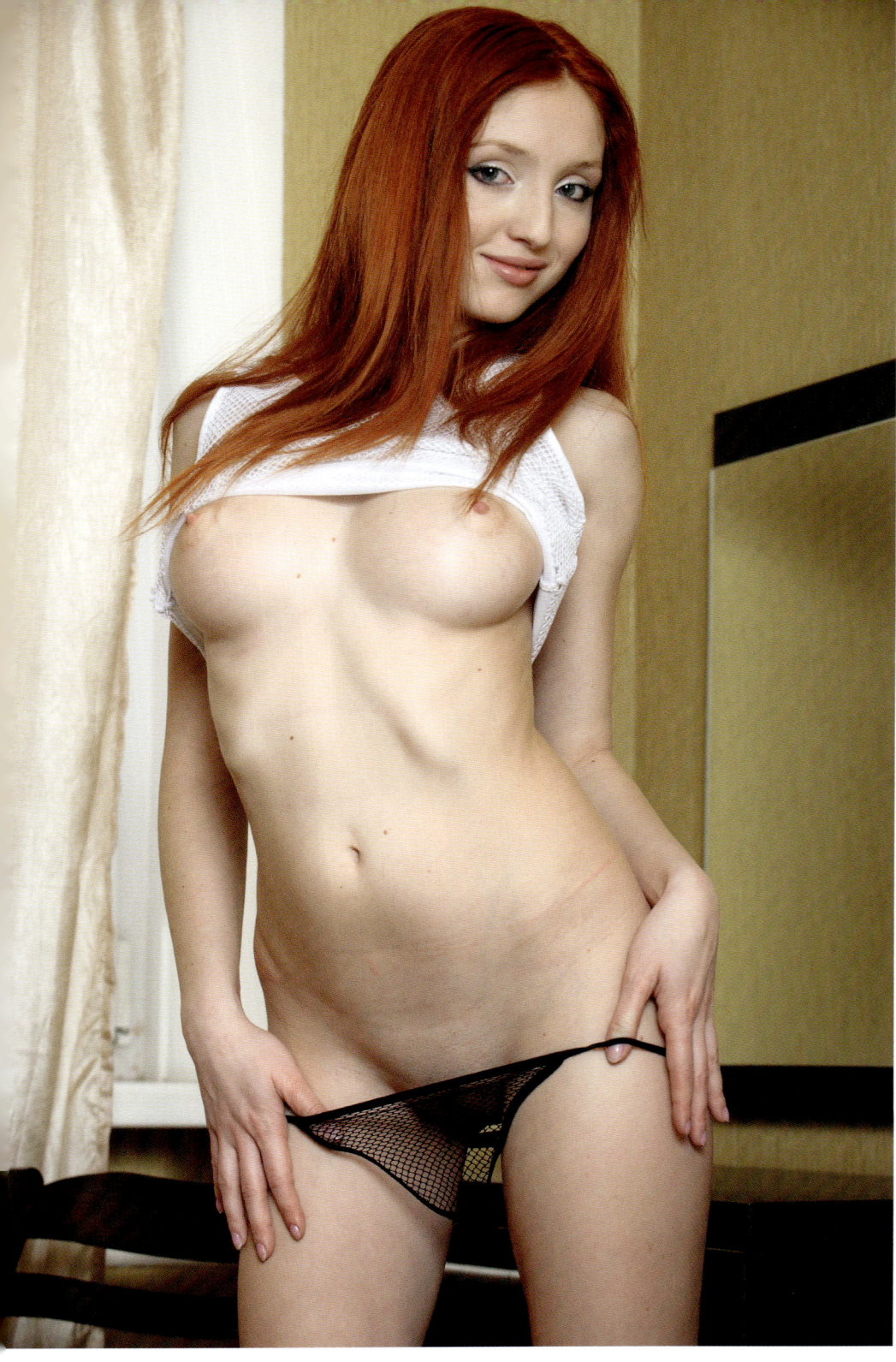

70

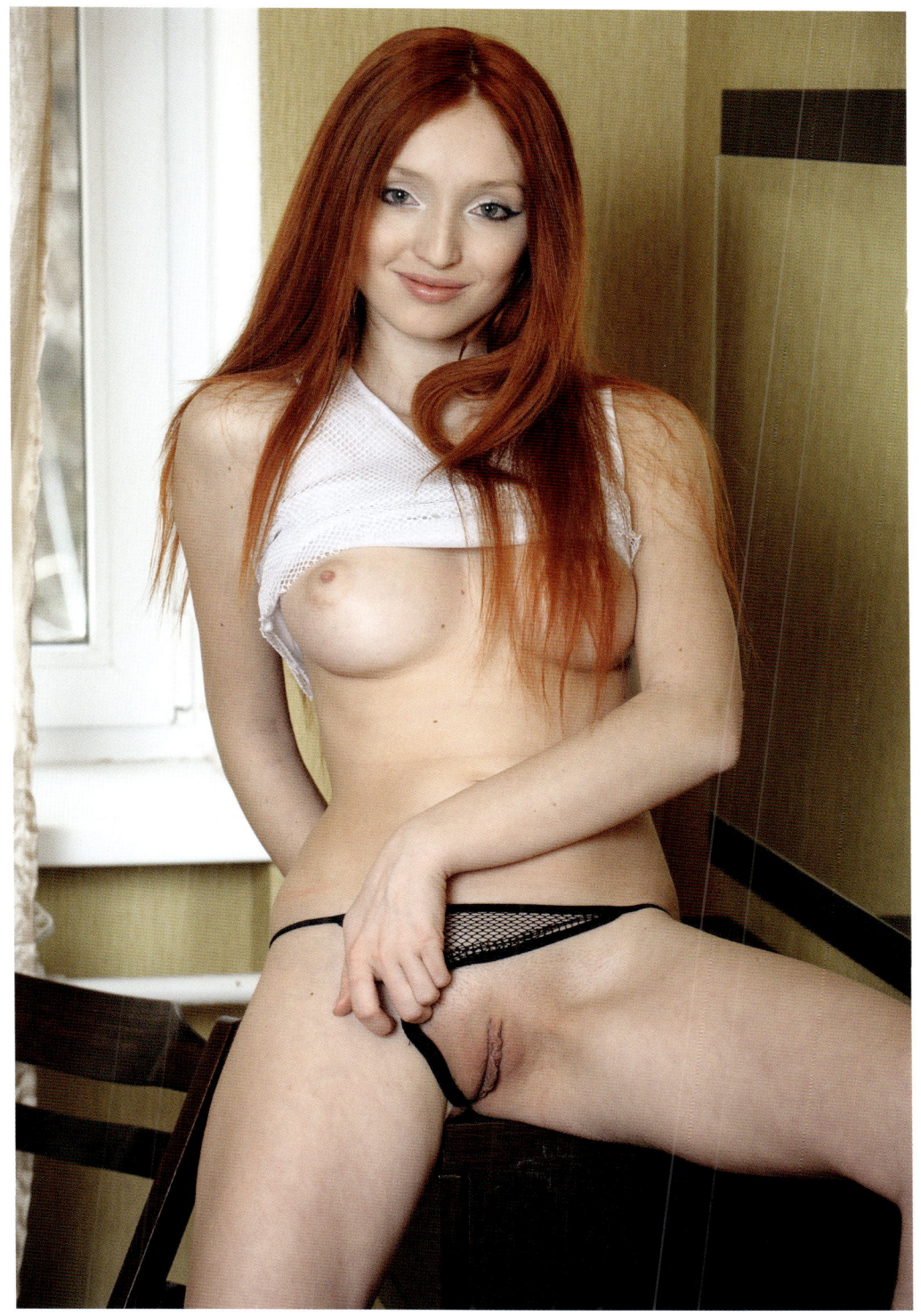

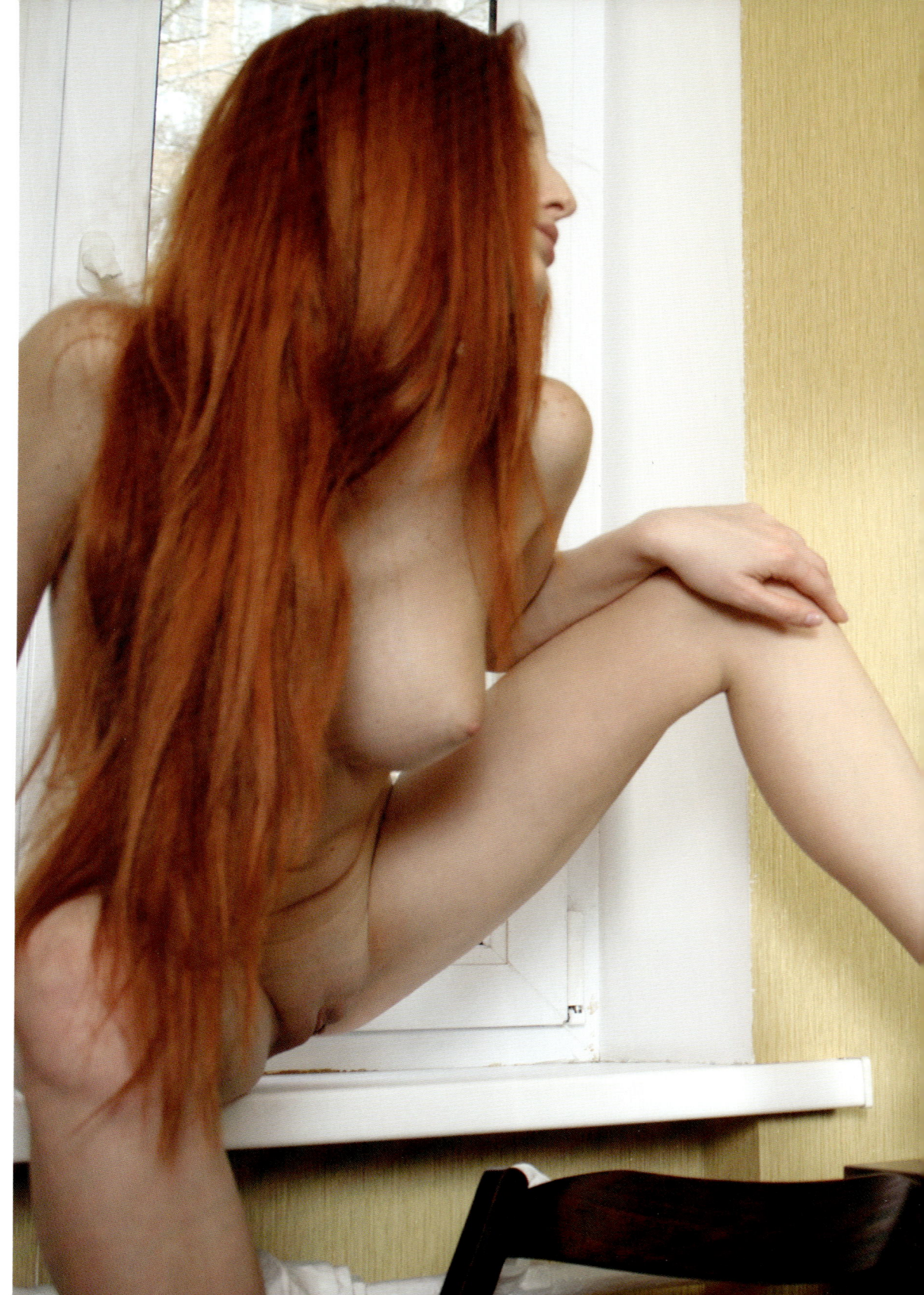

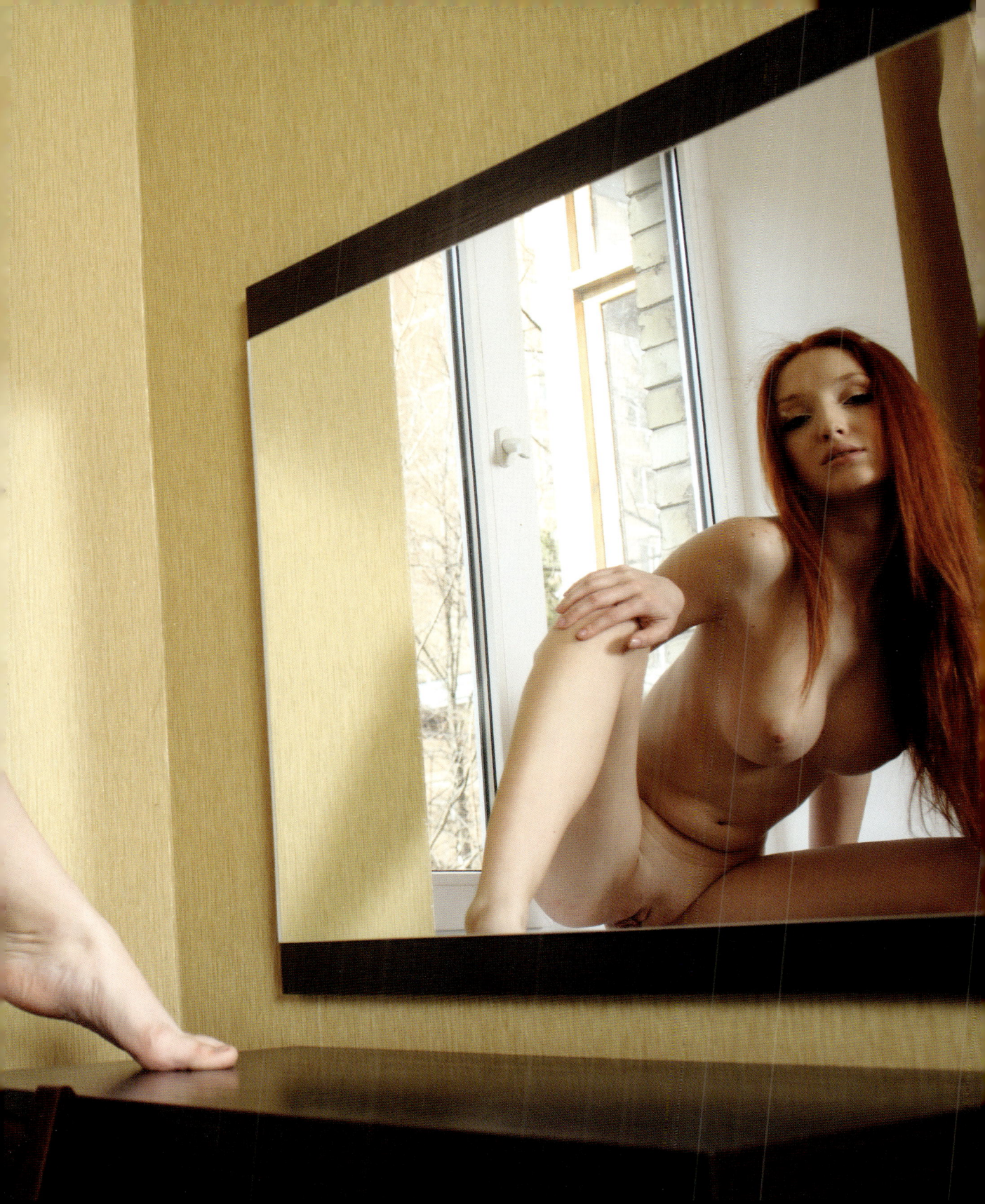

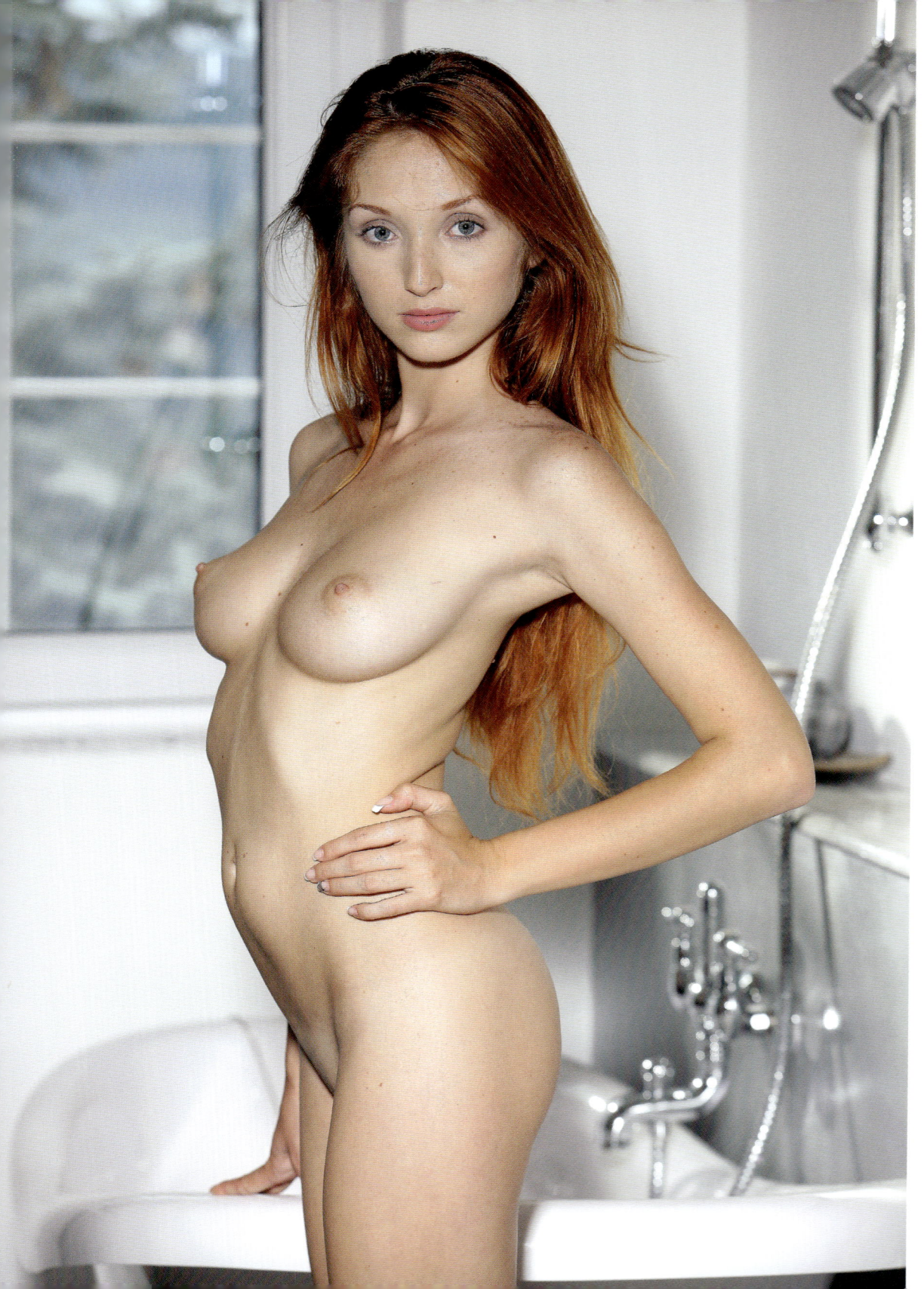

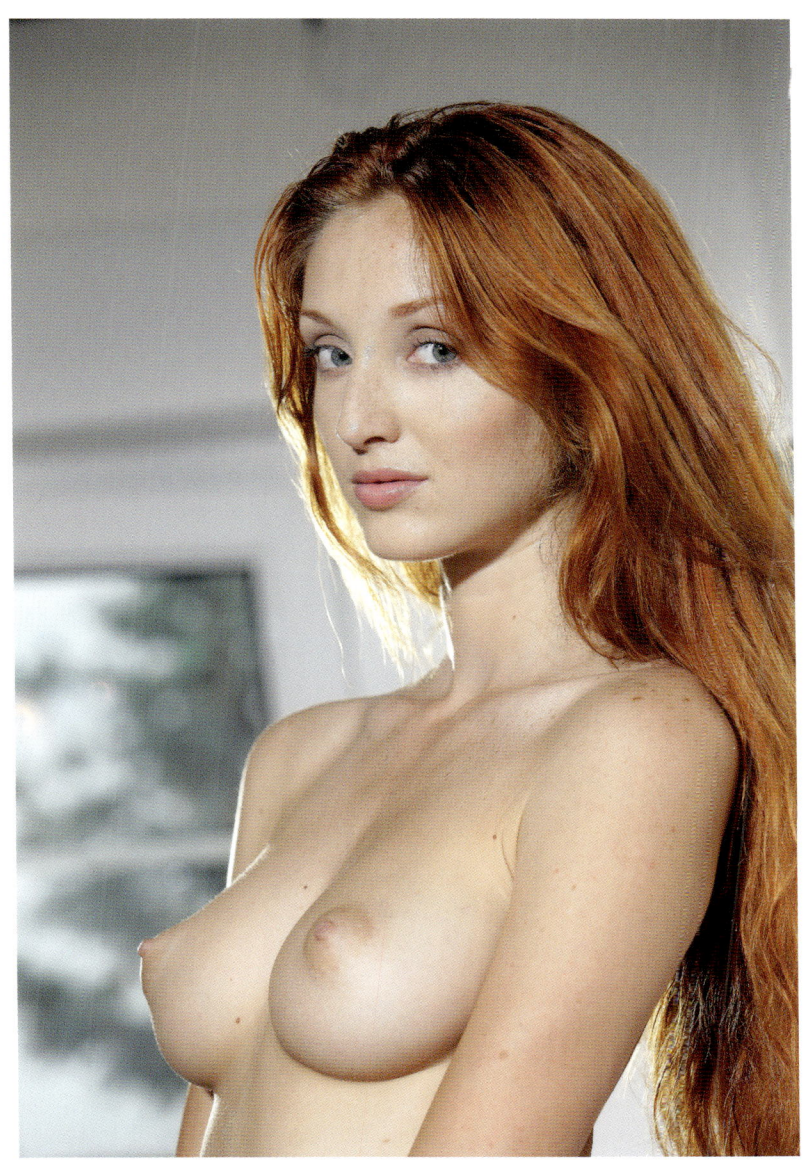

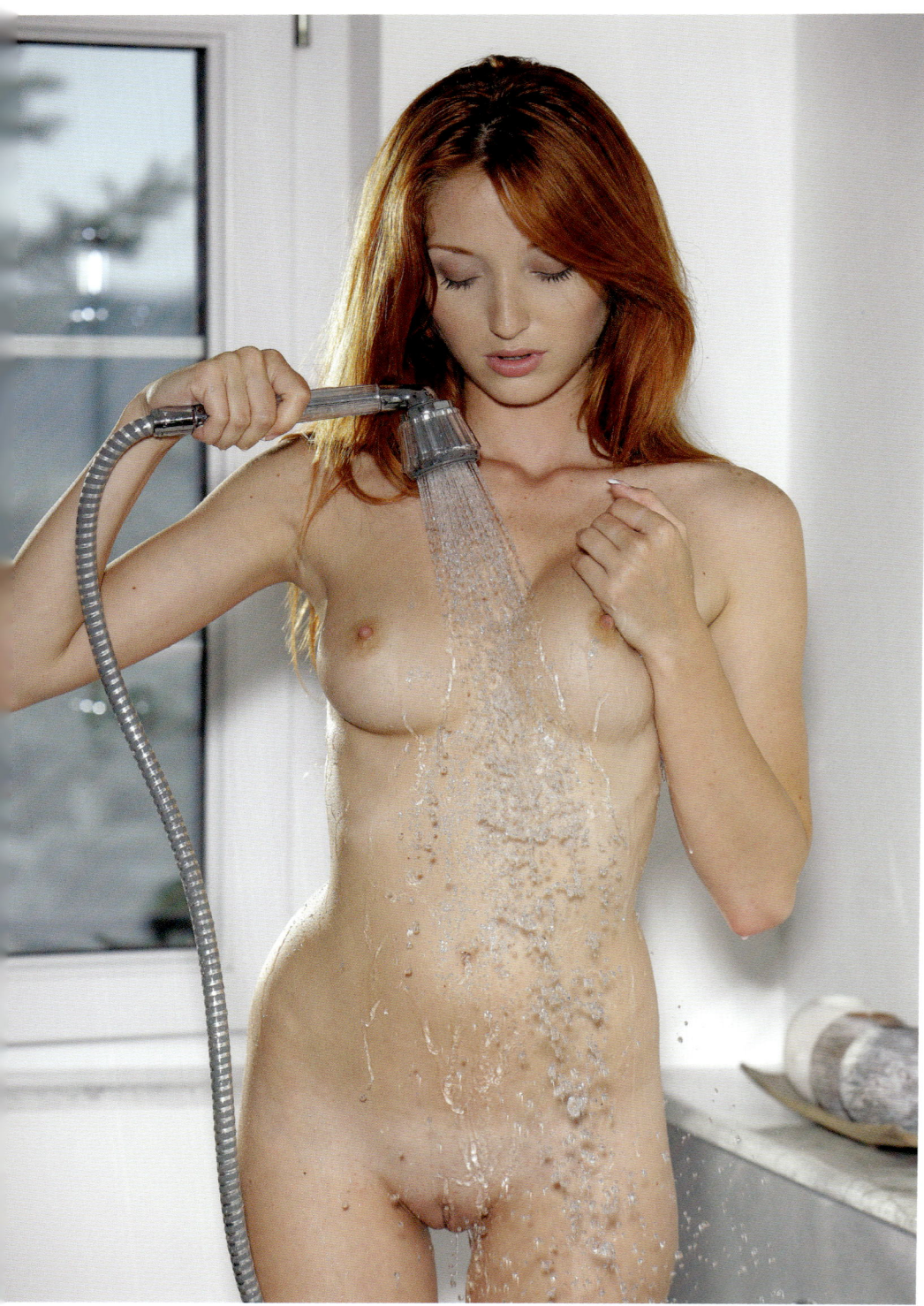

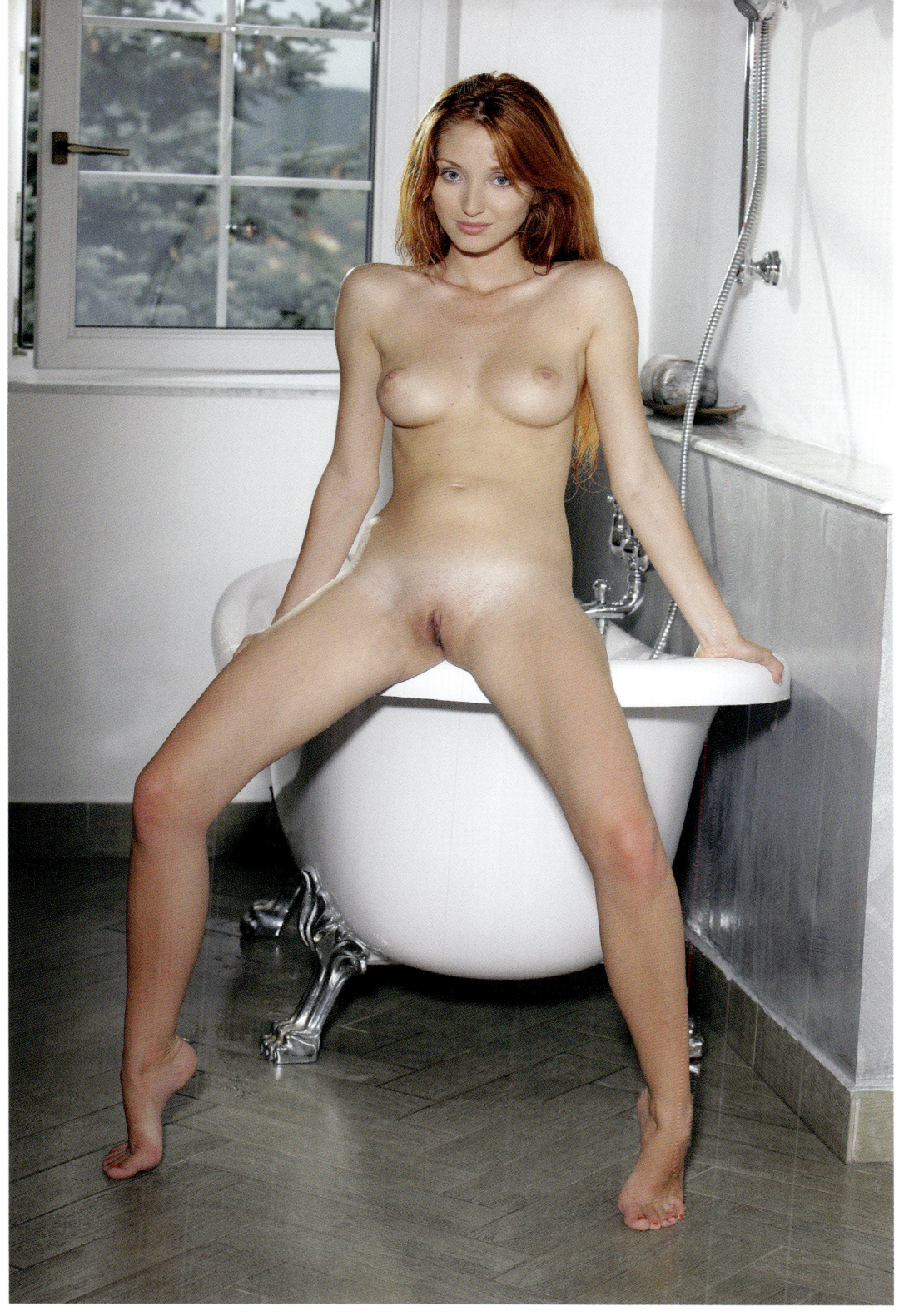

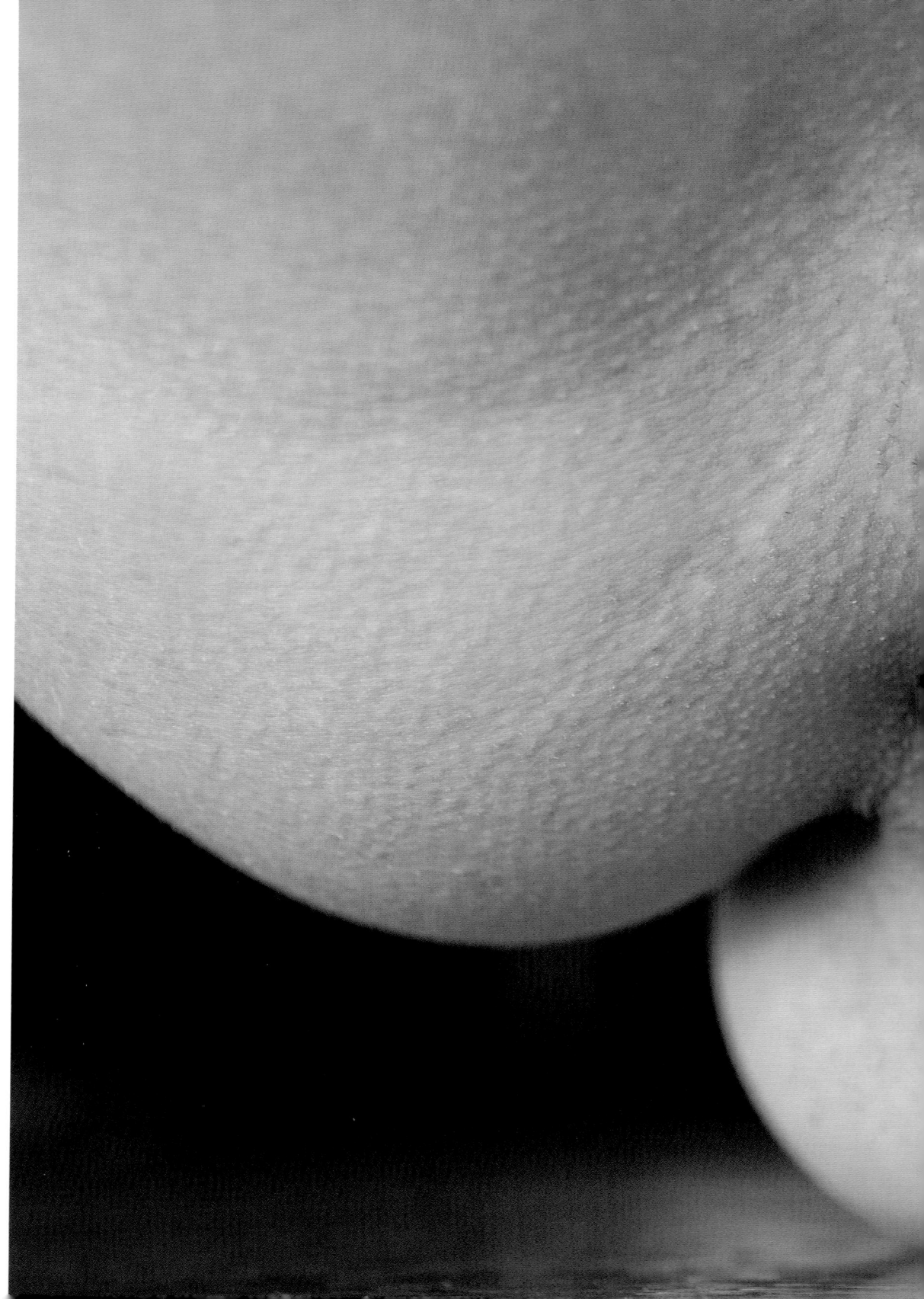

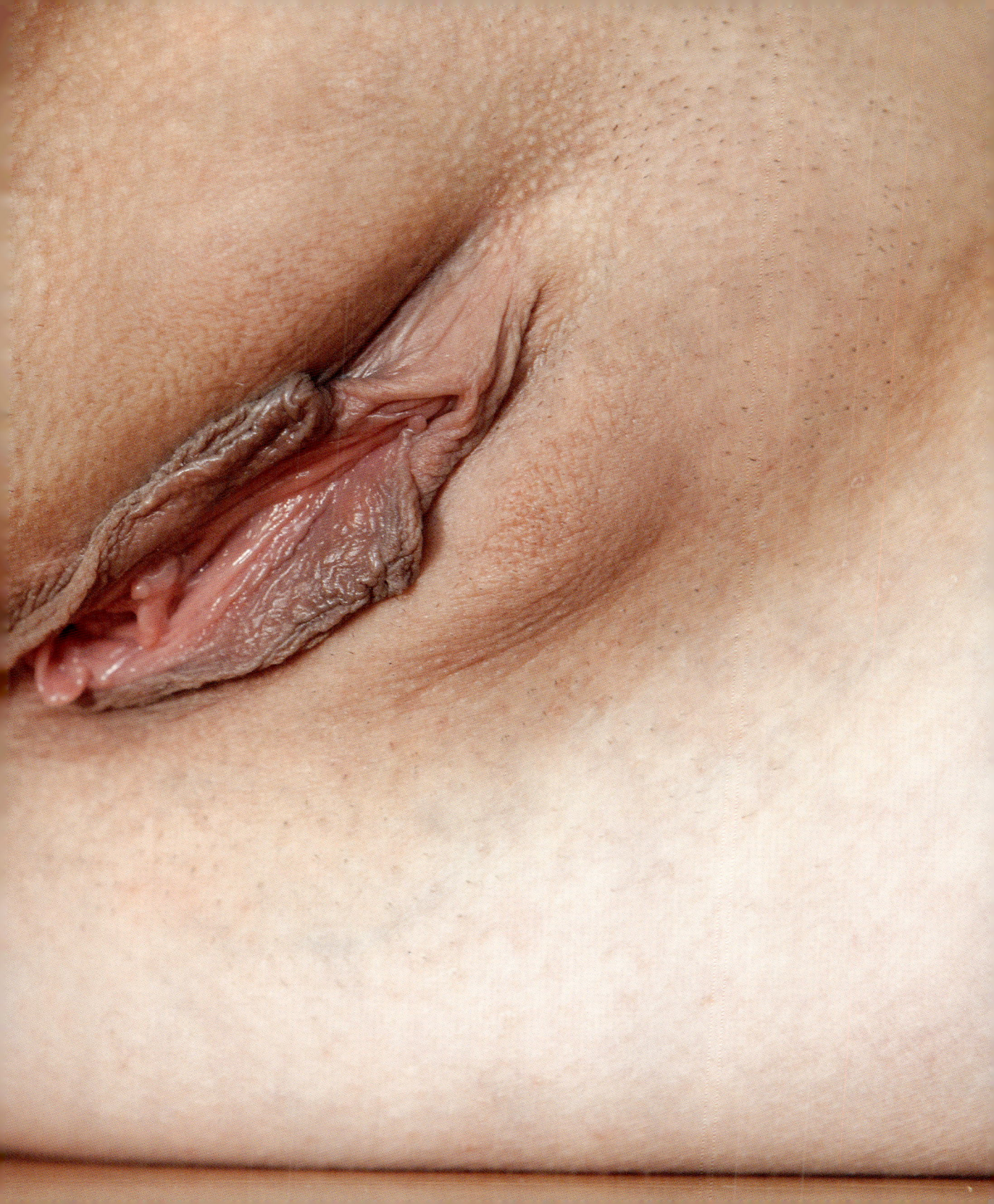

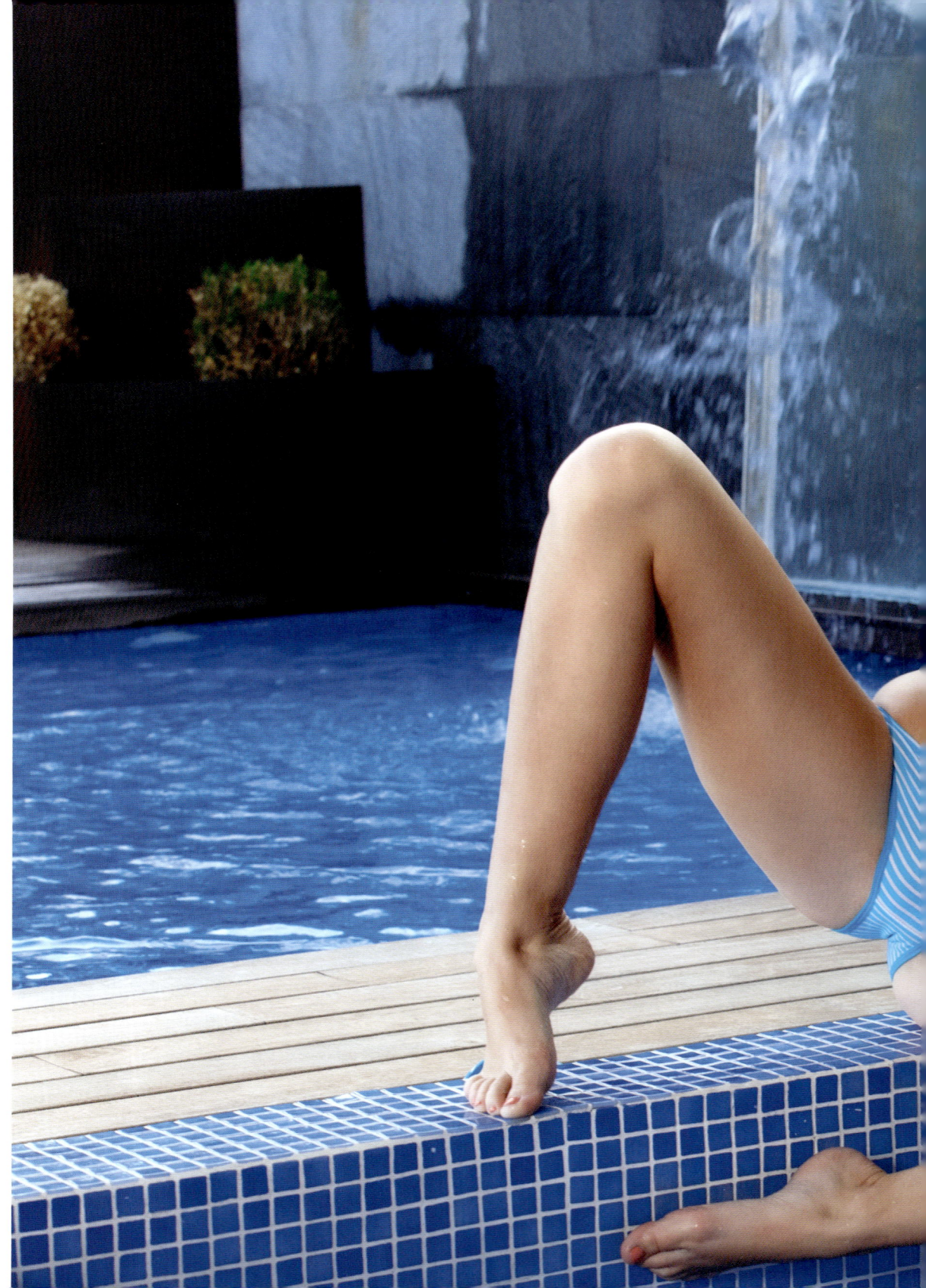

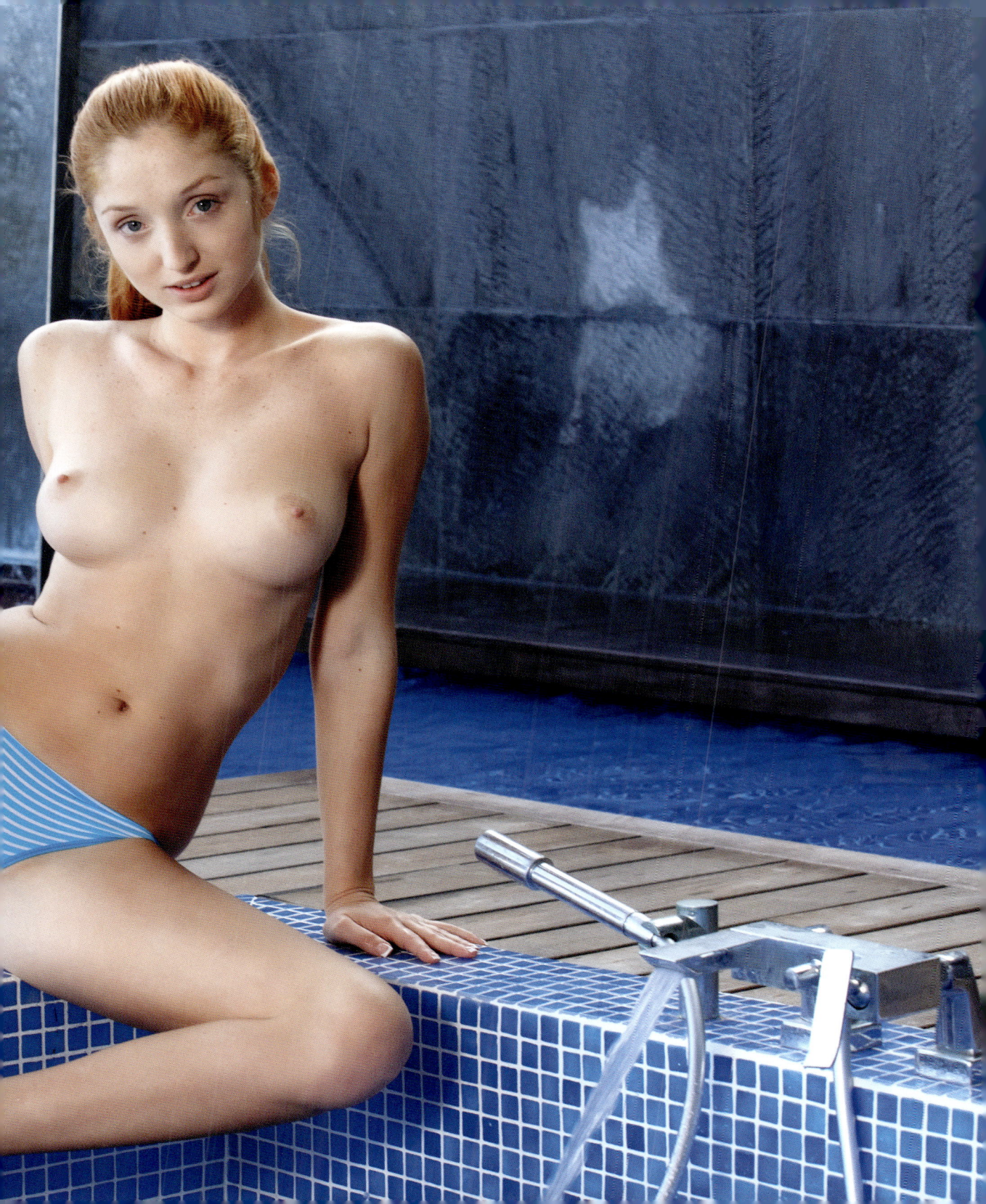

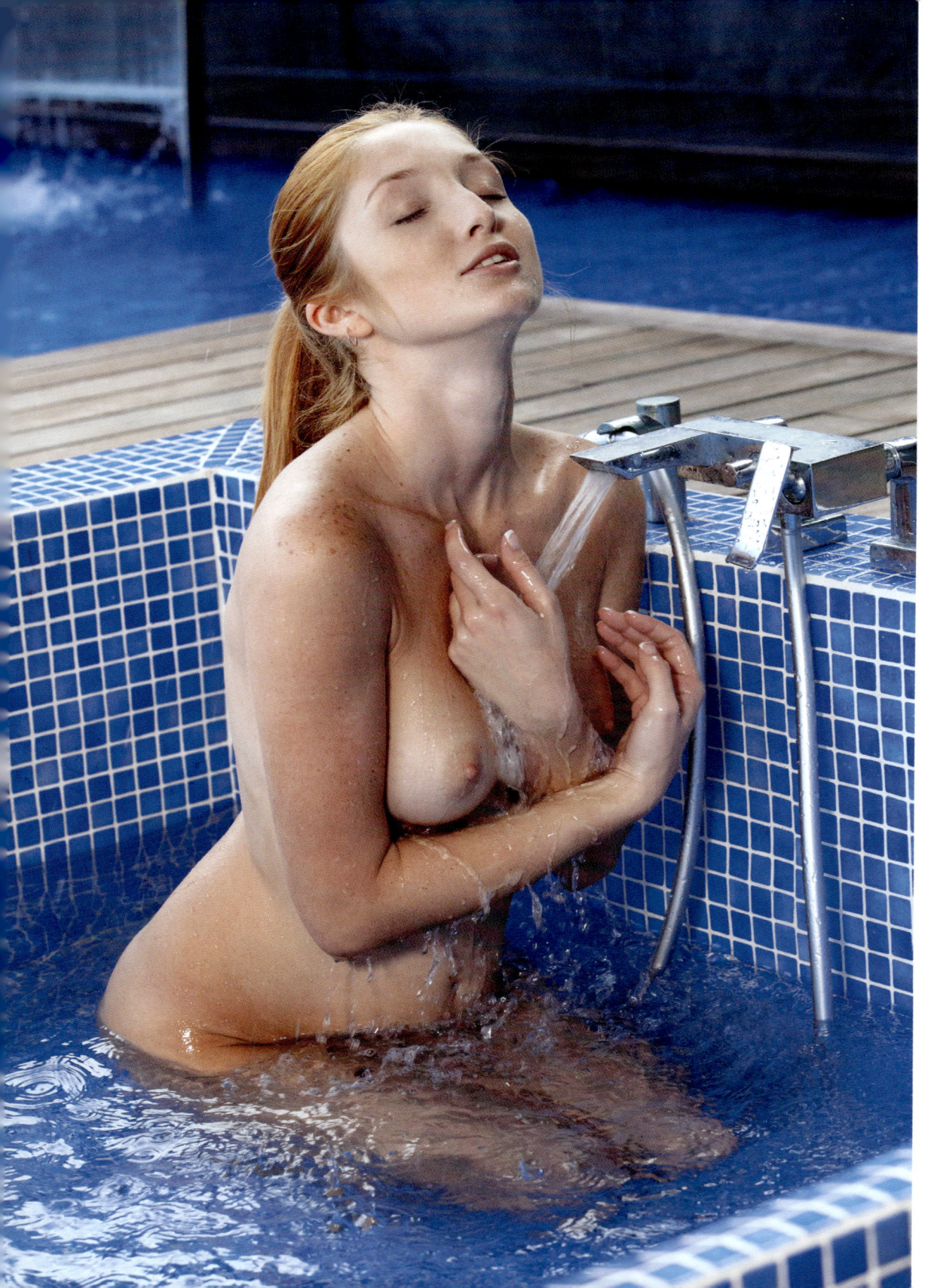

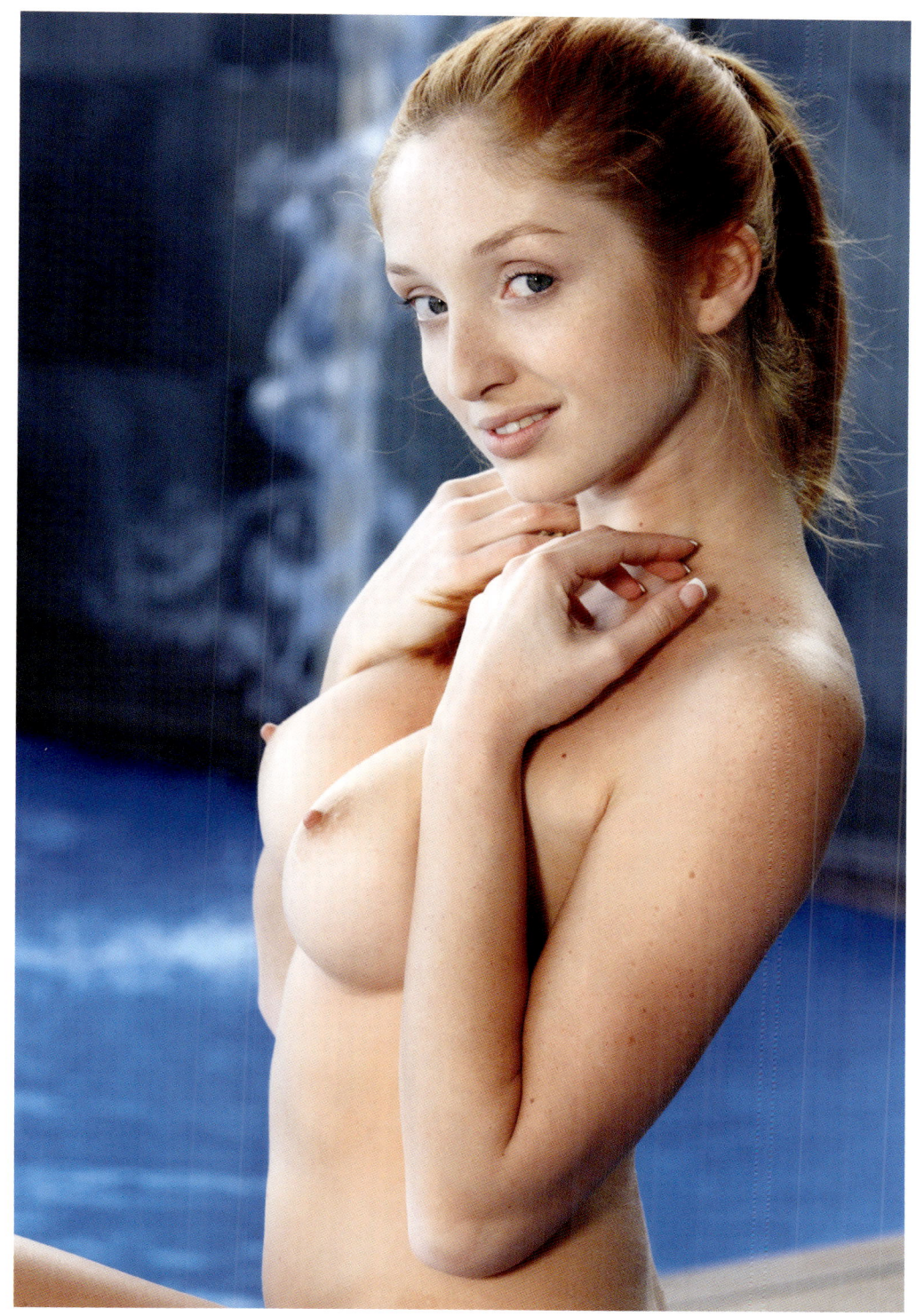

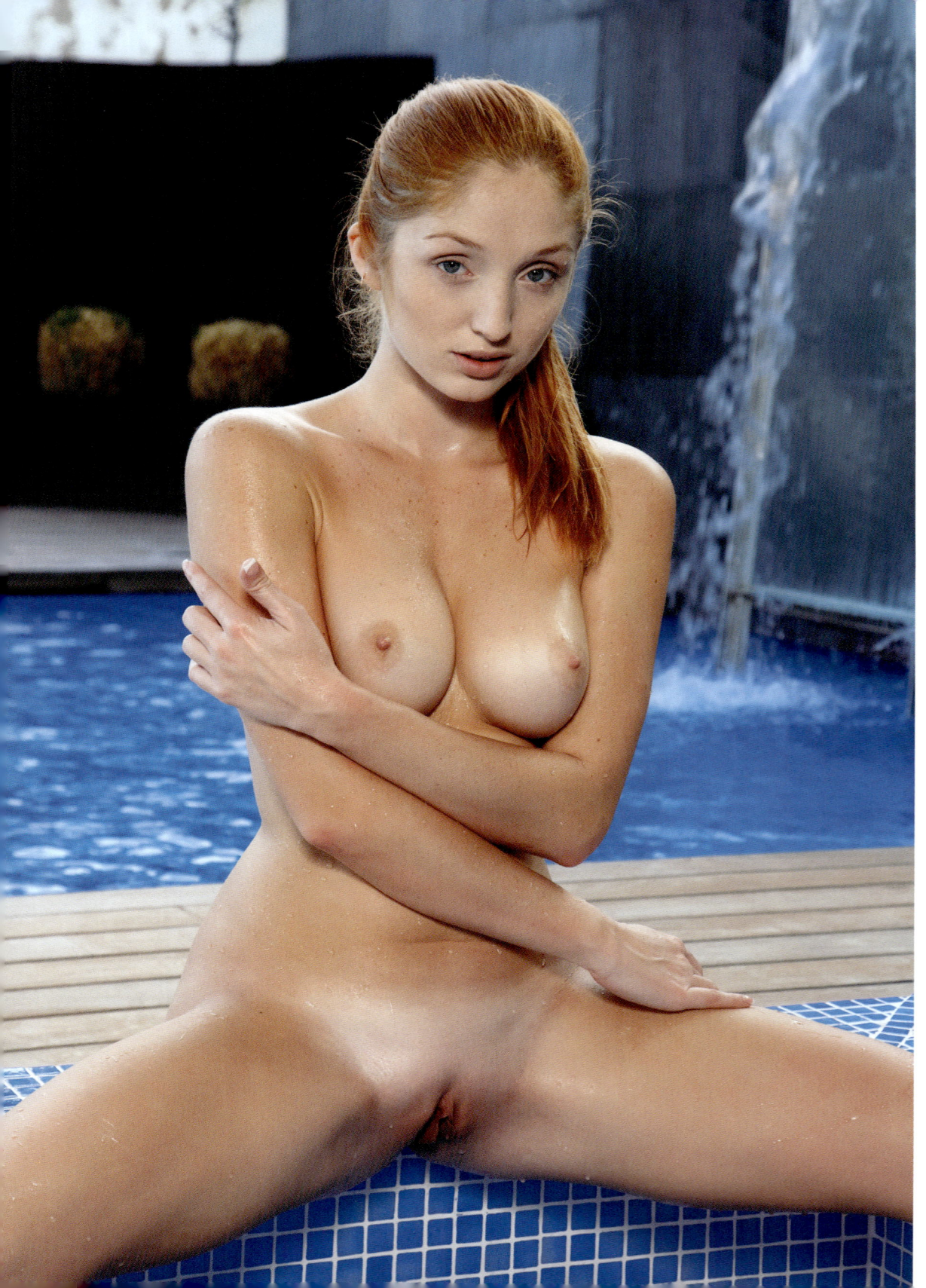

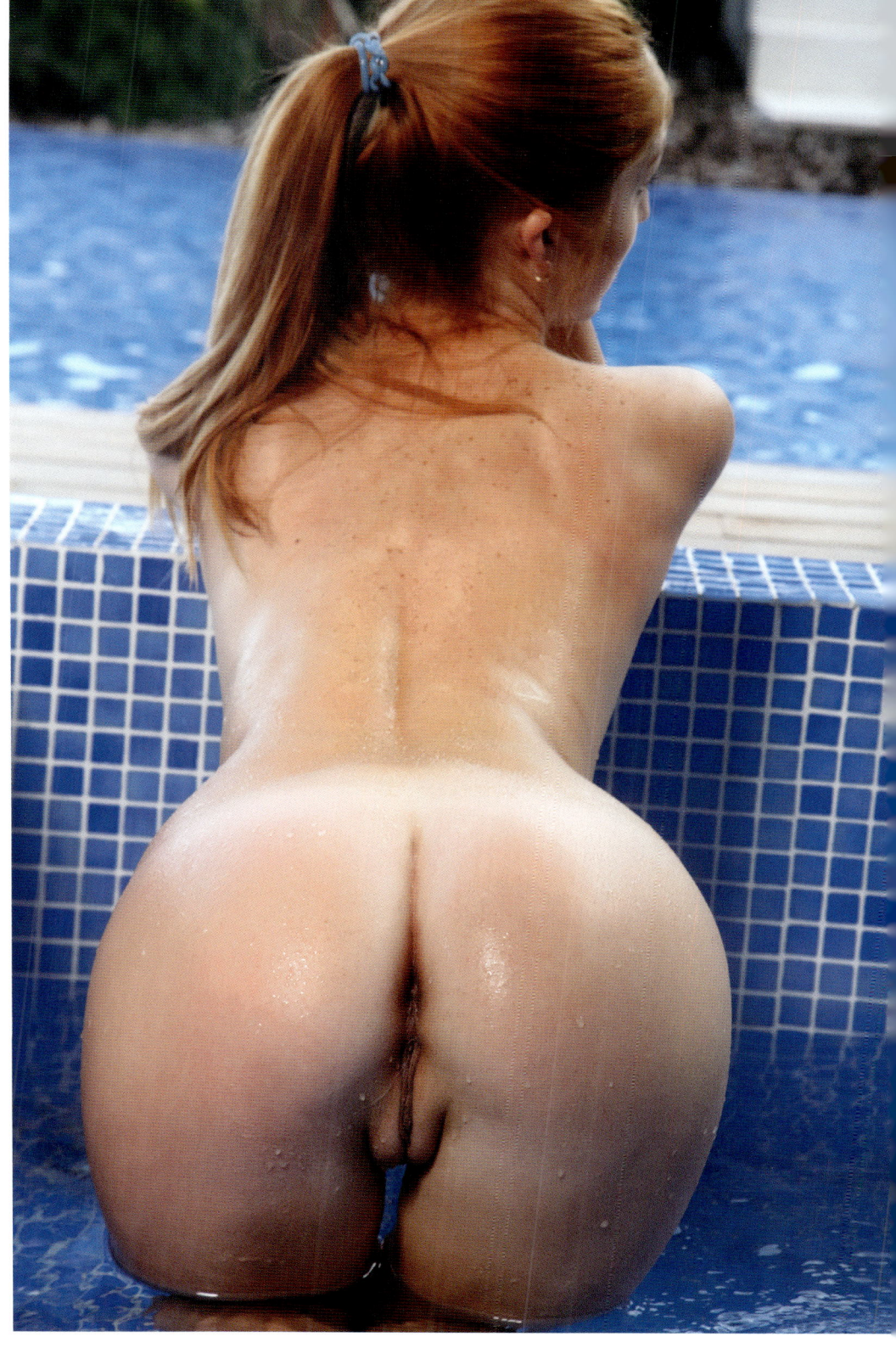

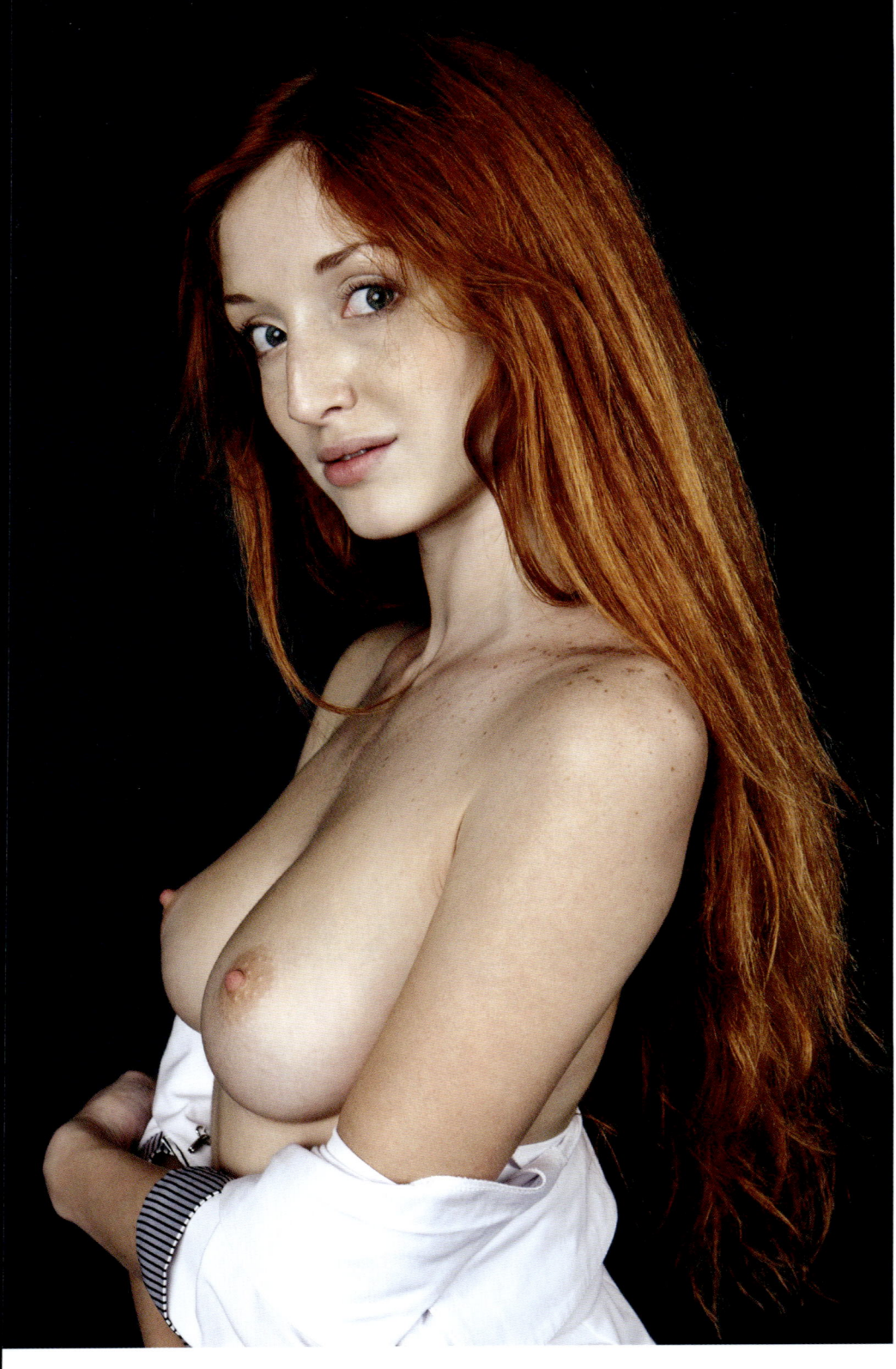

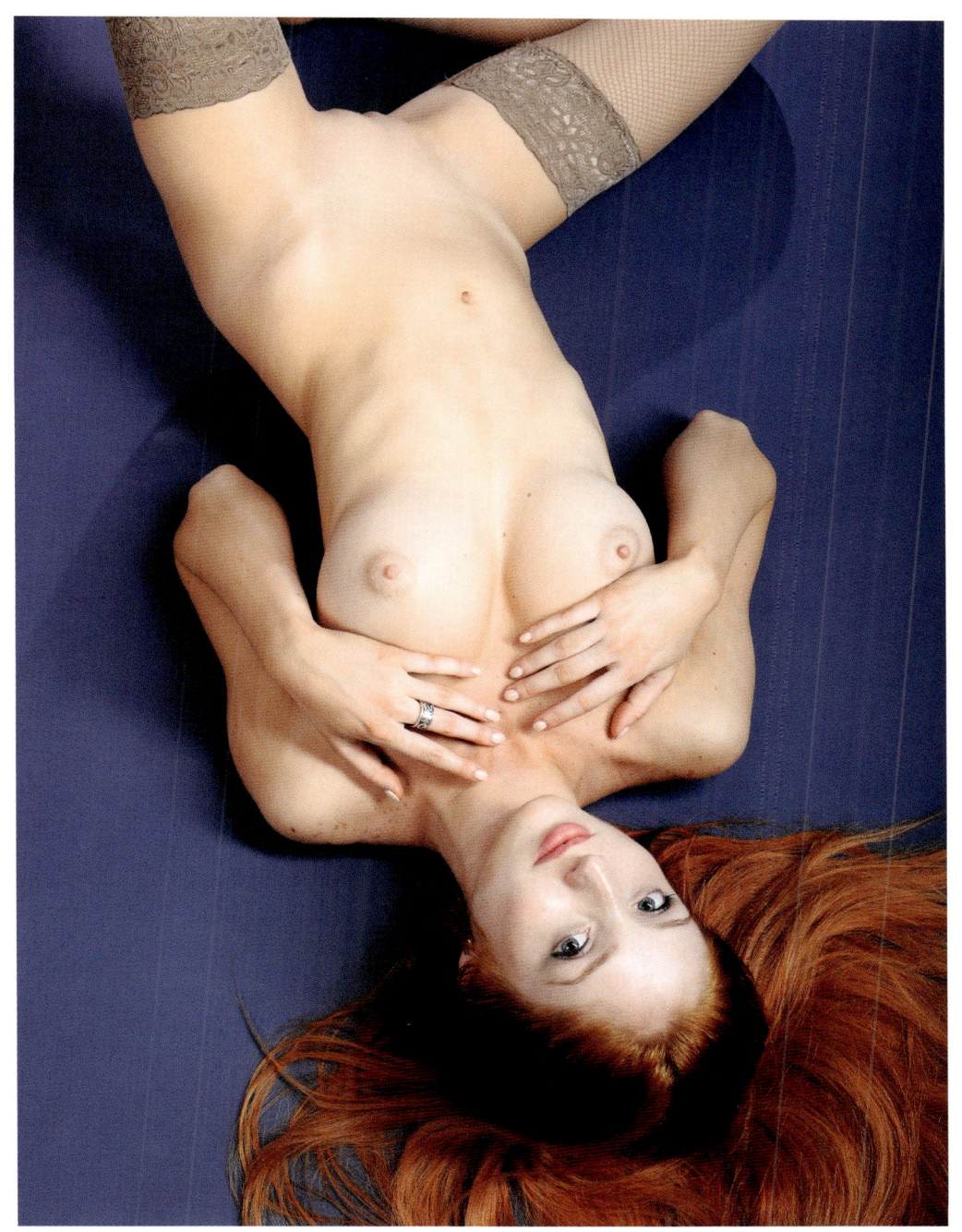

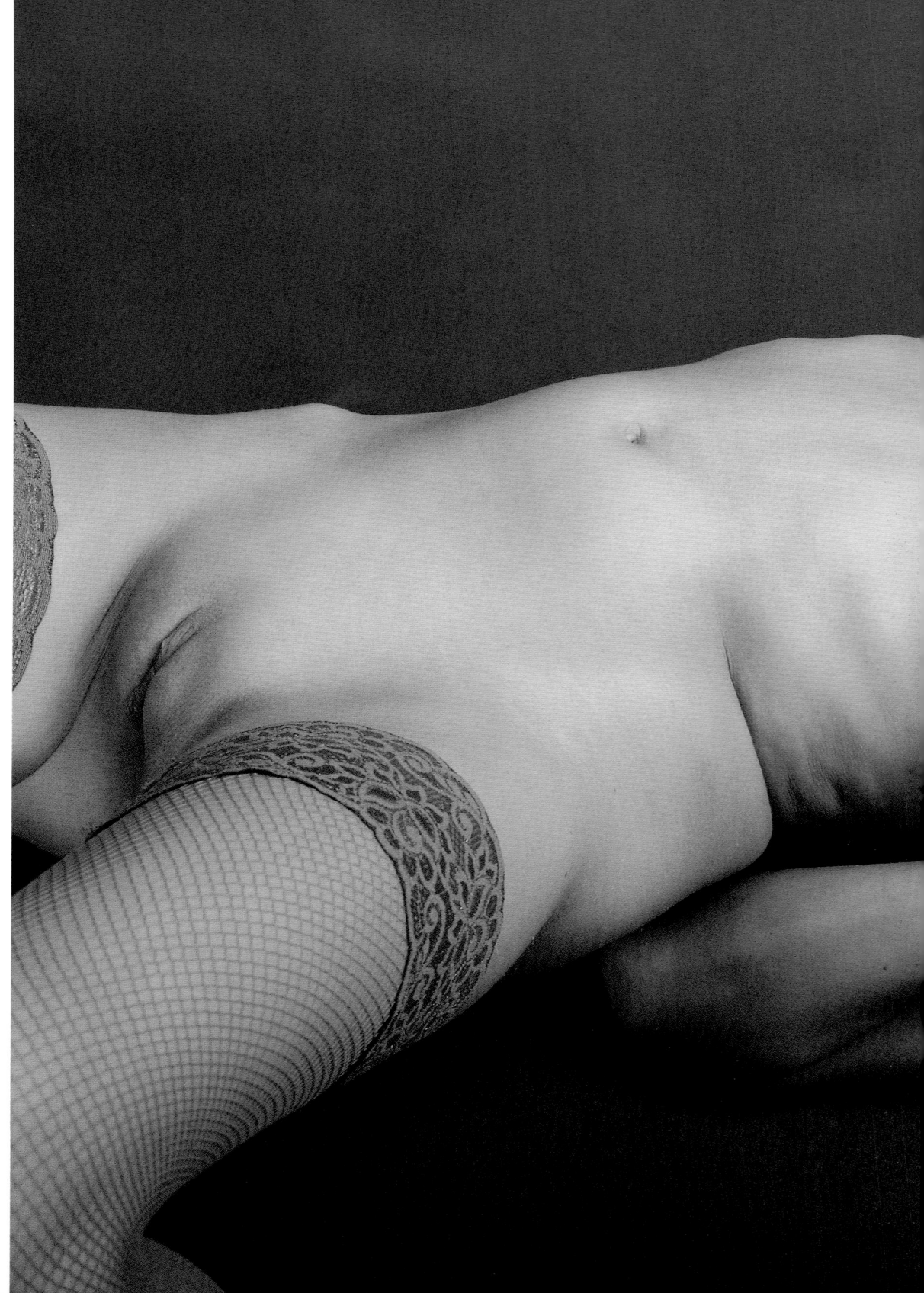

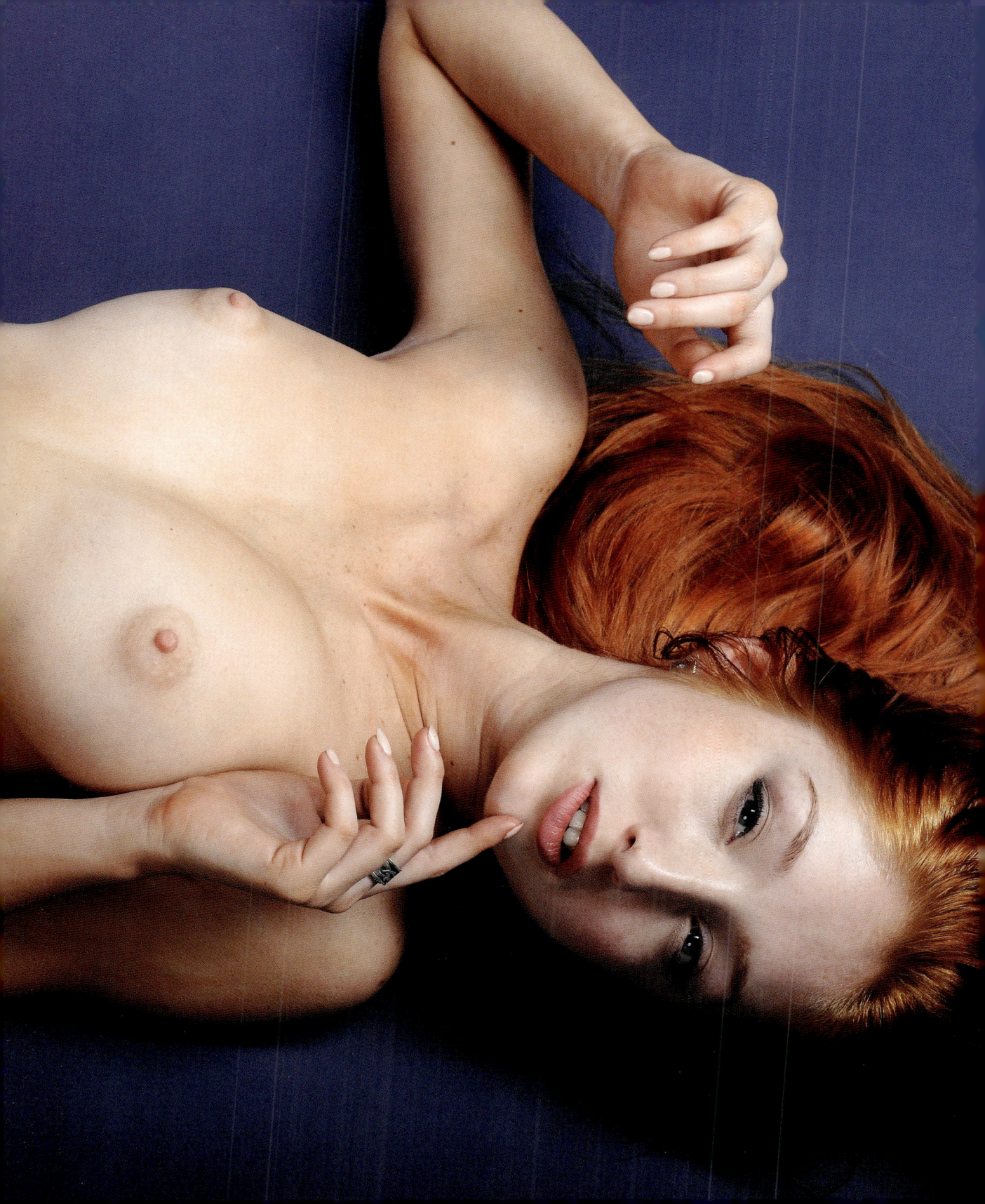

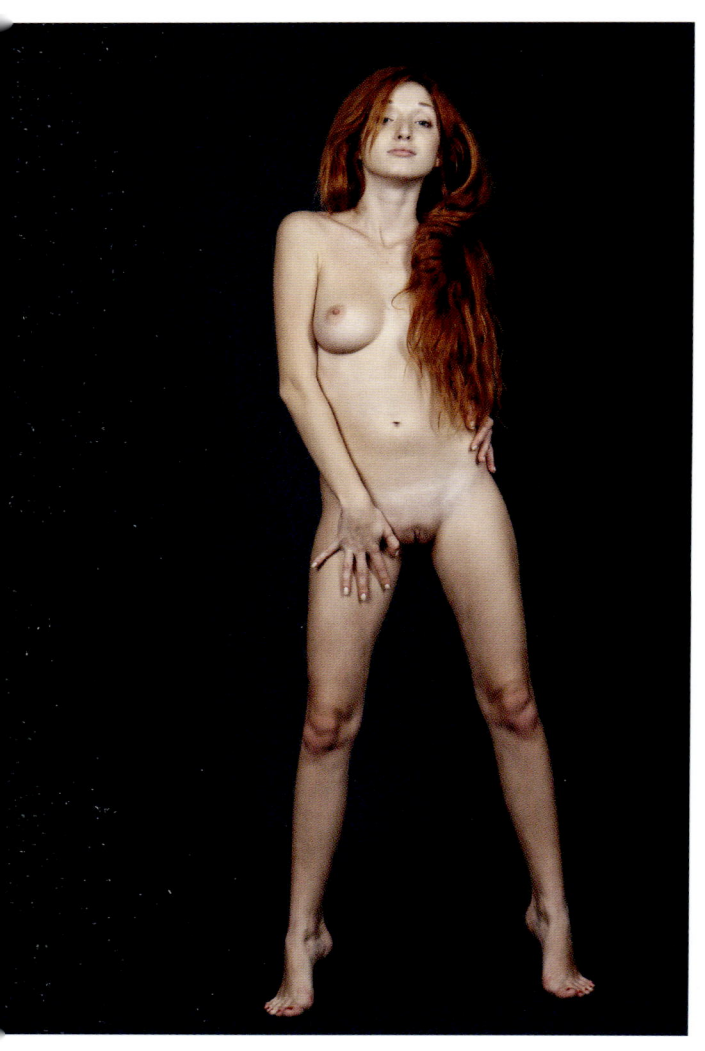
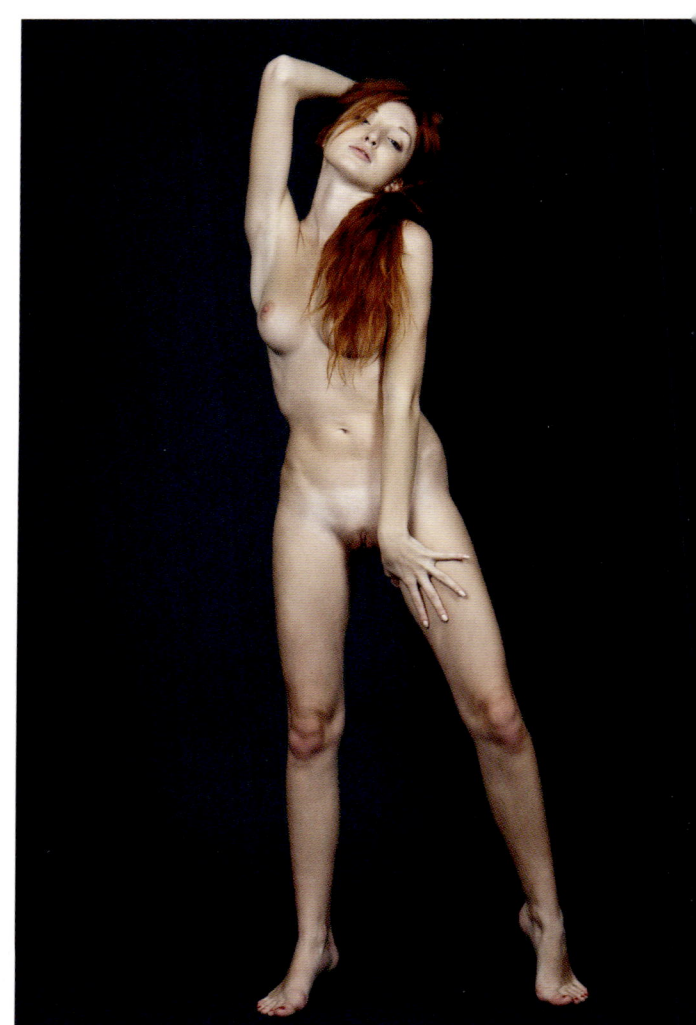

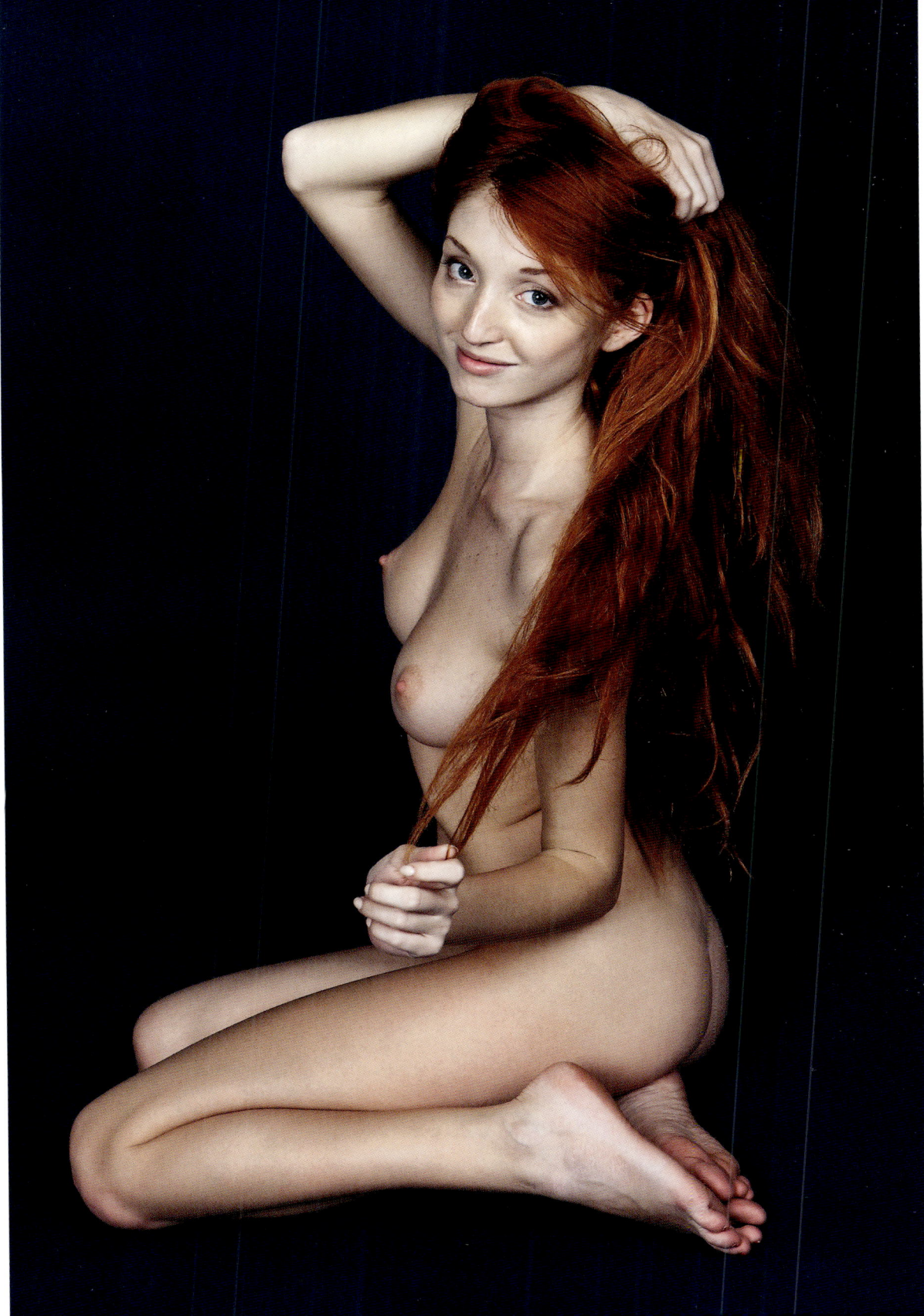

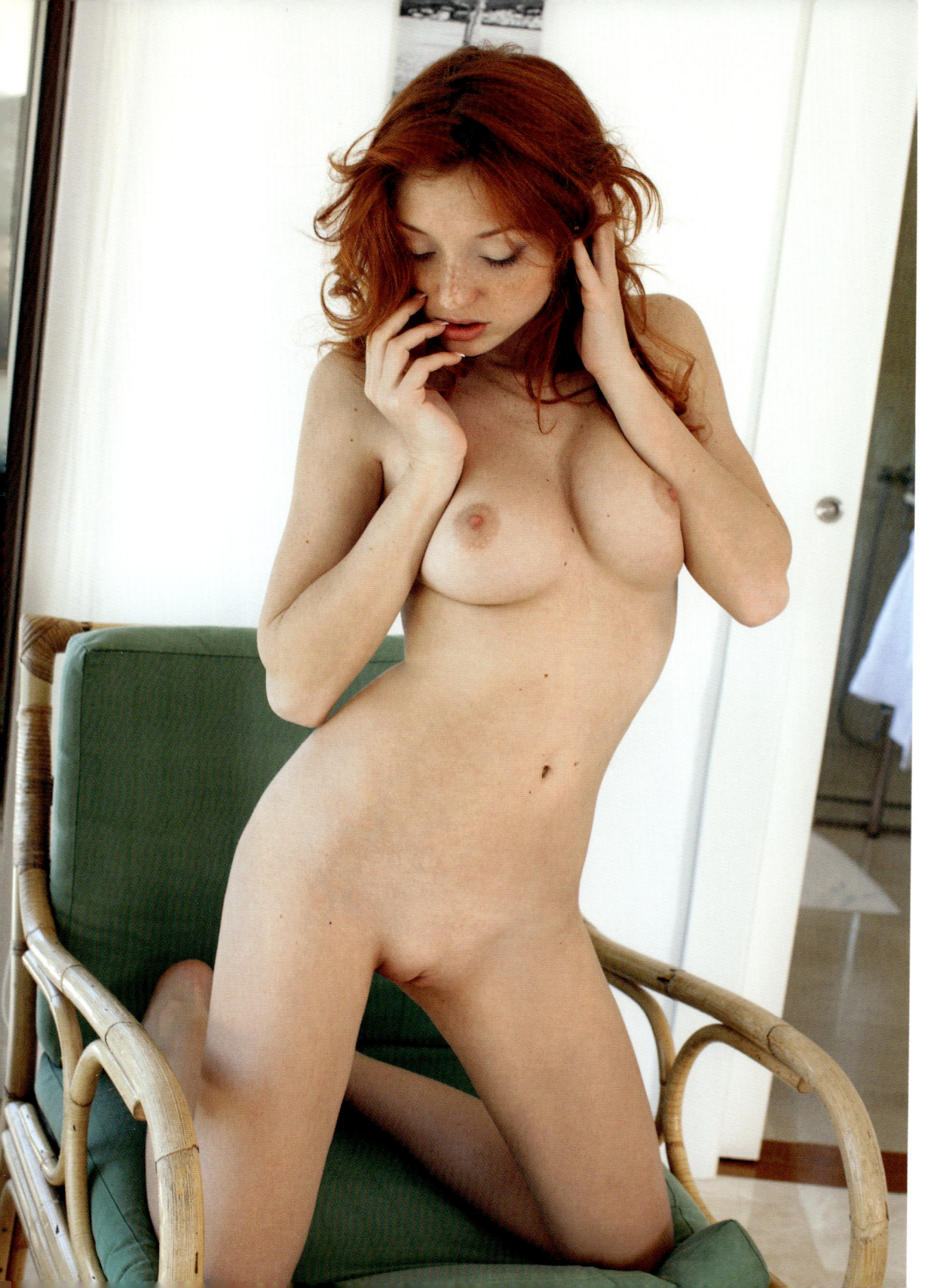

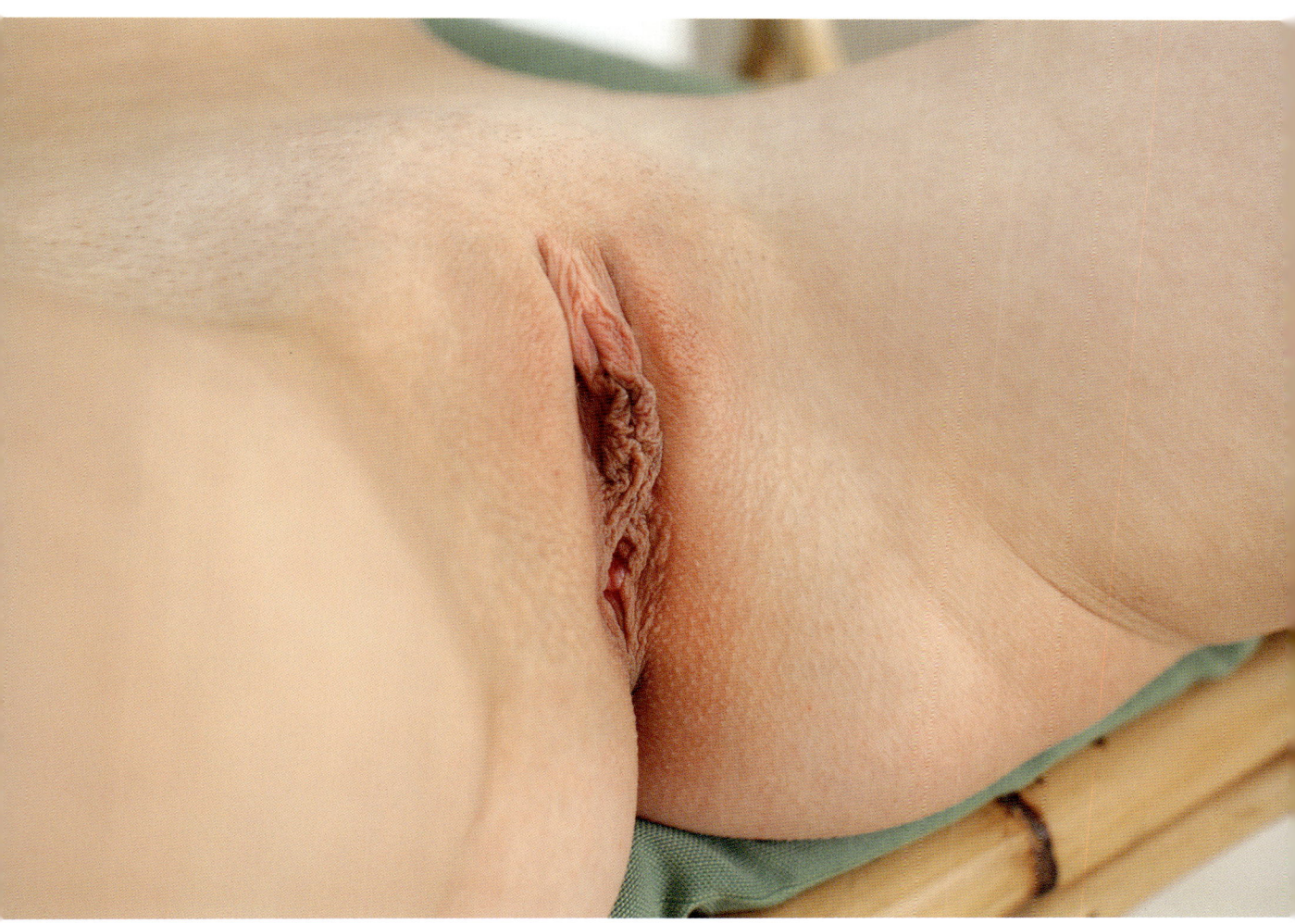

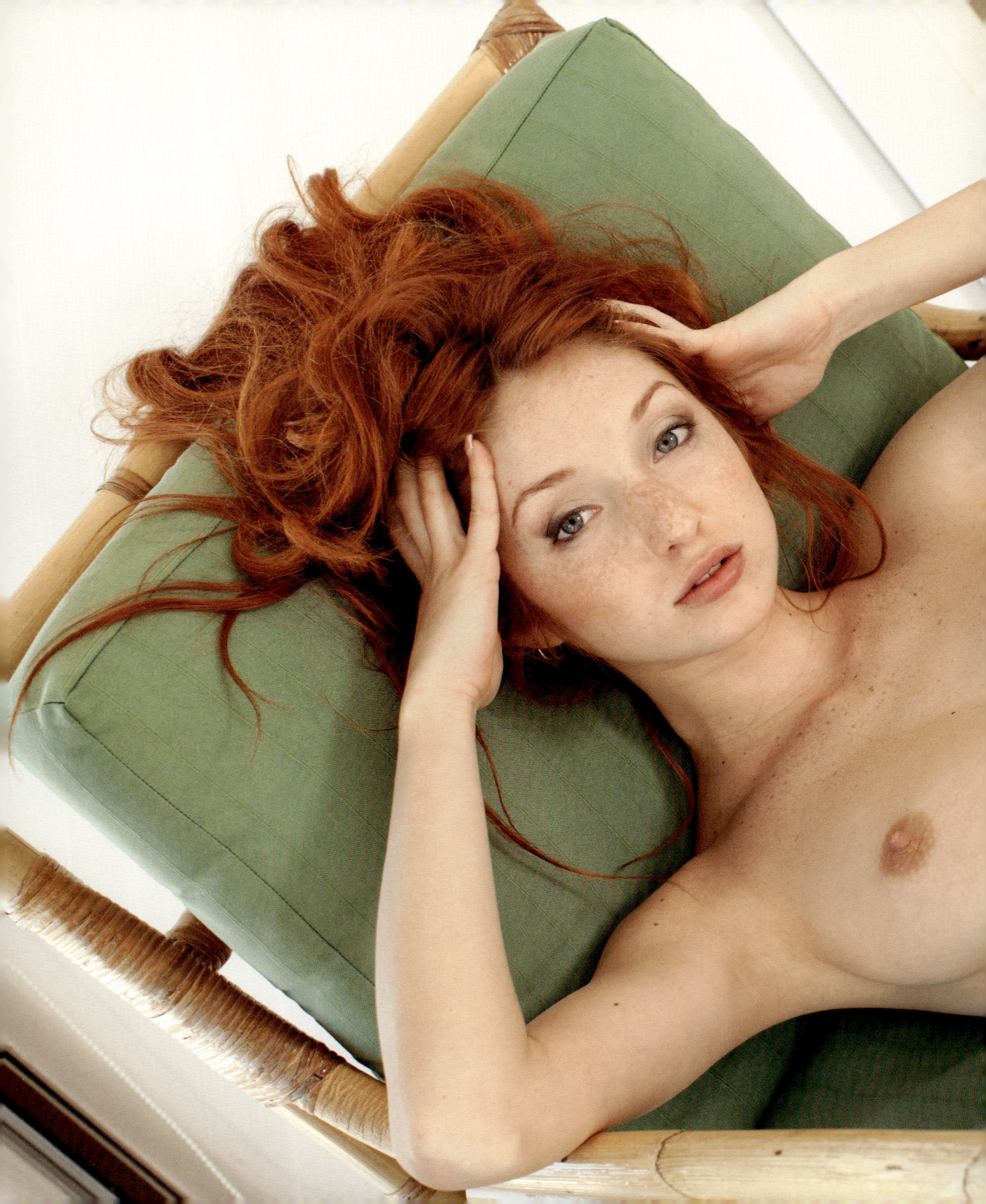

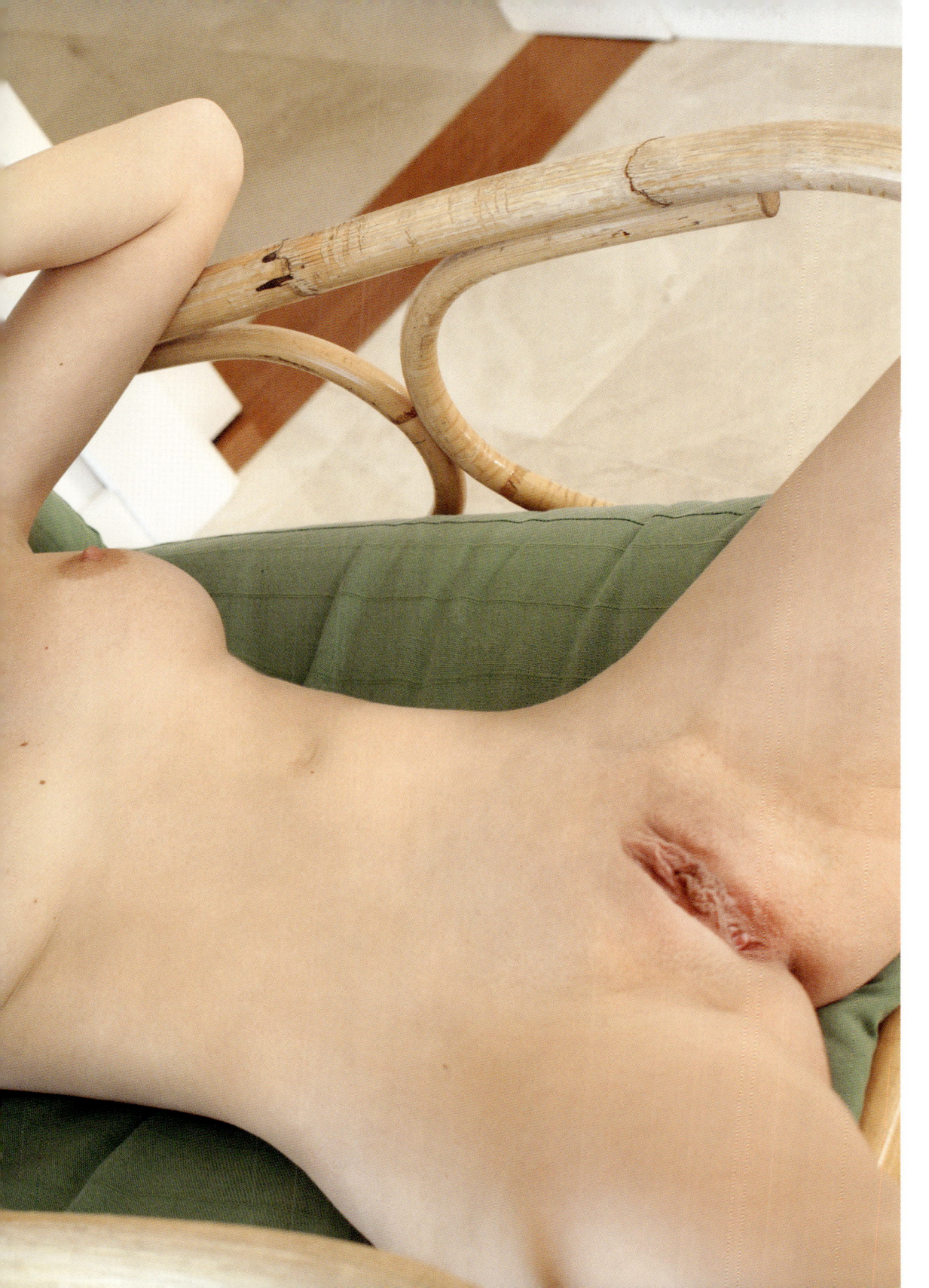

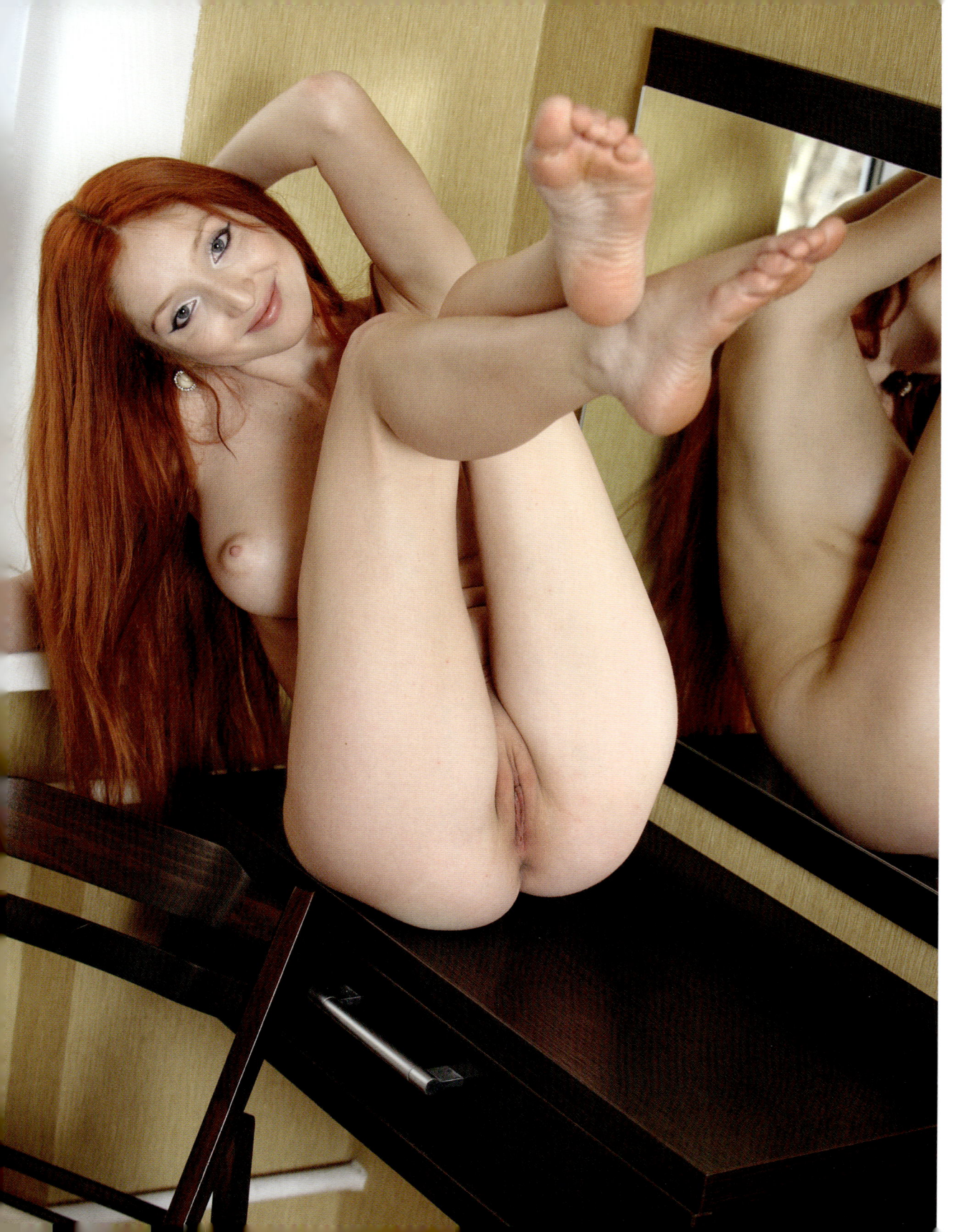

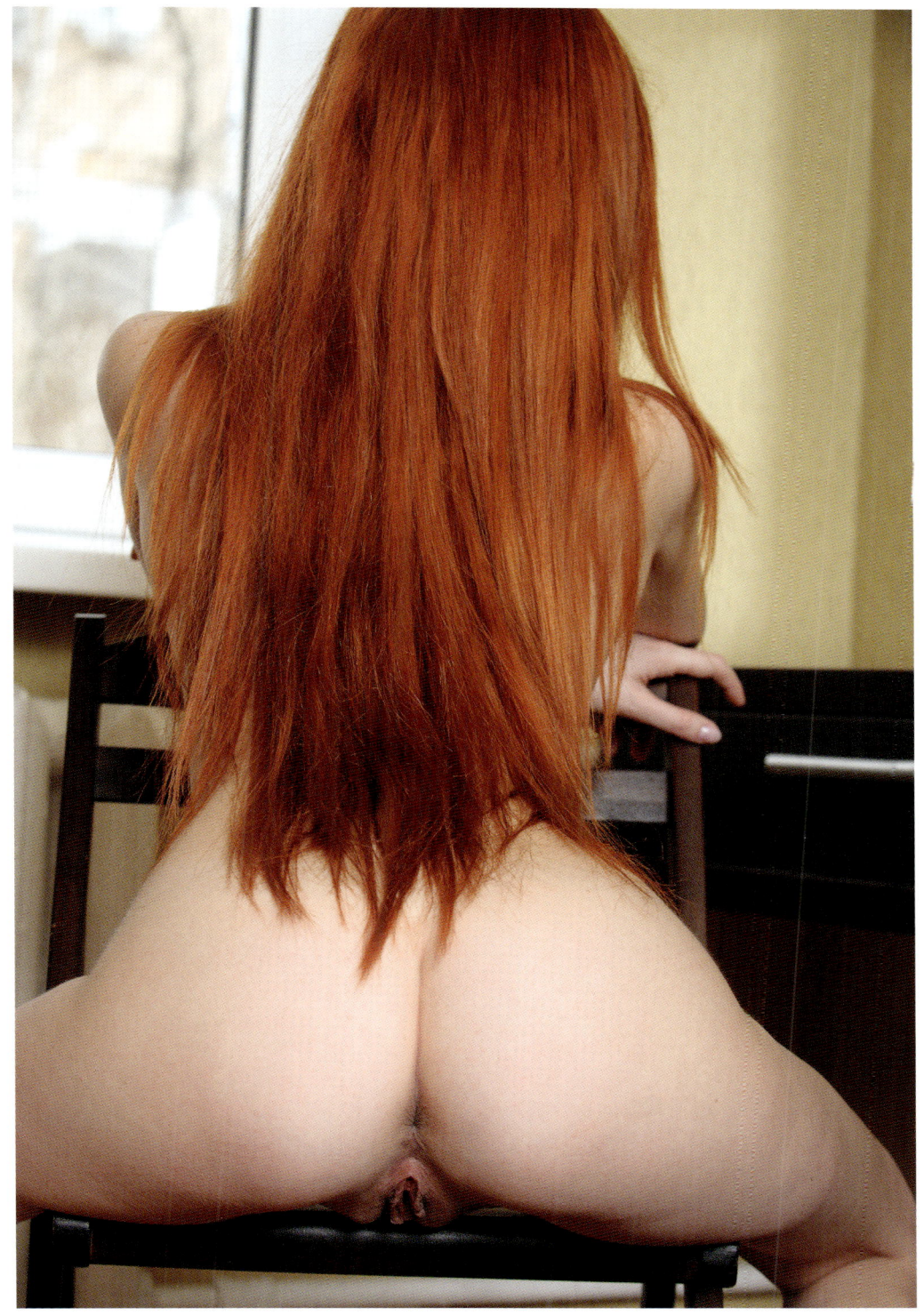

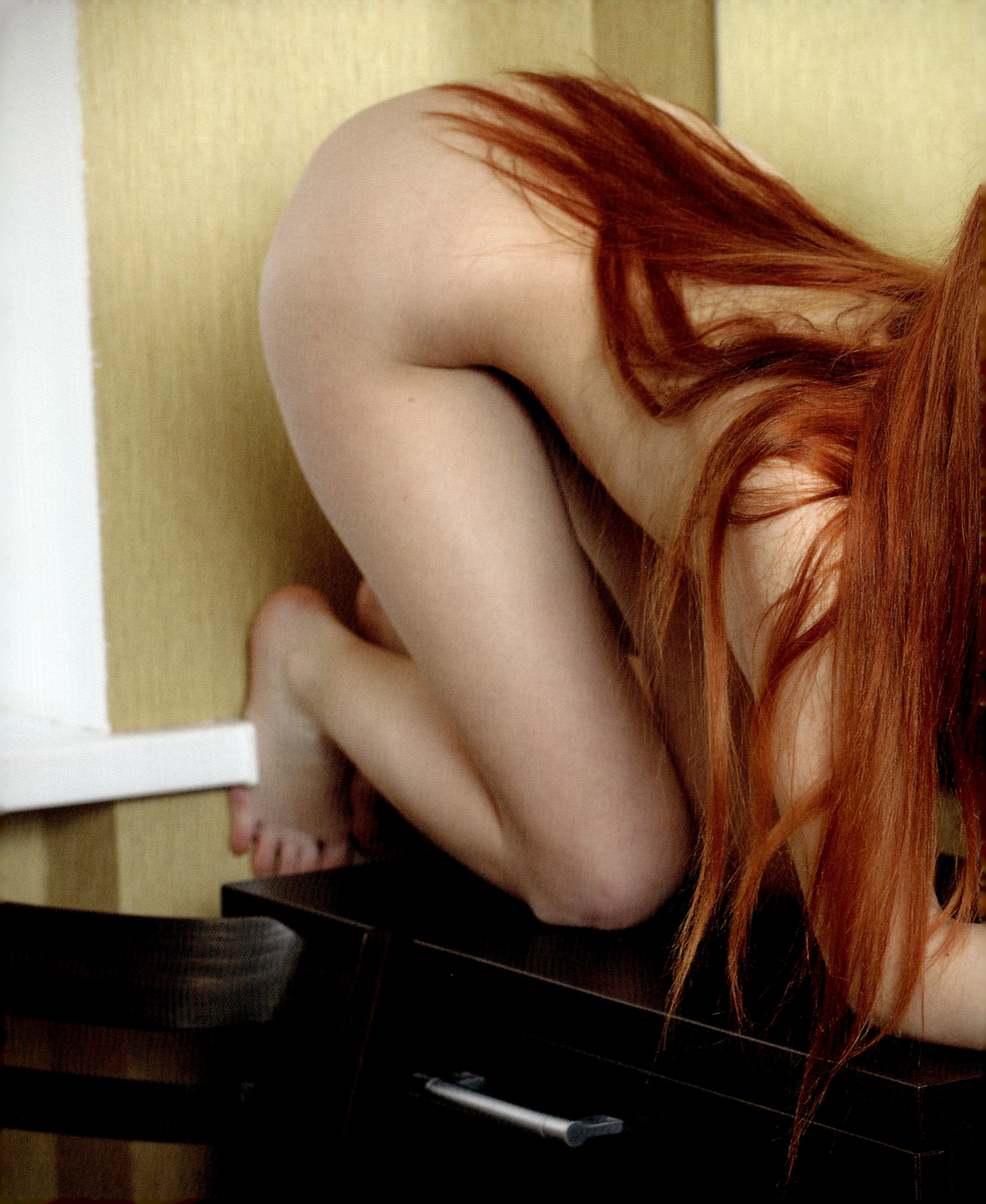

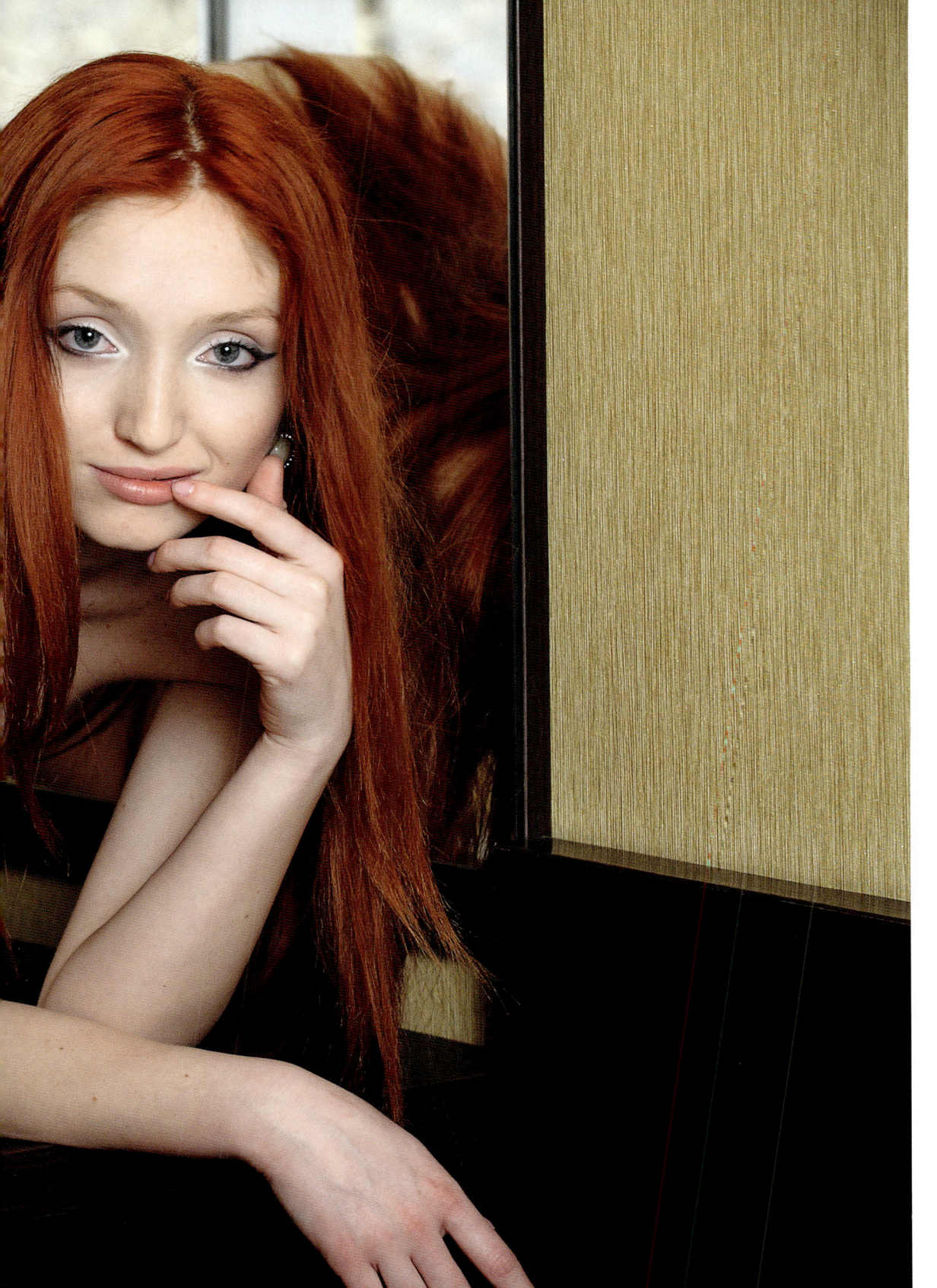

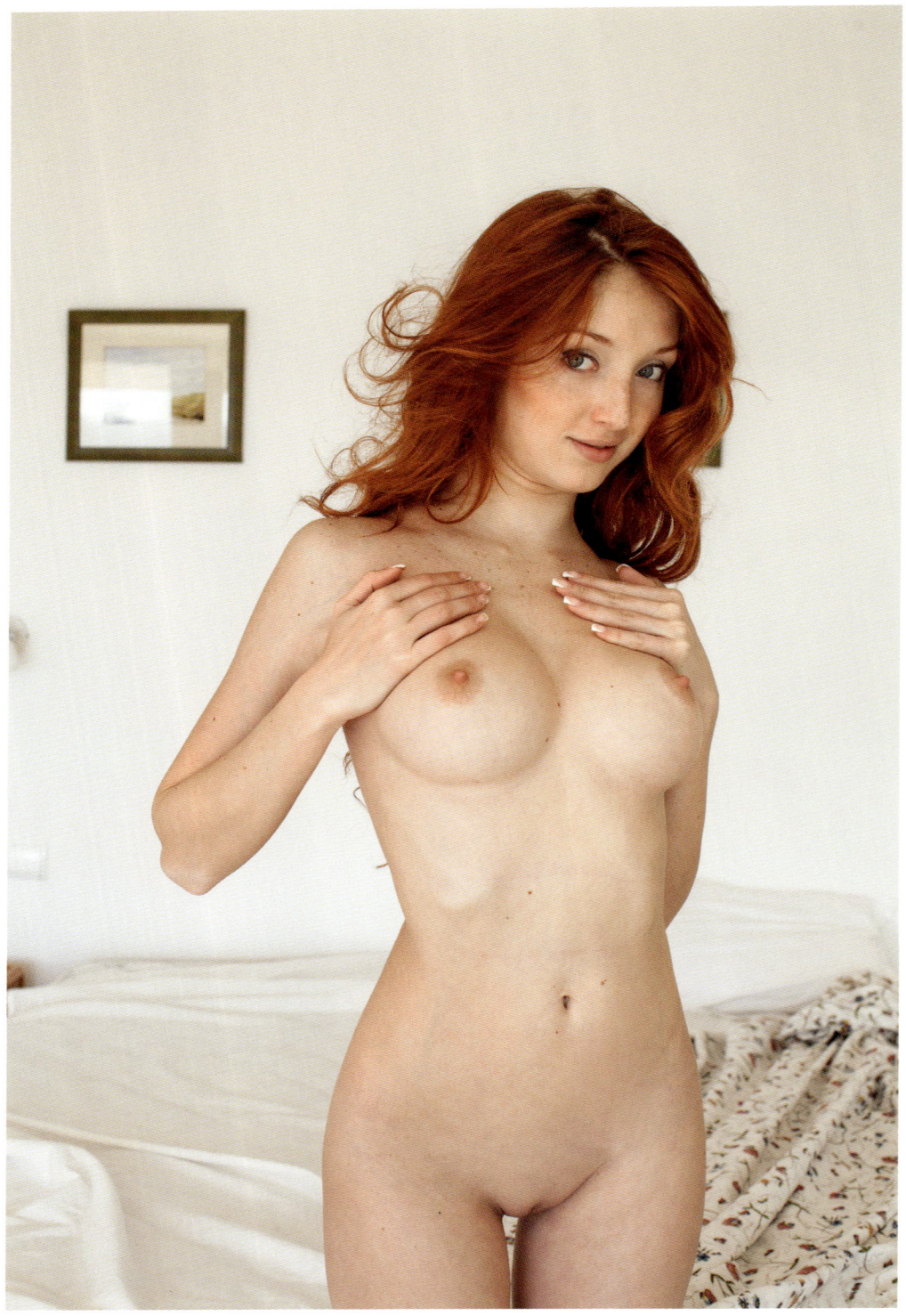

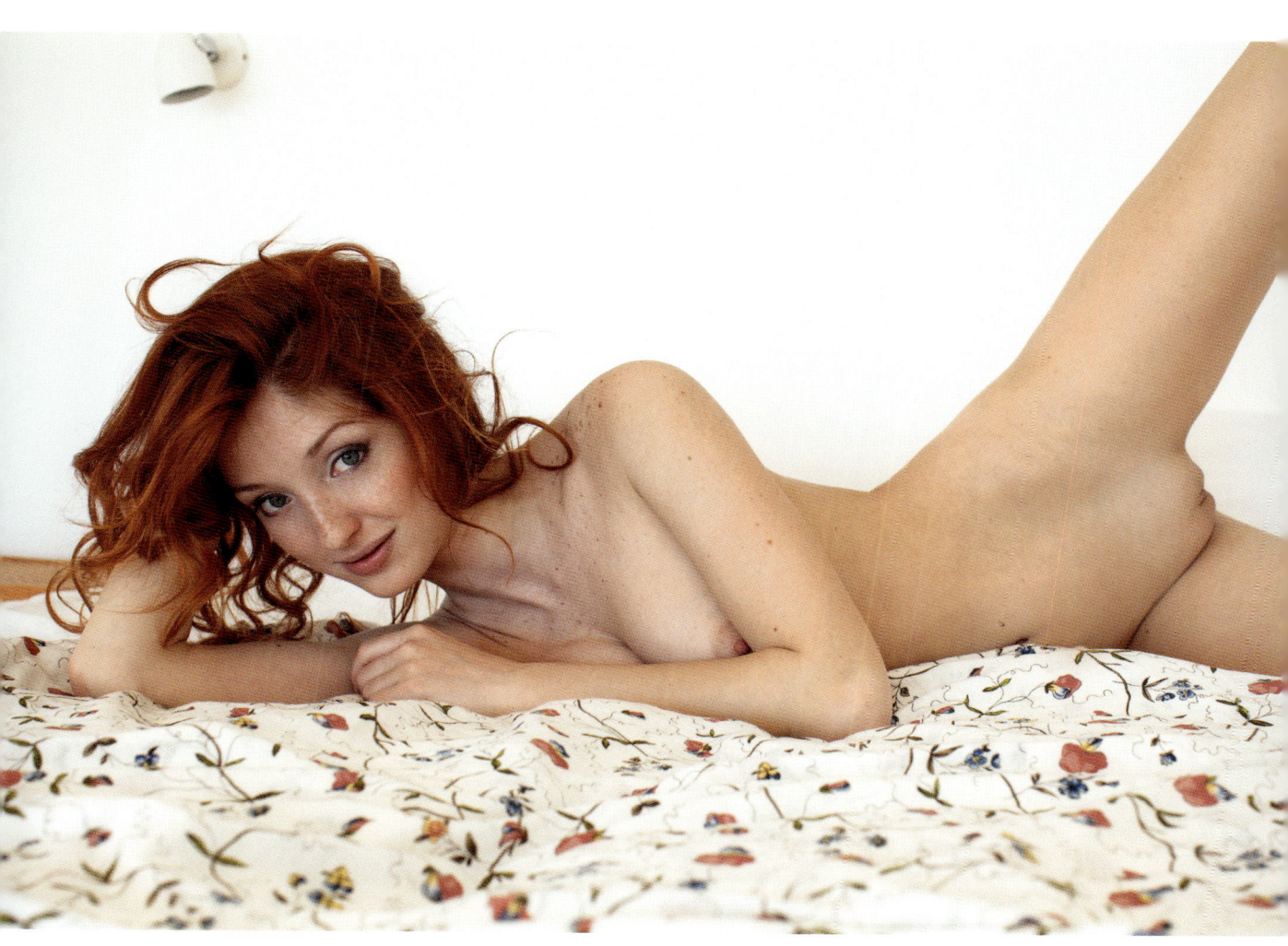

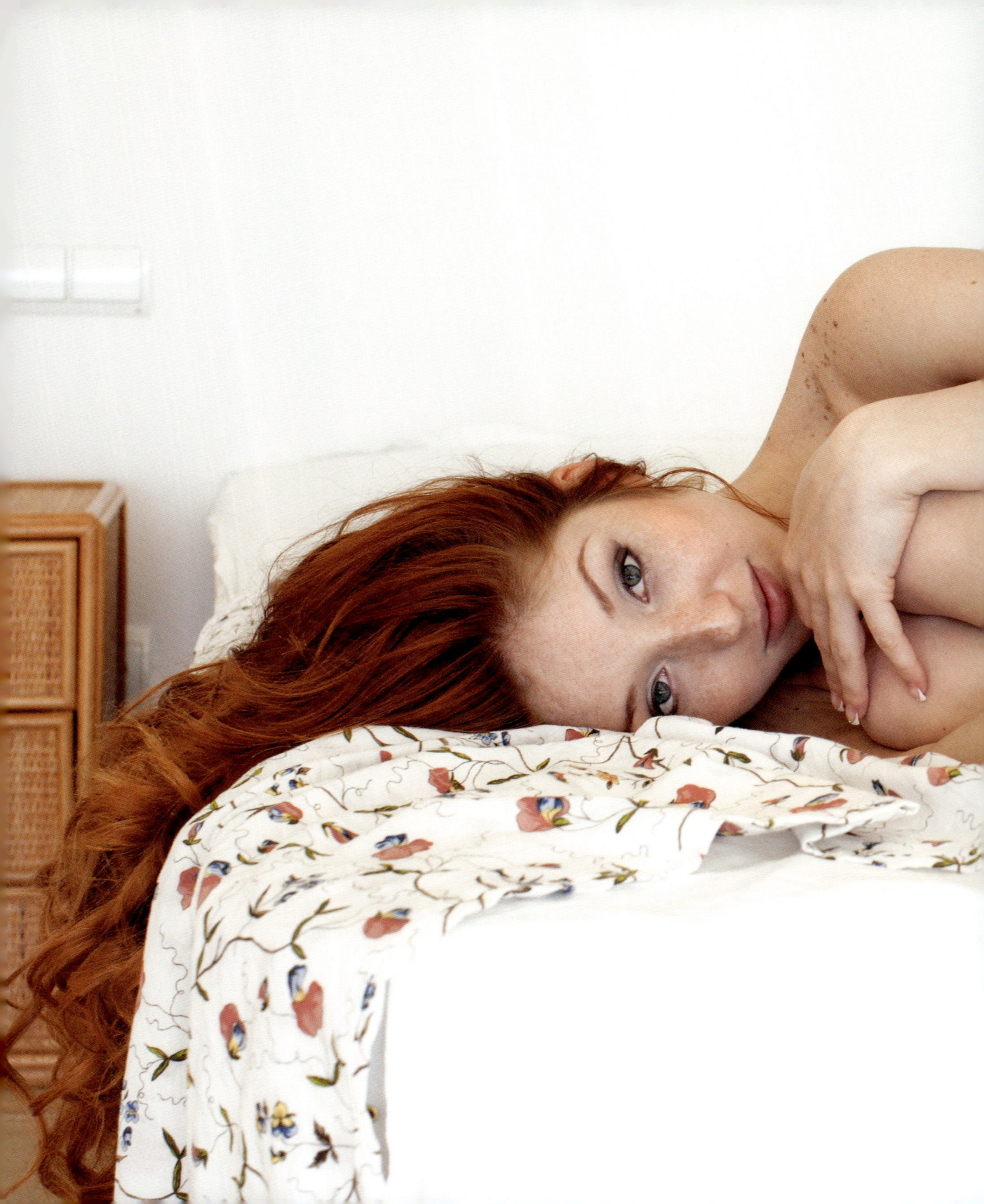

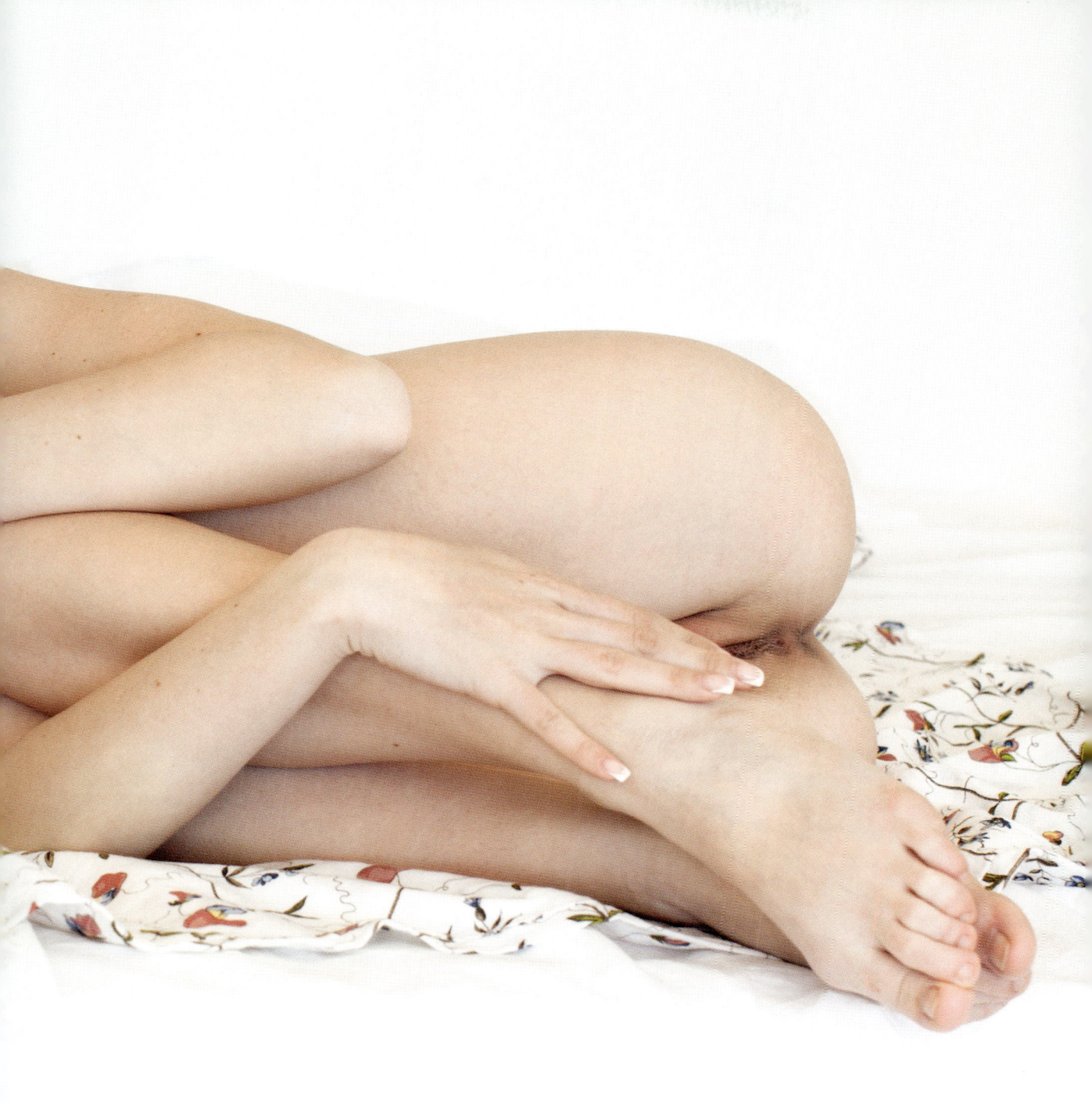

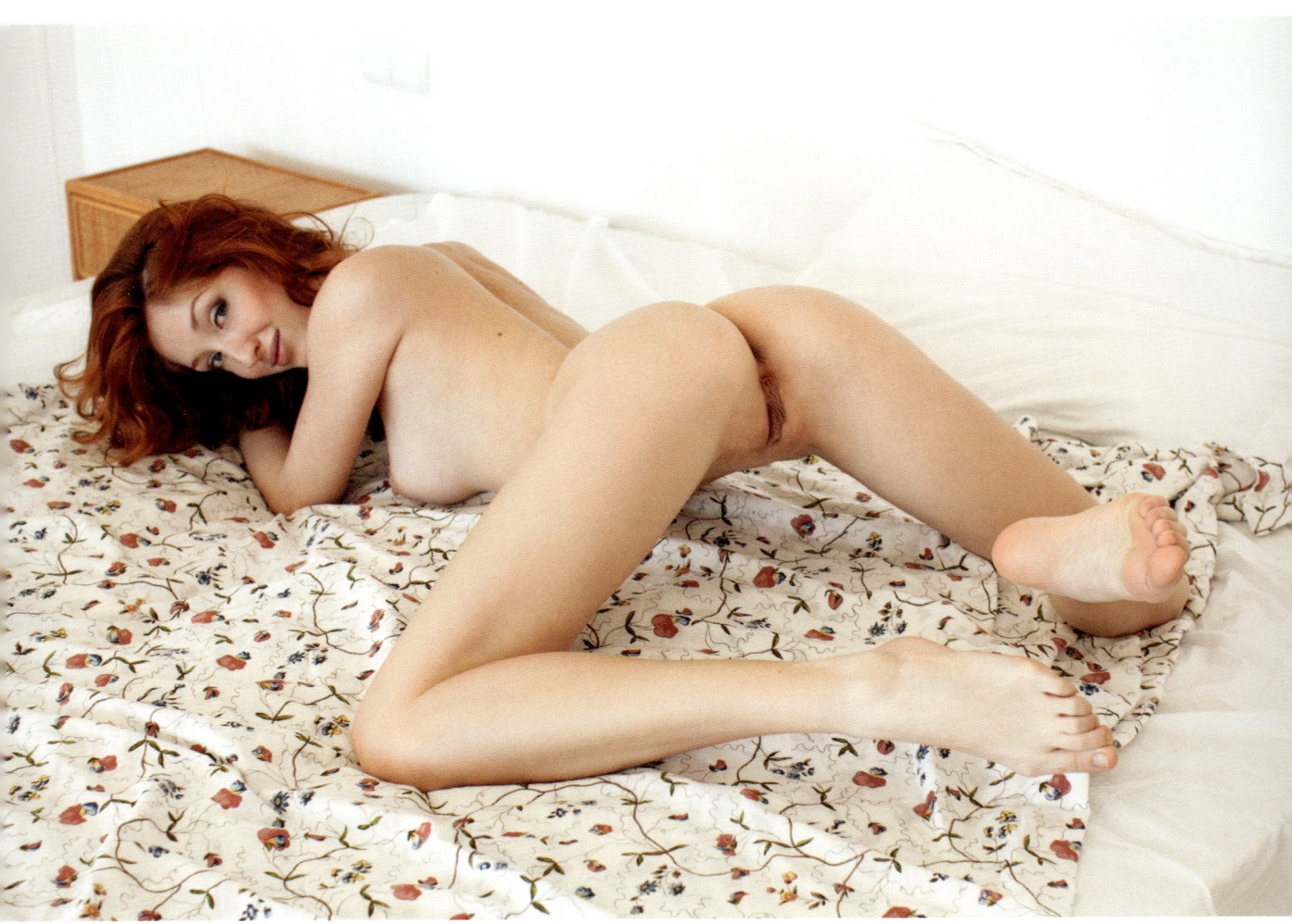

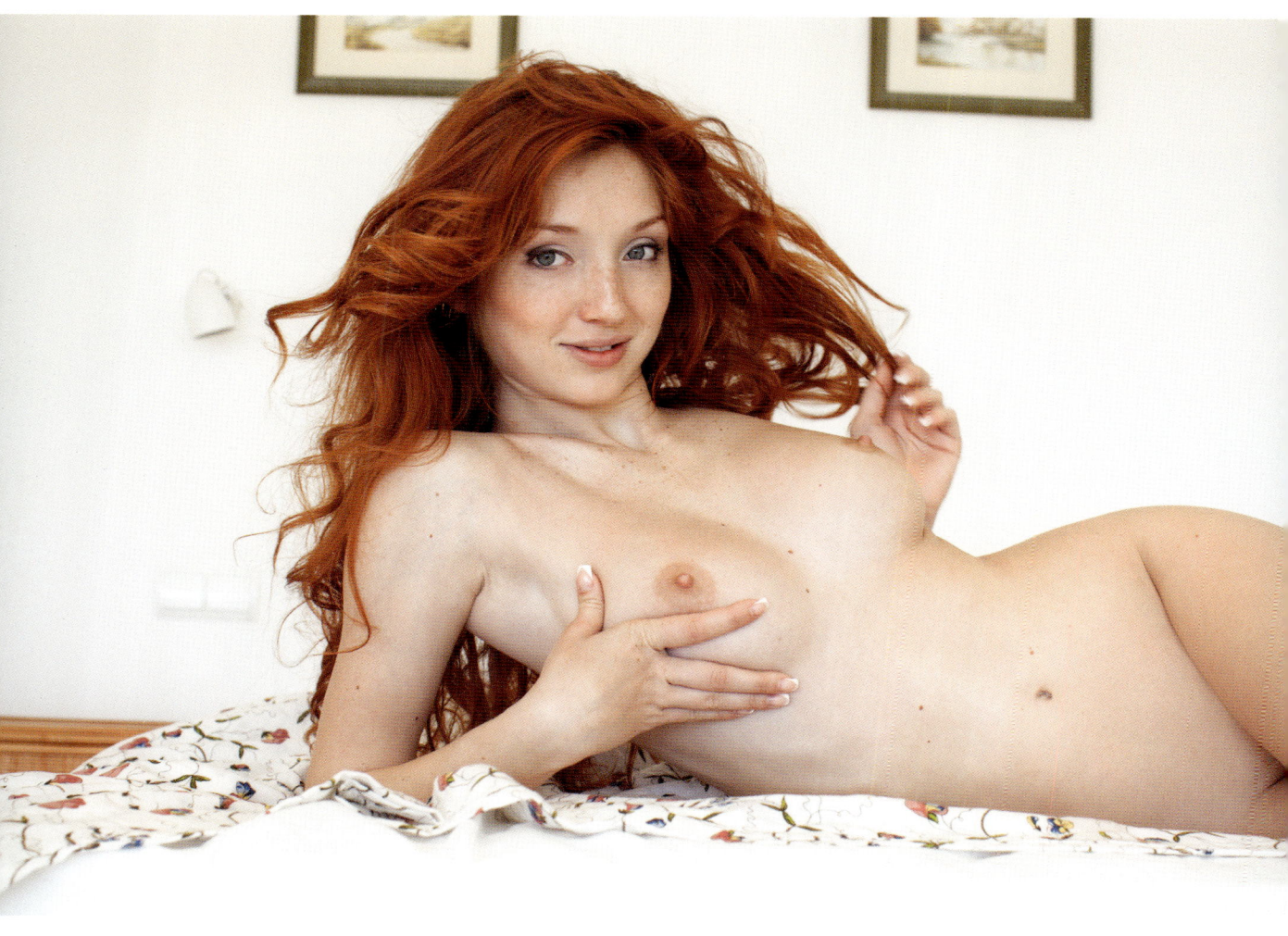

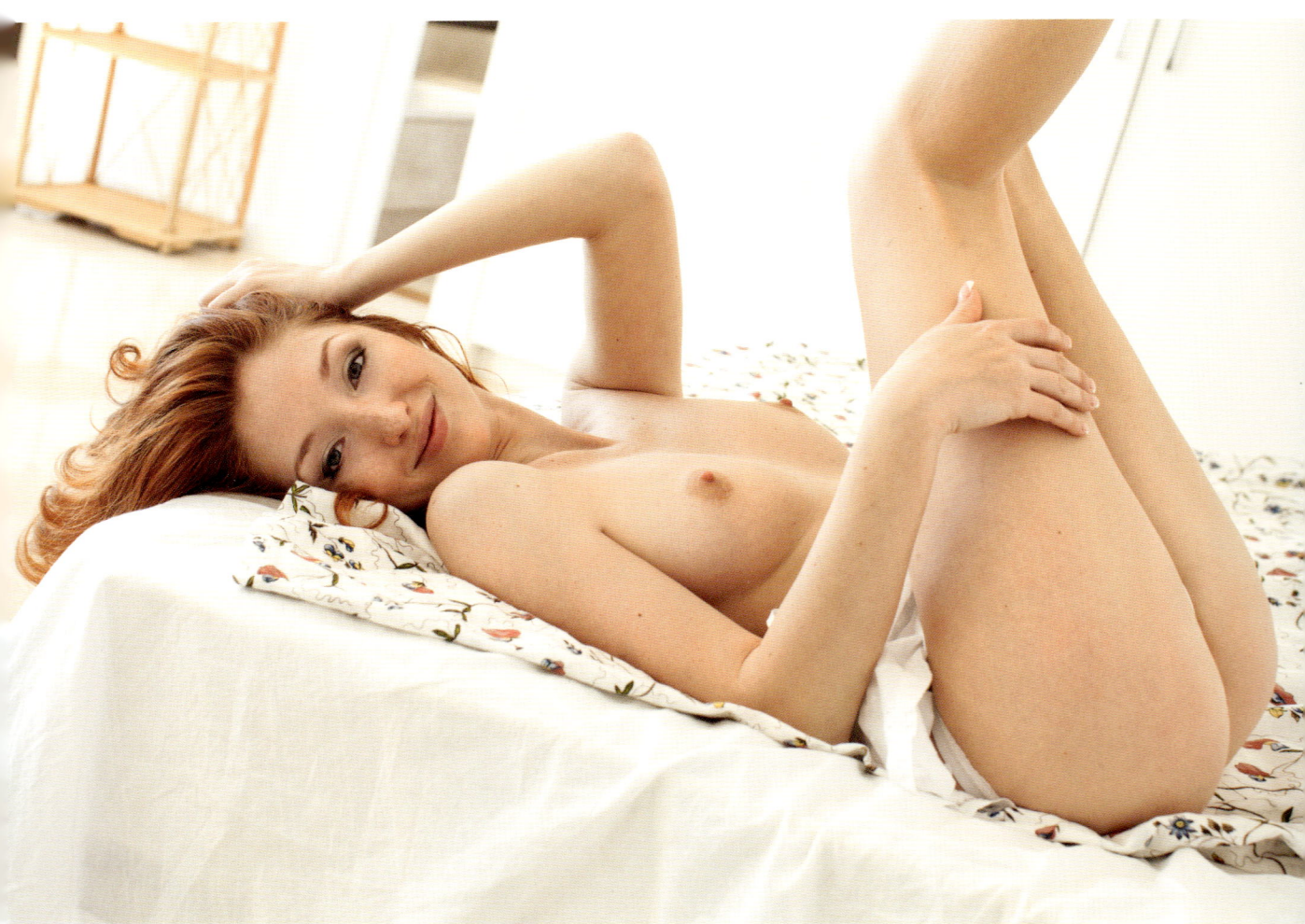

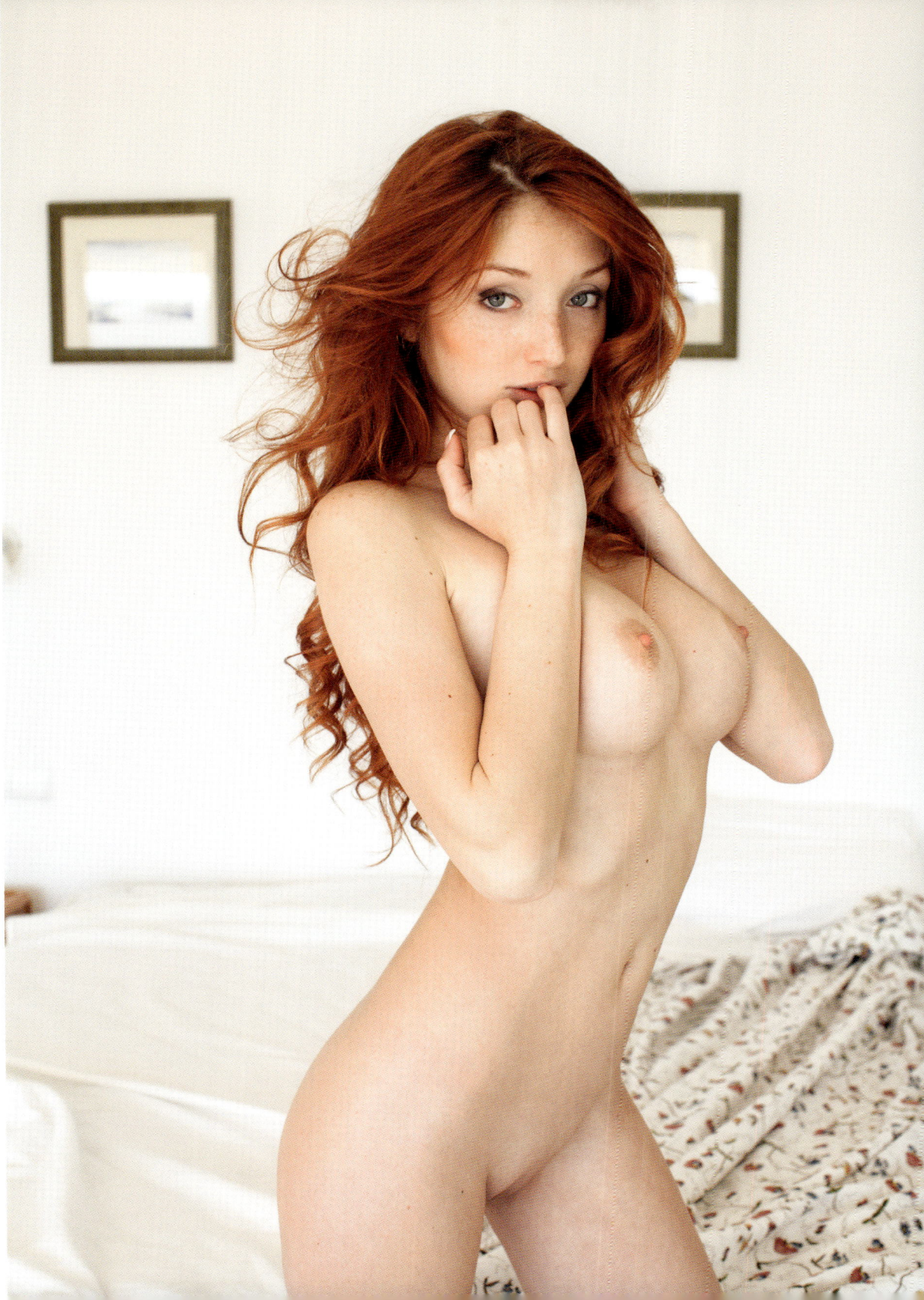

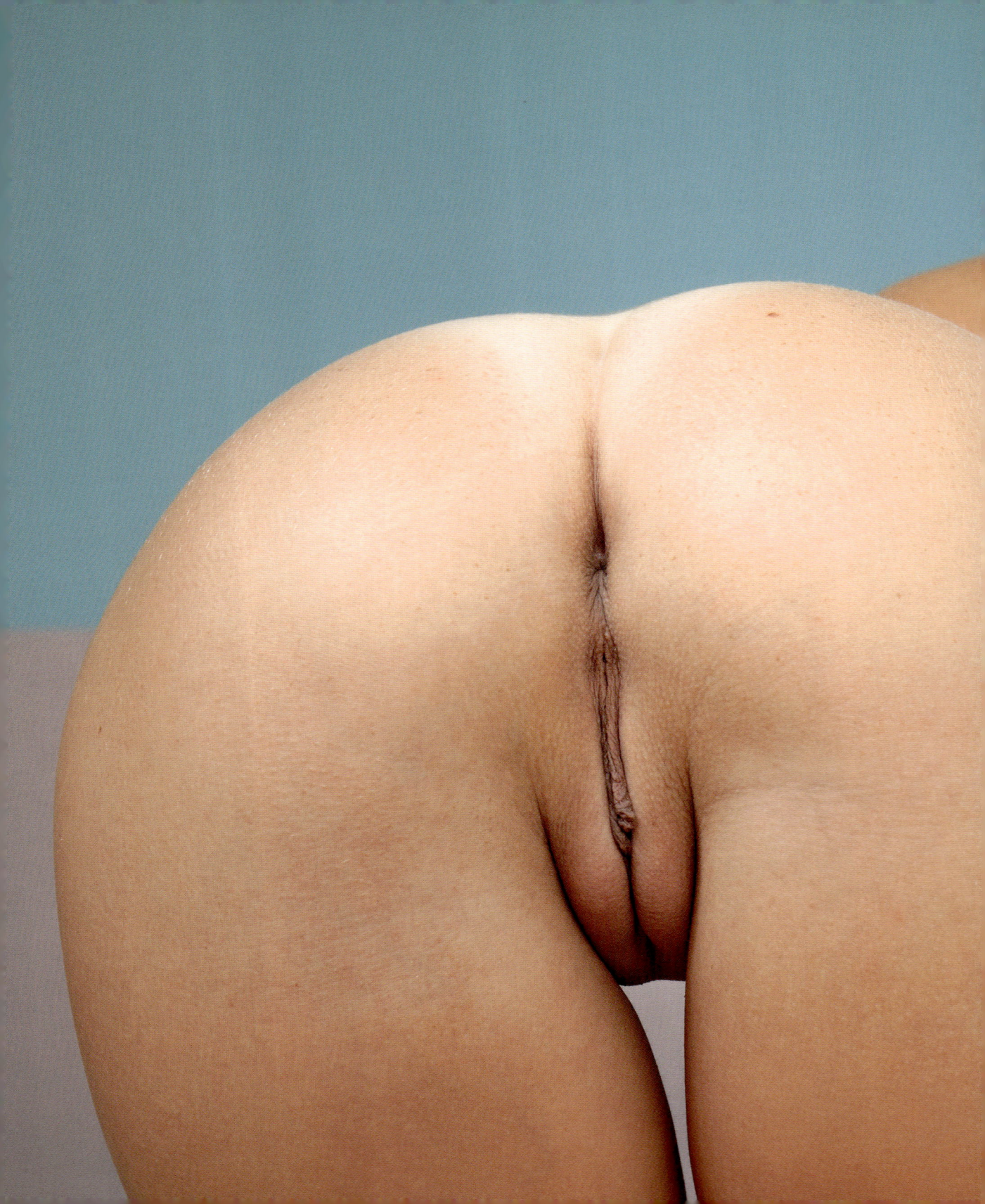

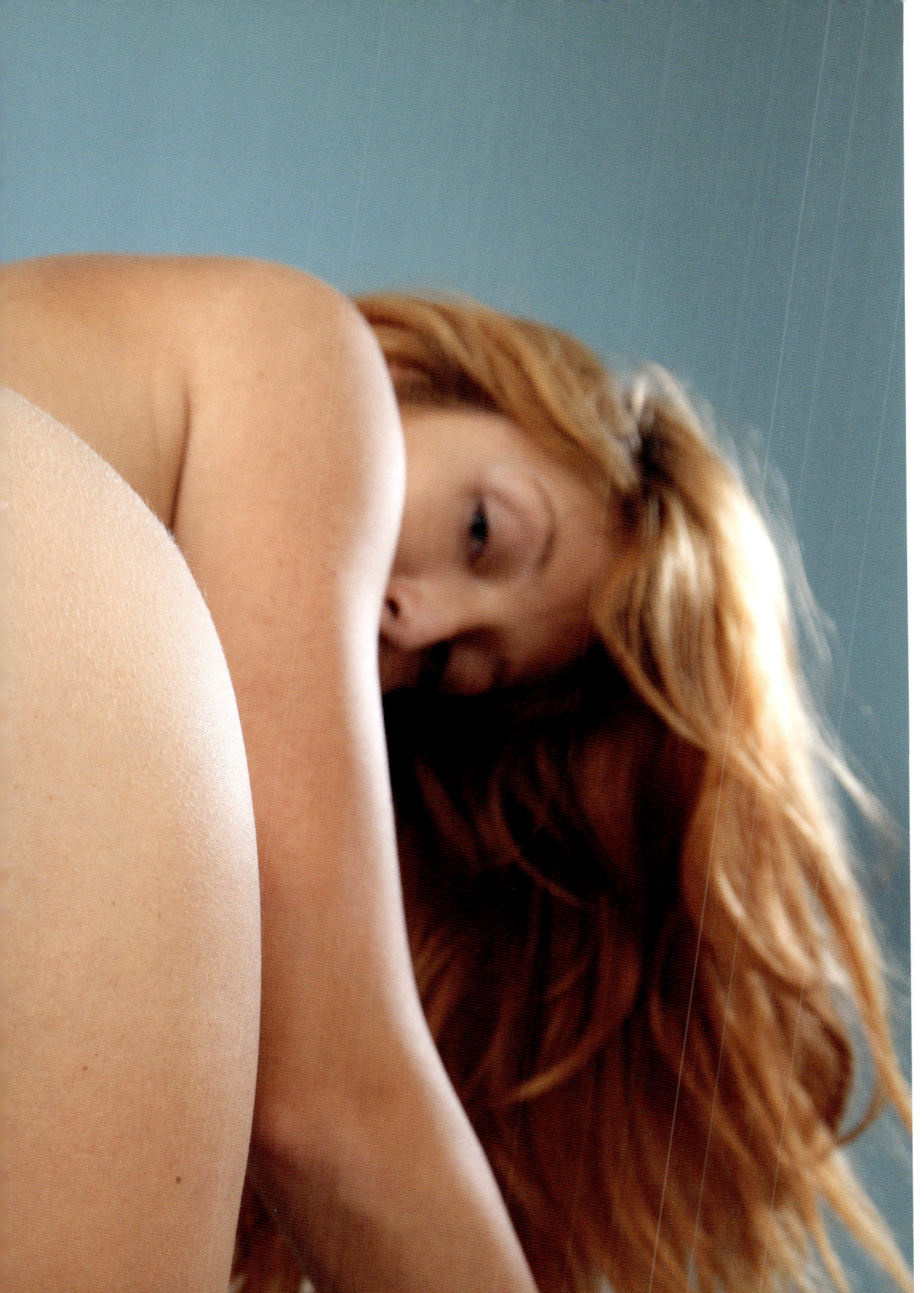

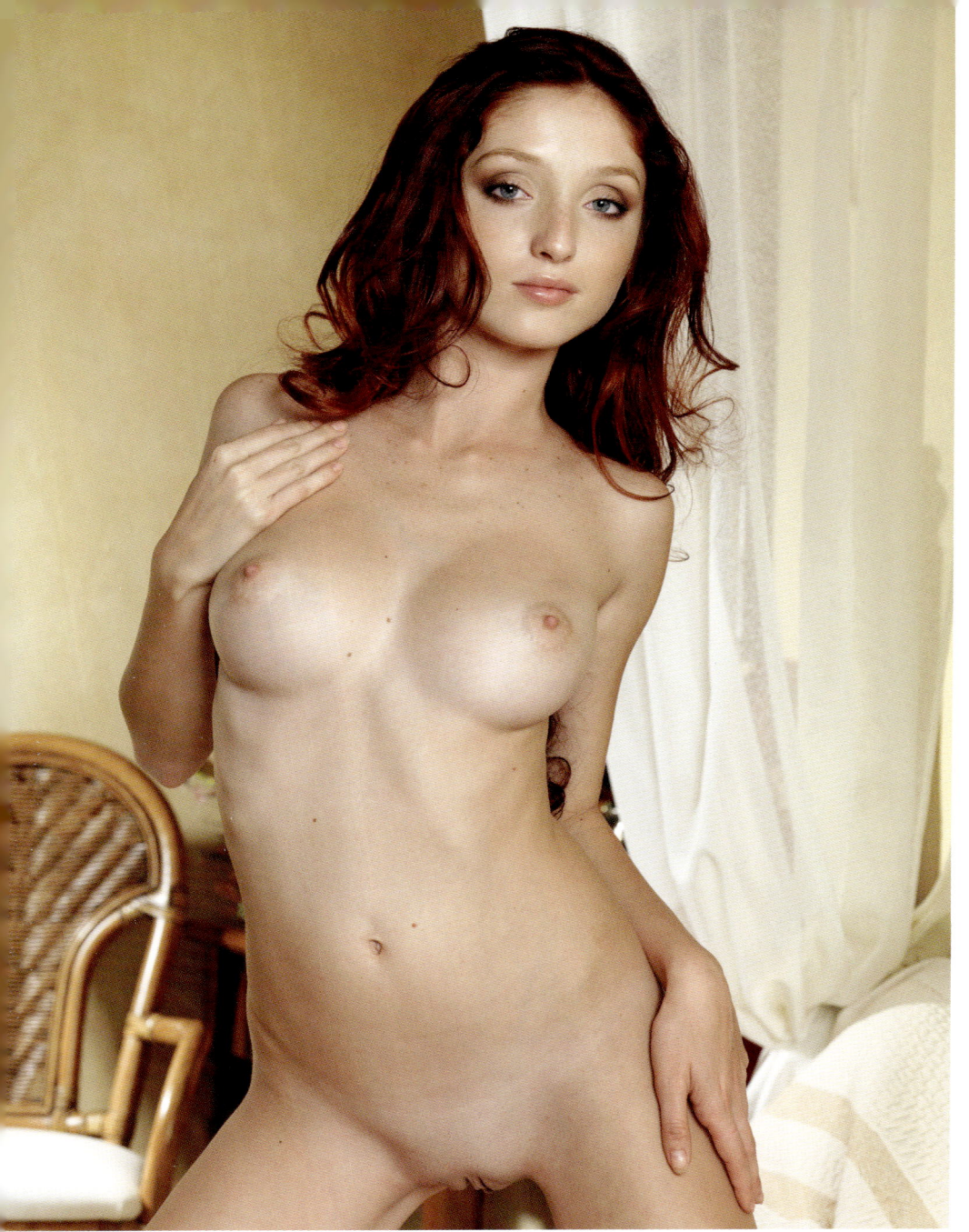

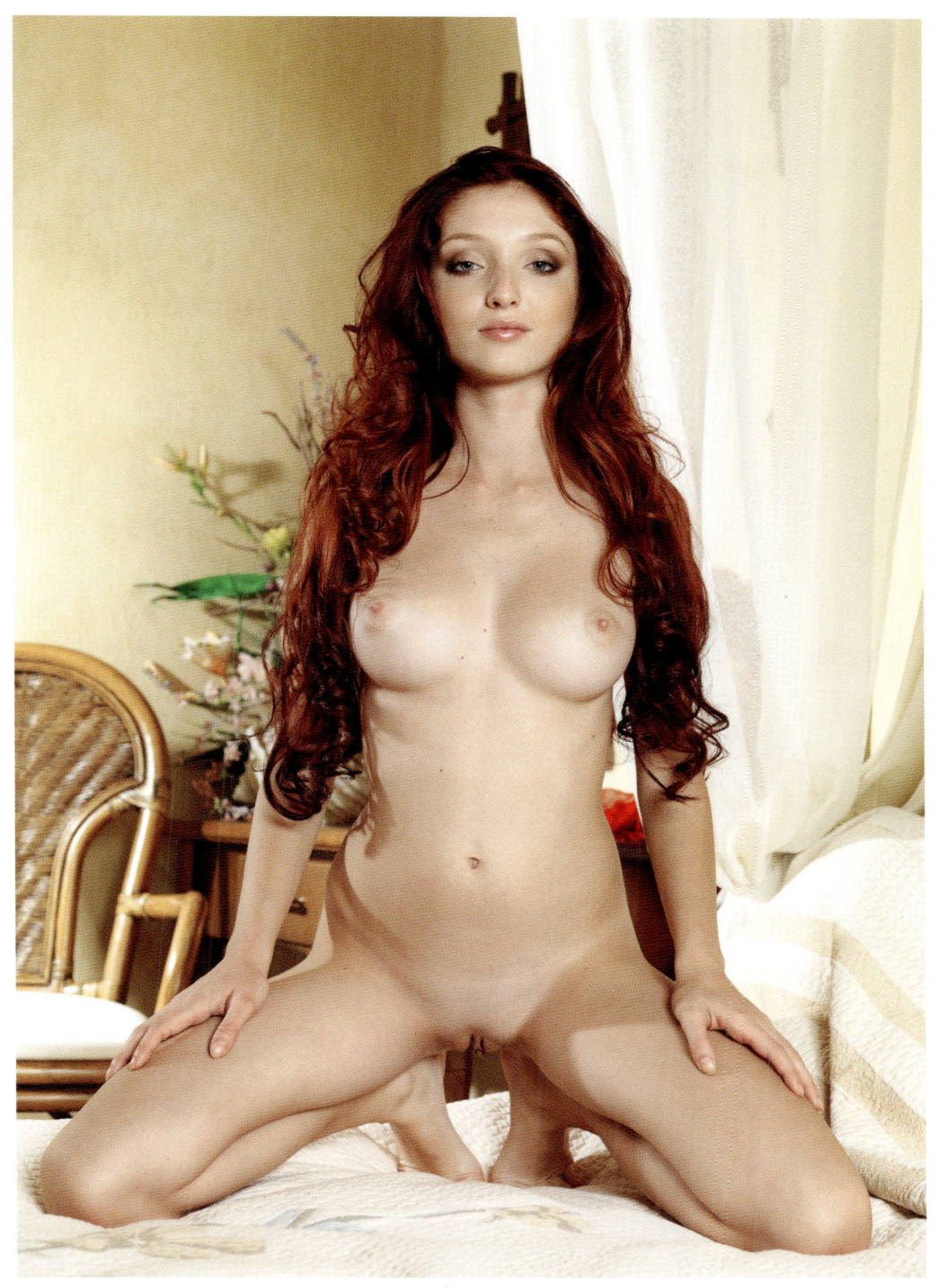

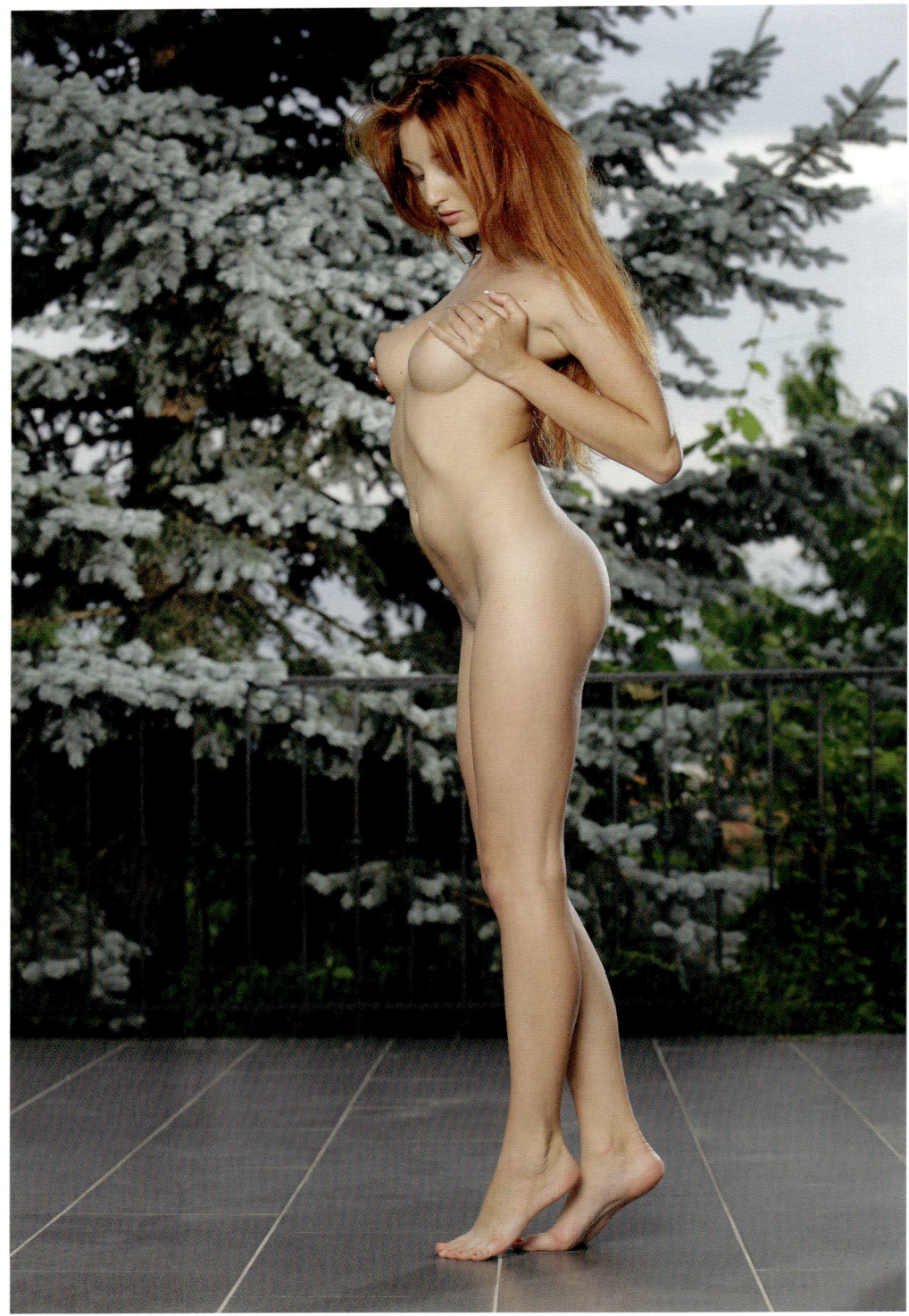

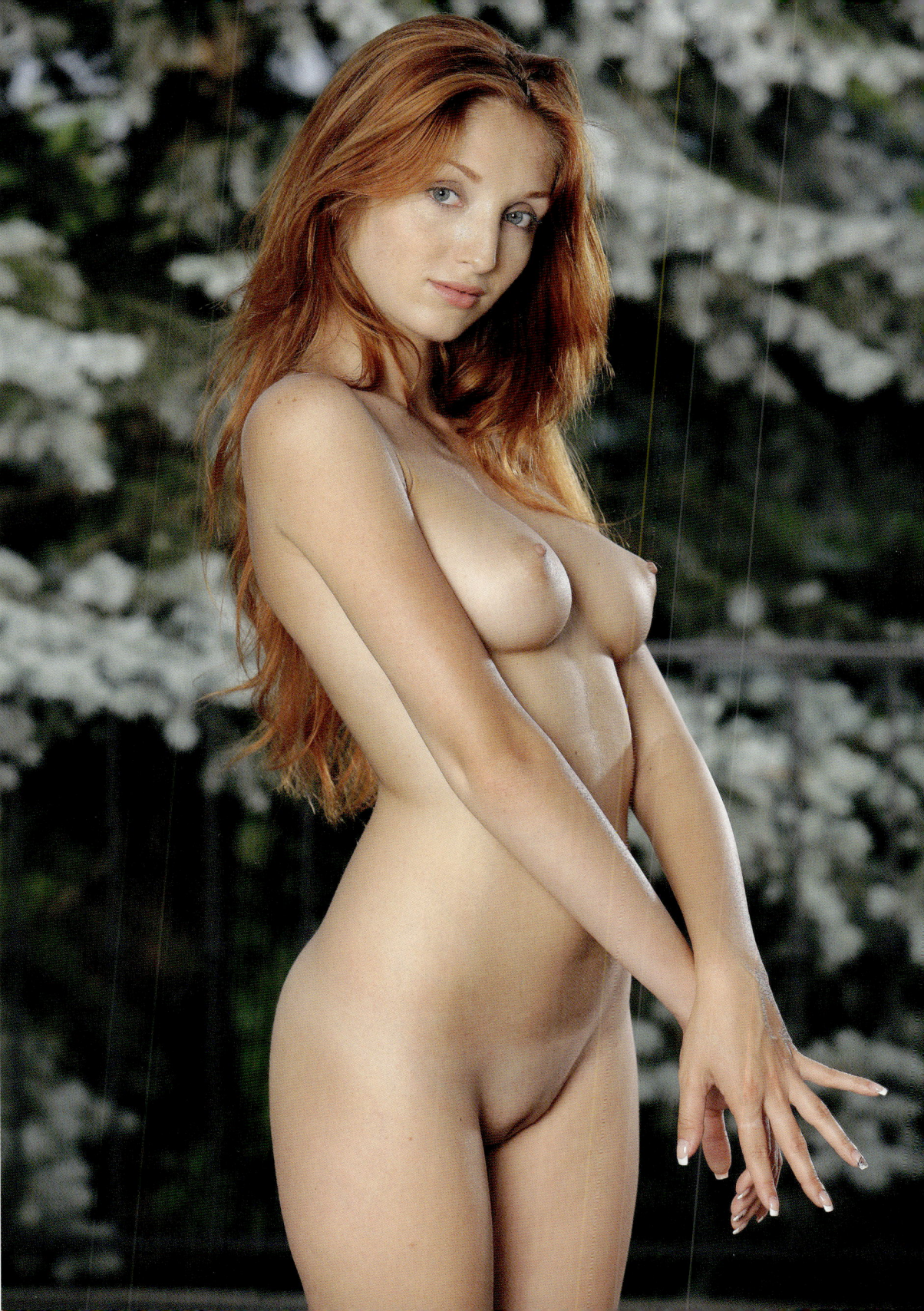

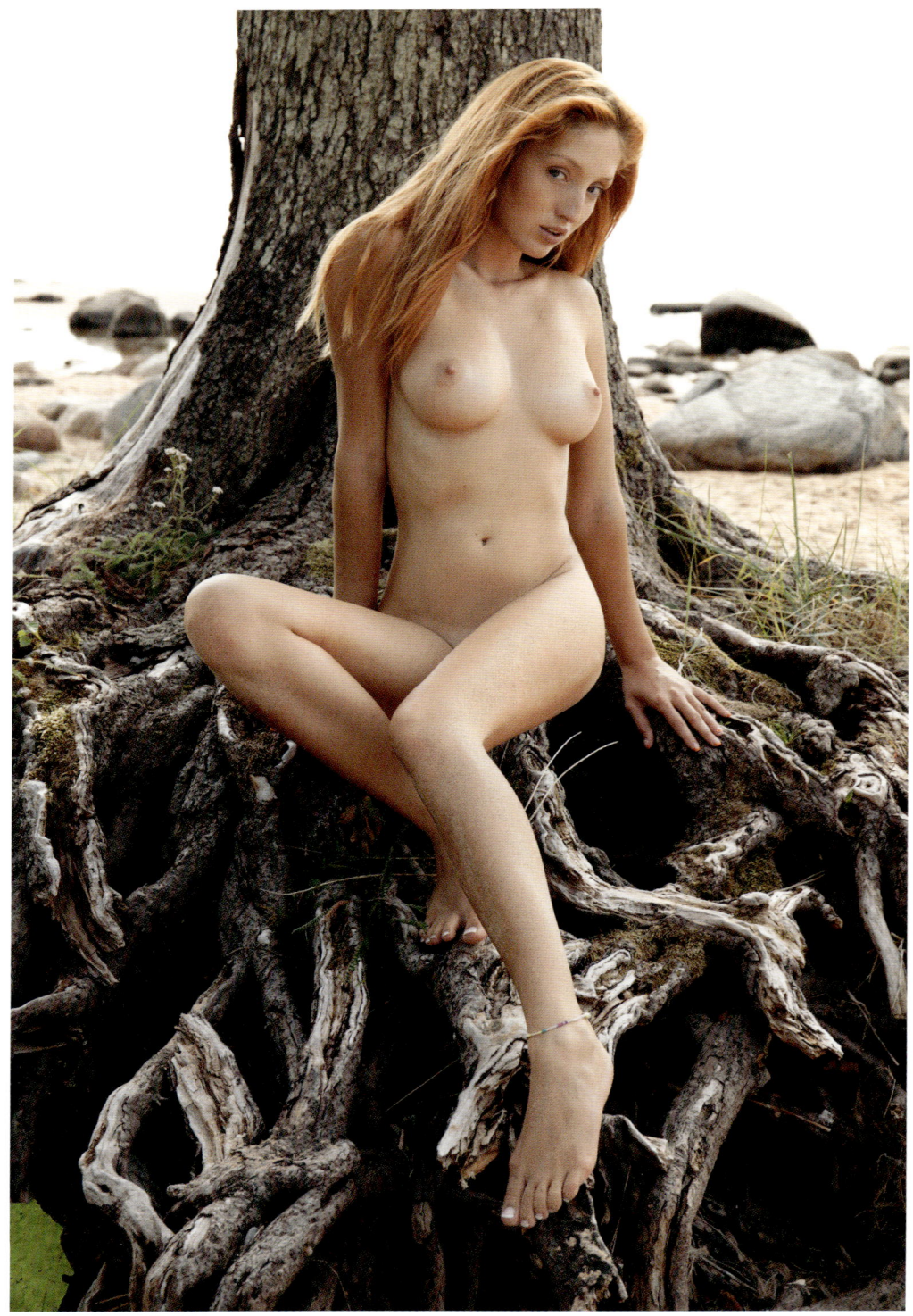

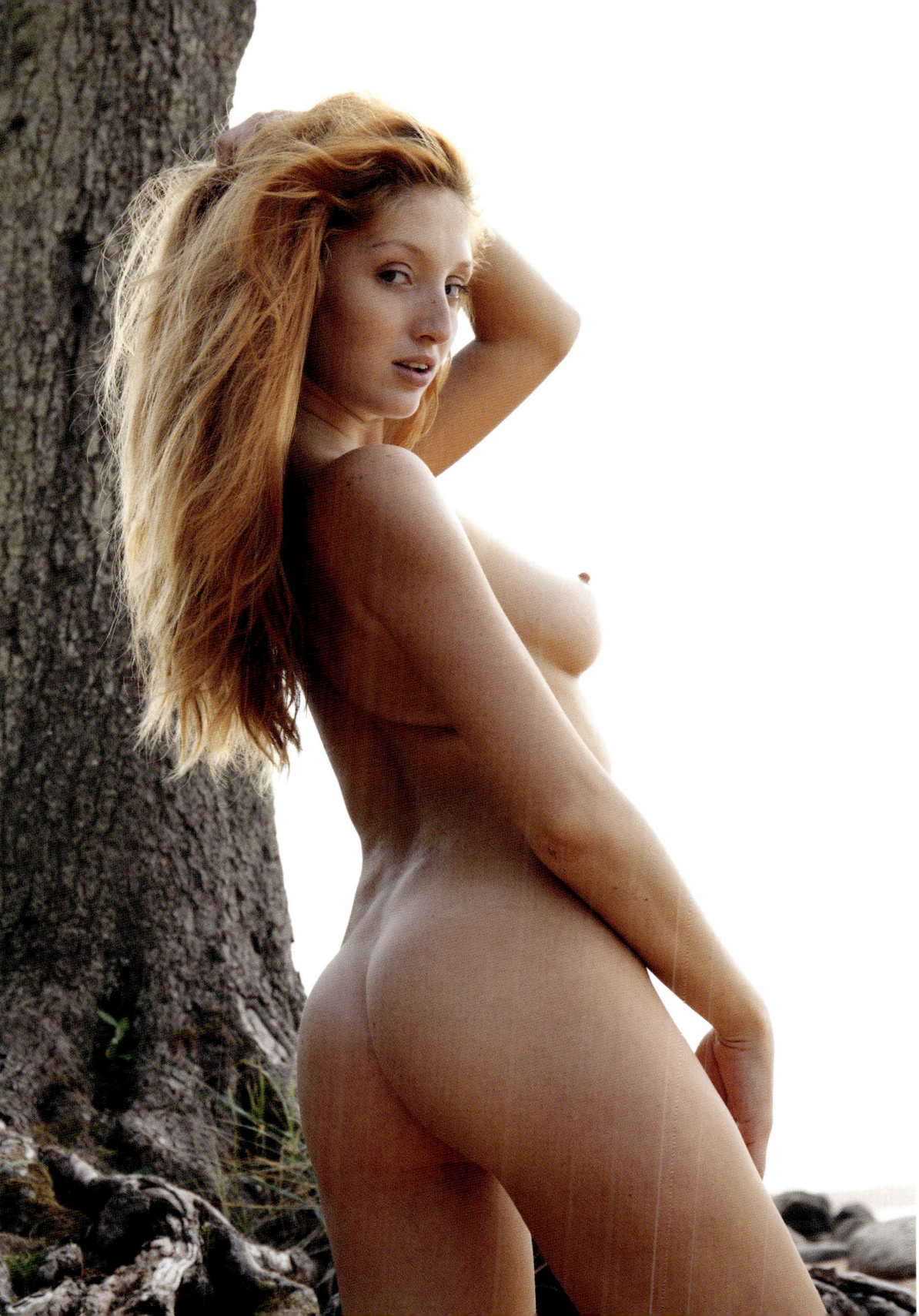

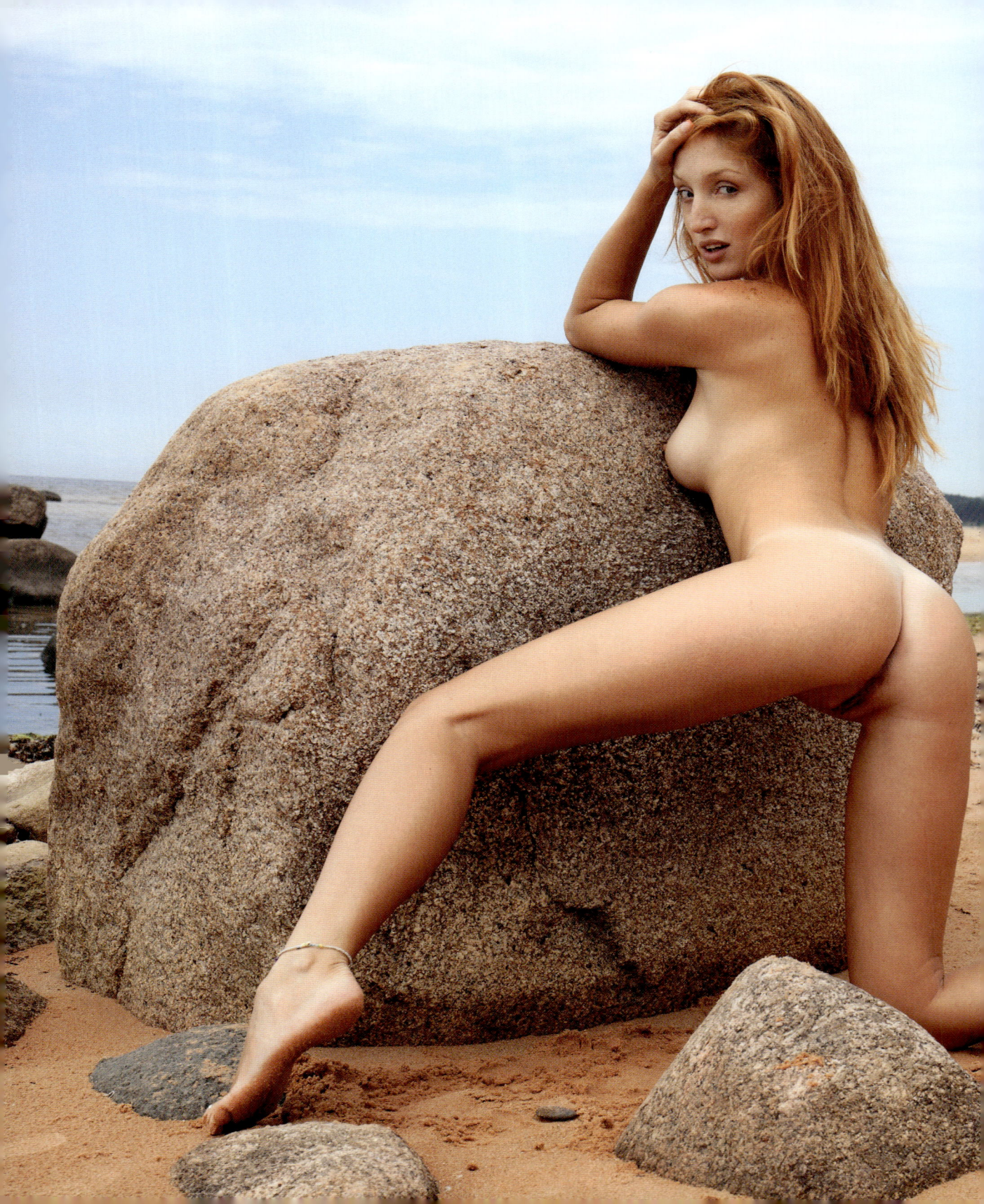

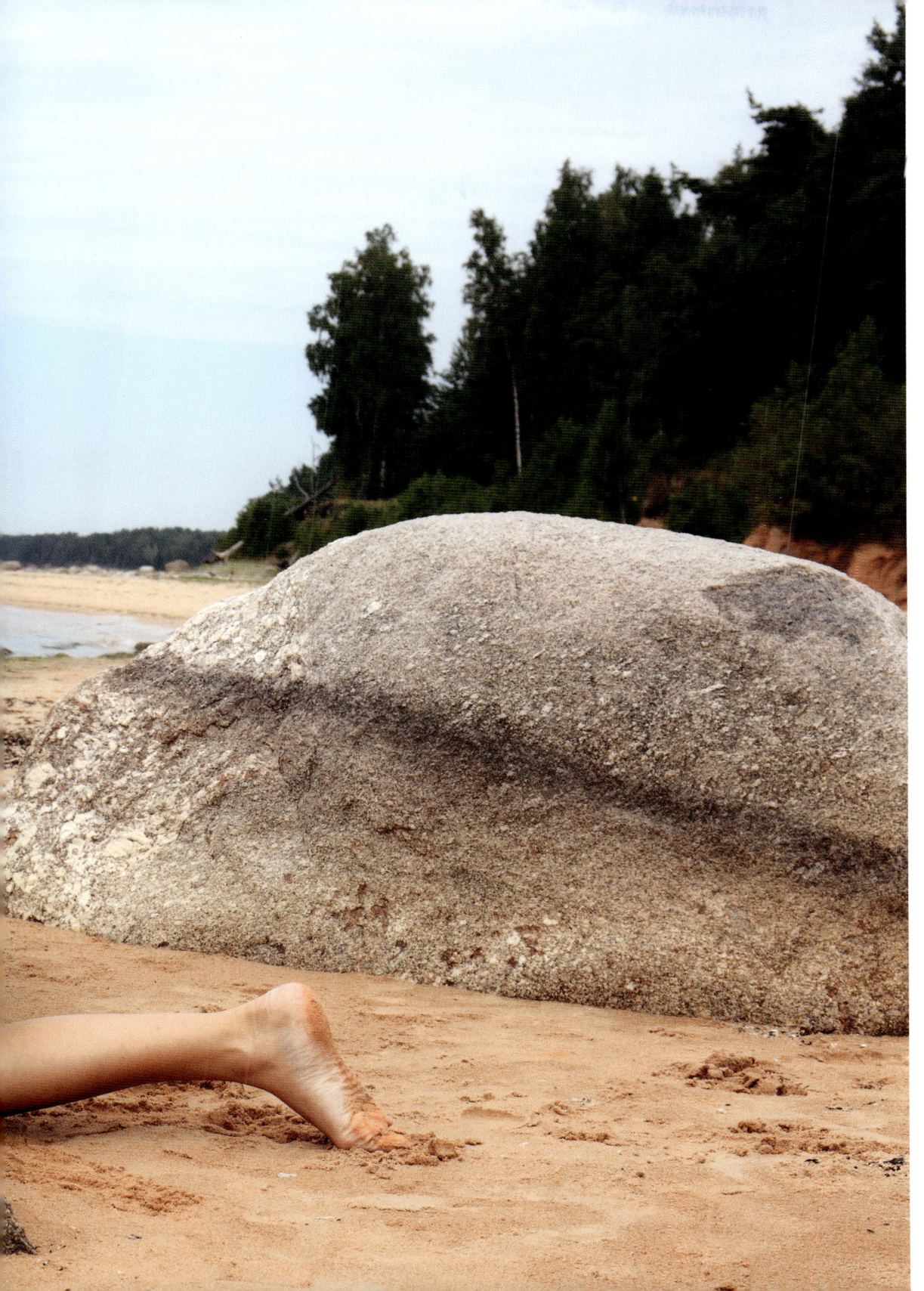

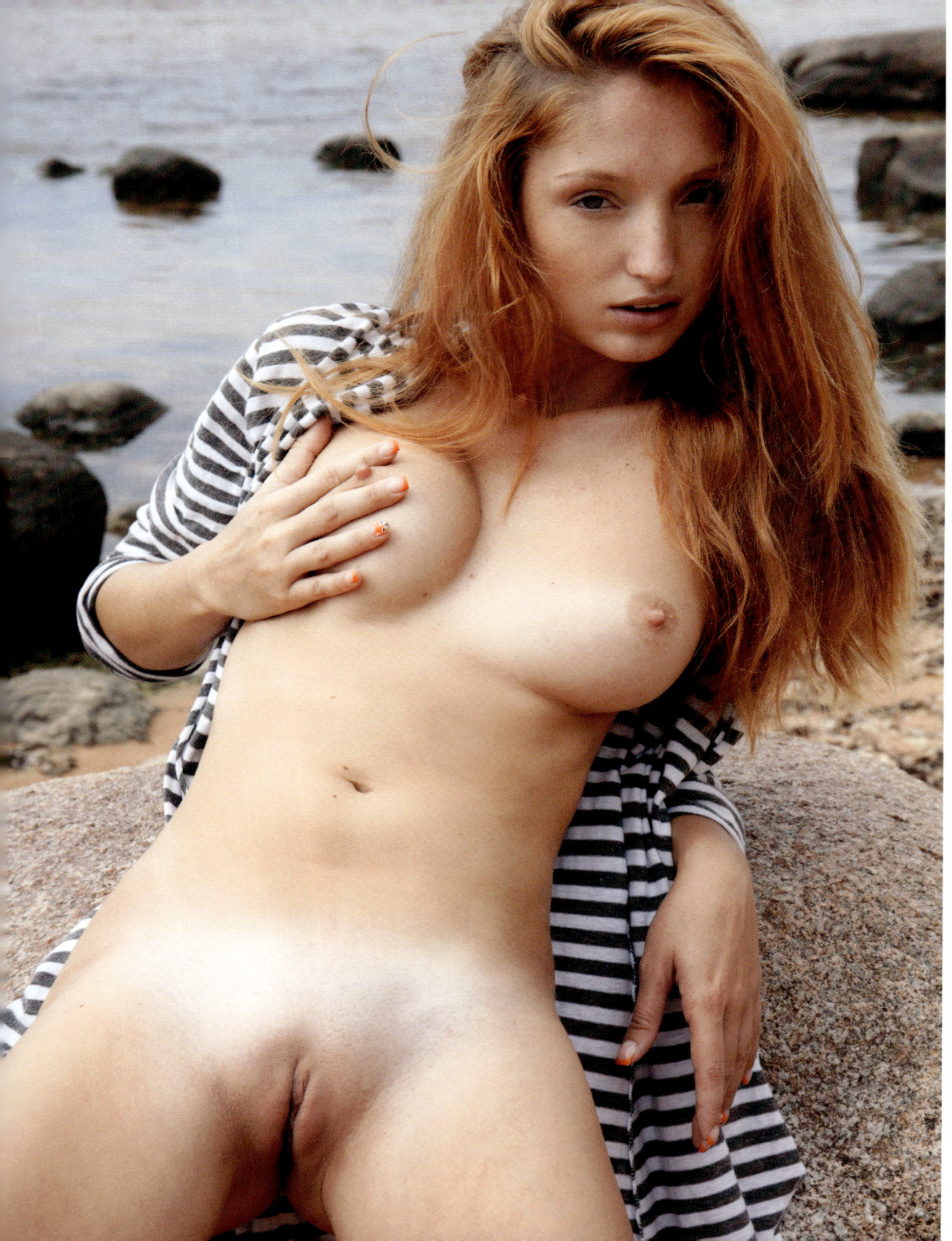

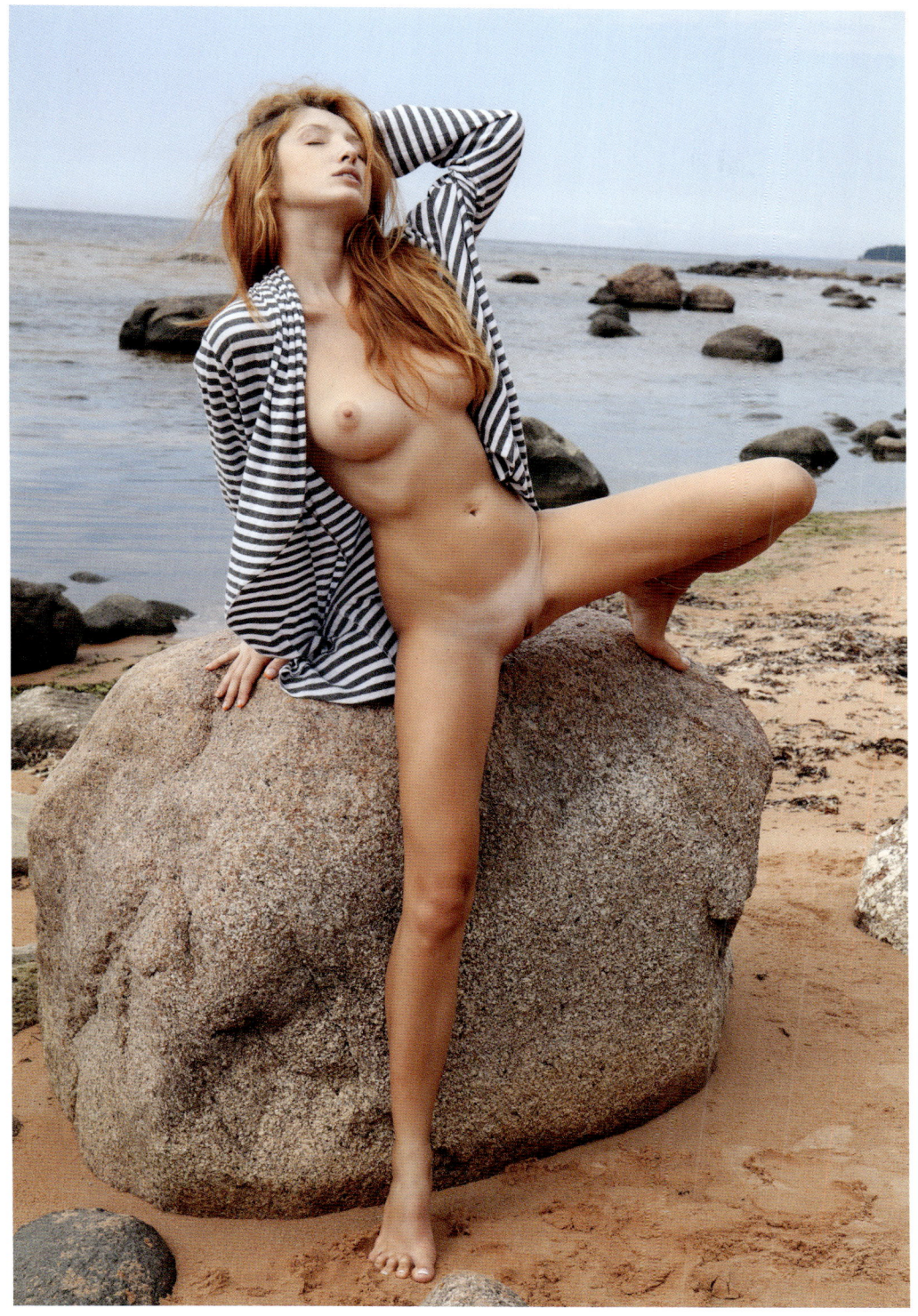

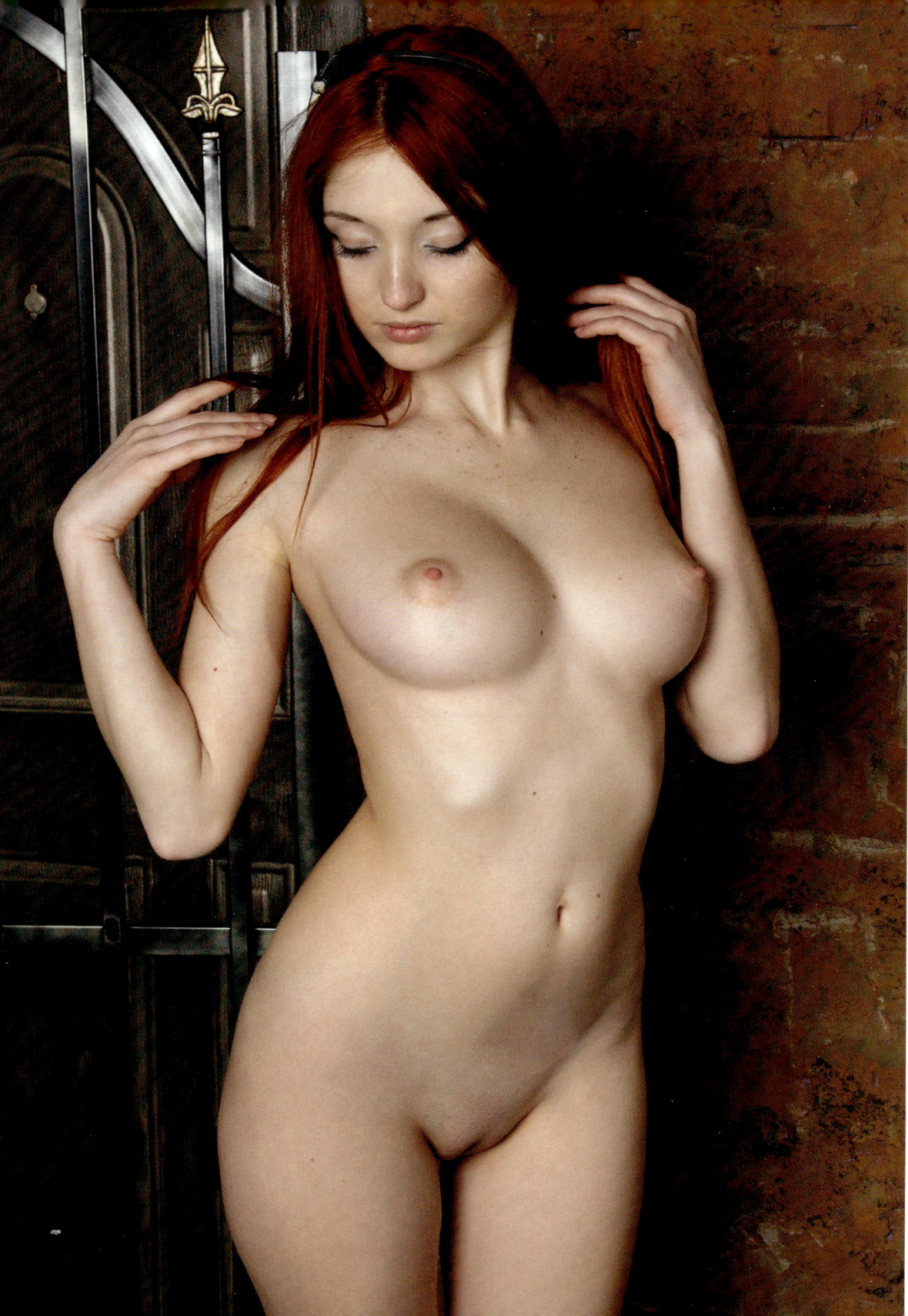

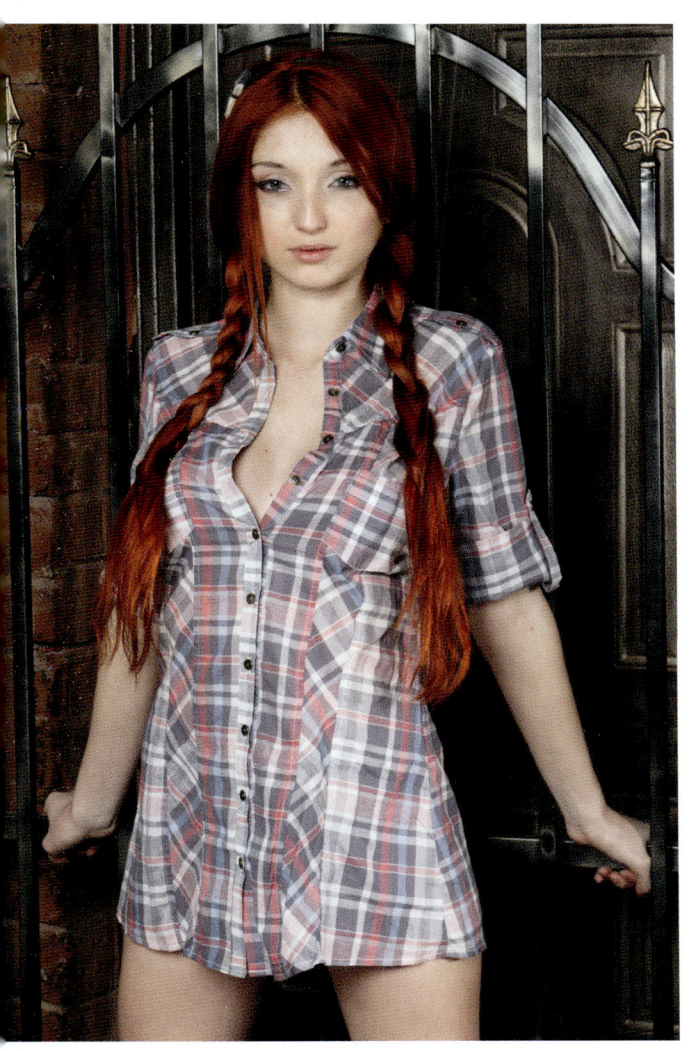
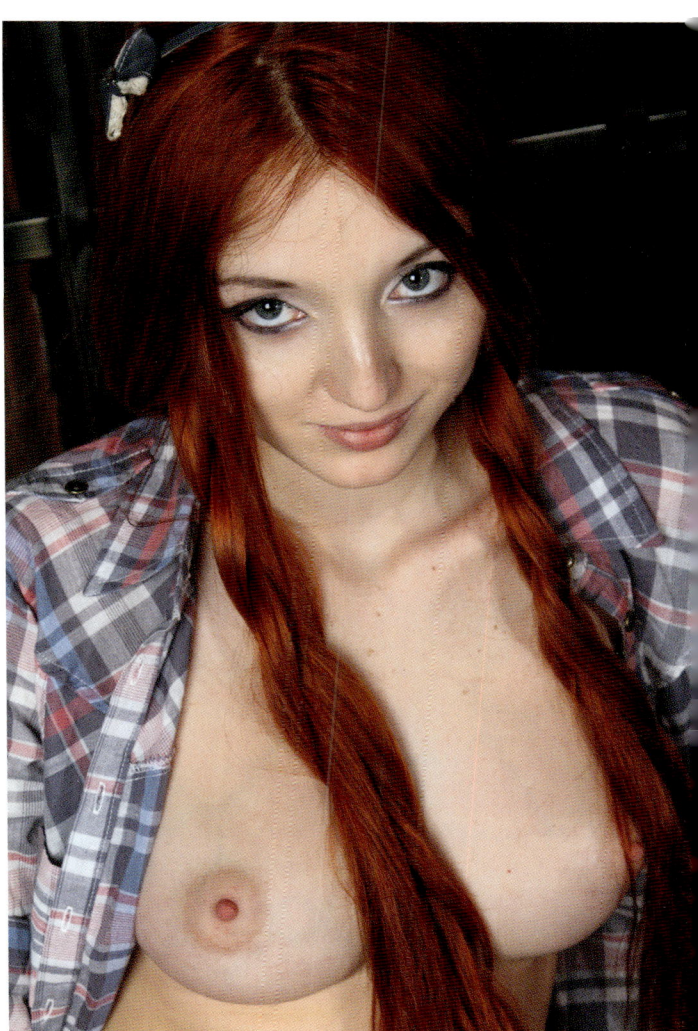

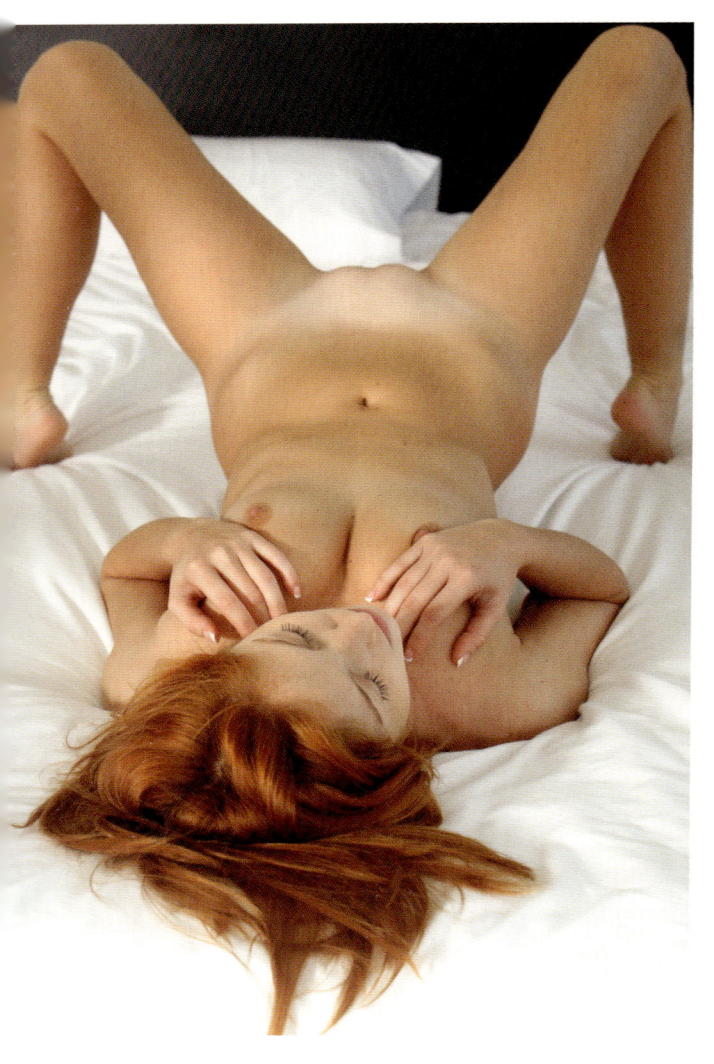
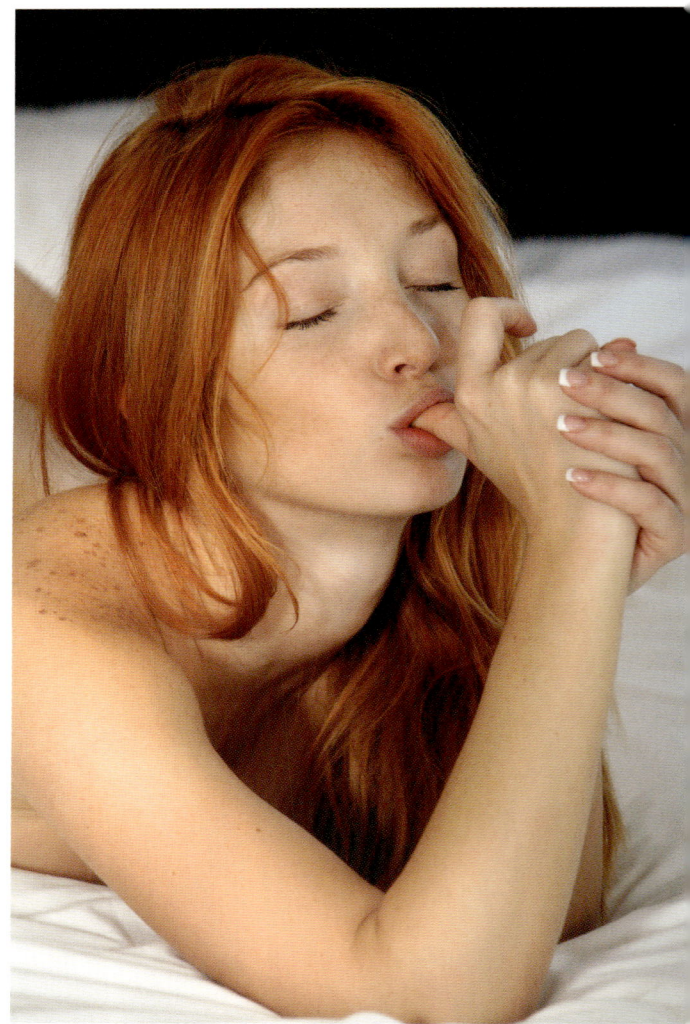

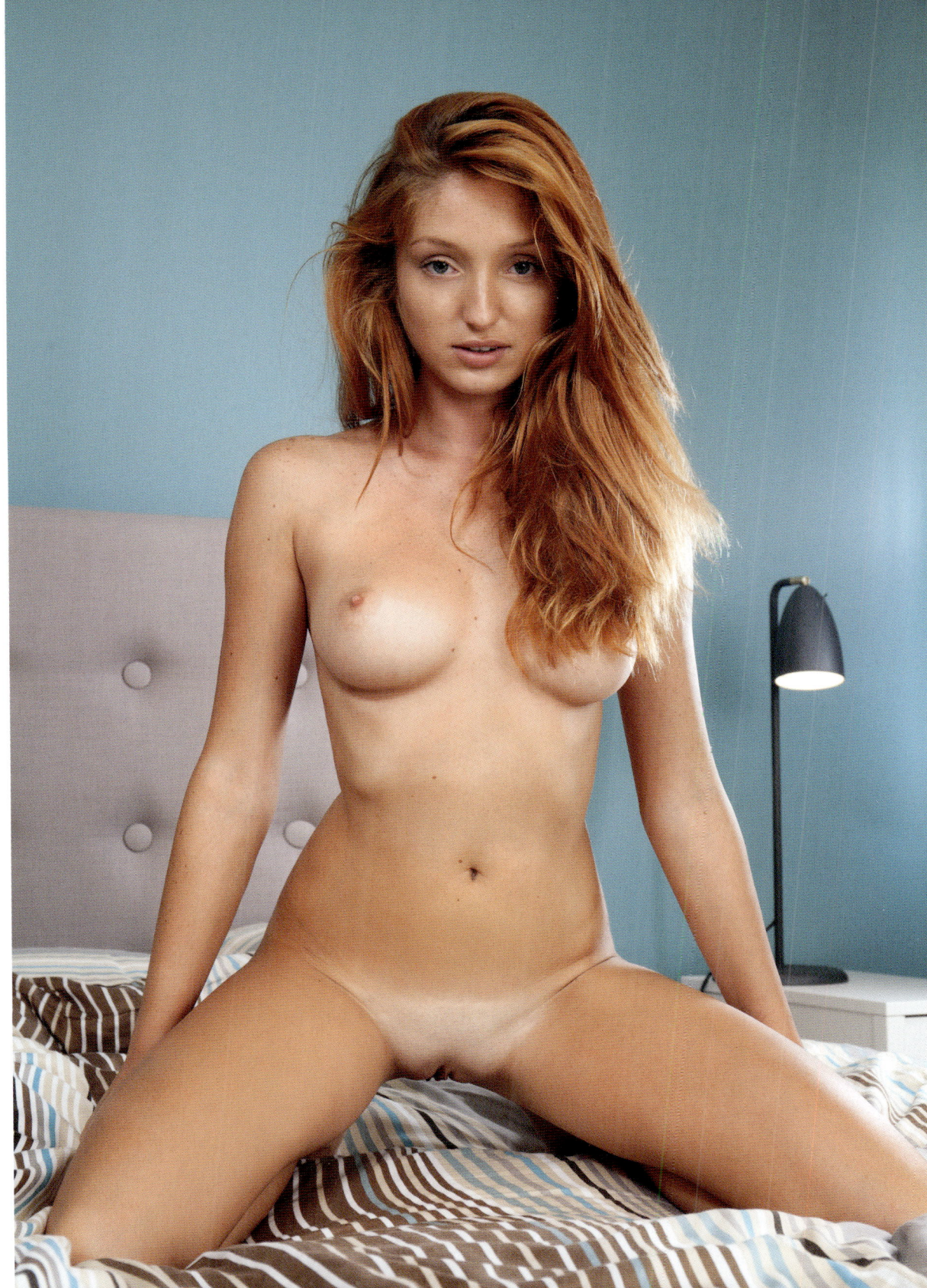

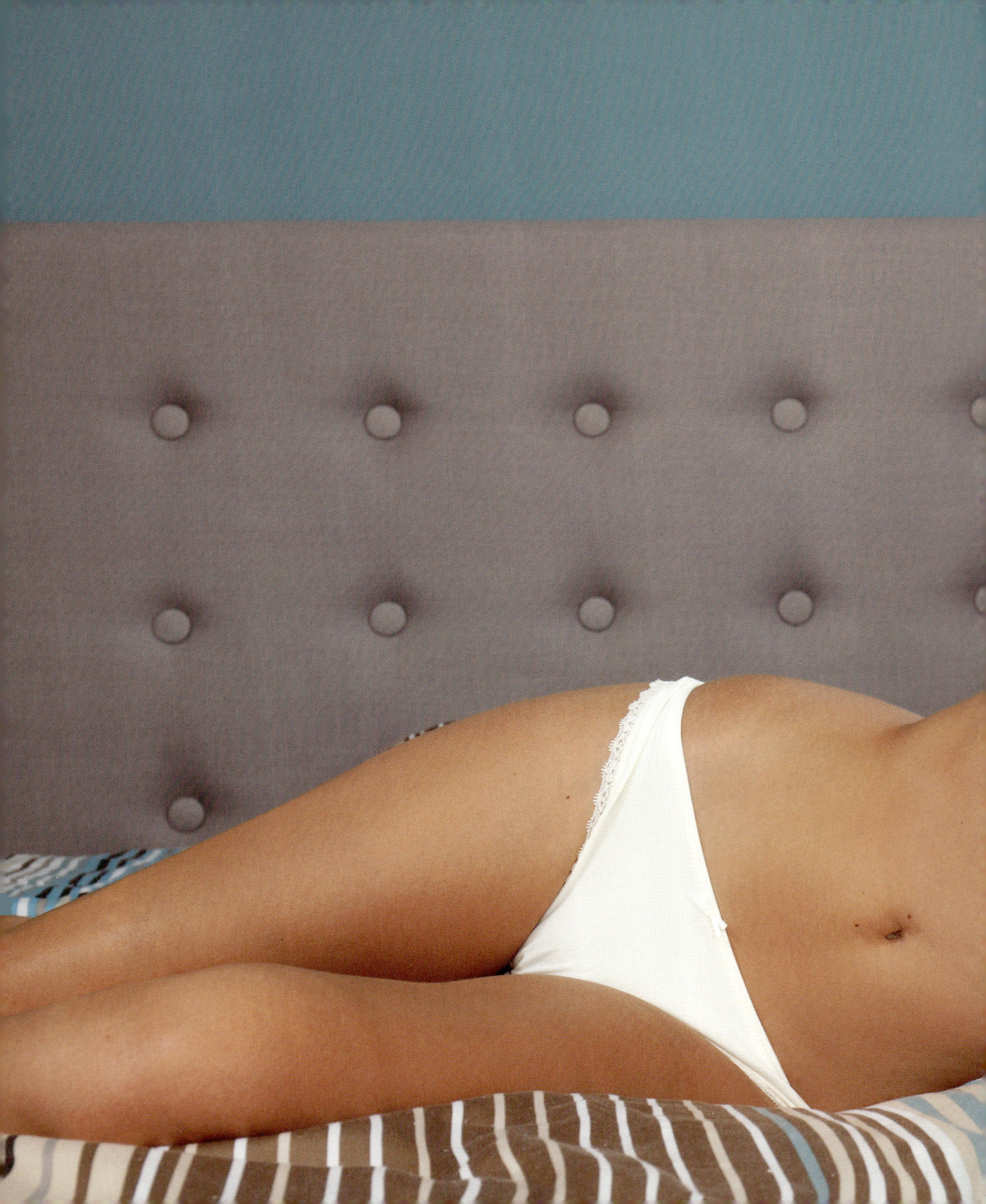

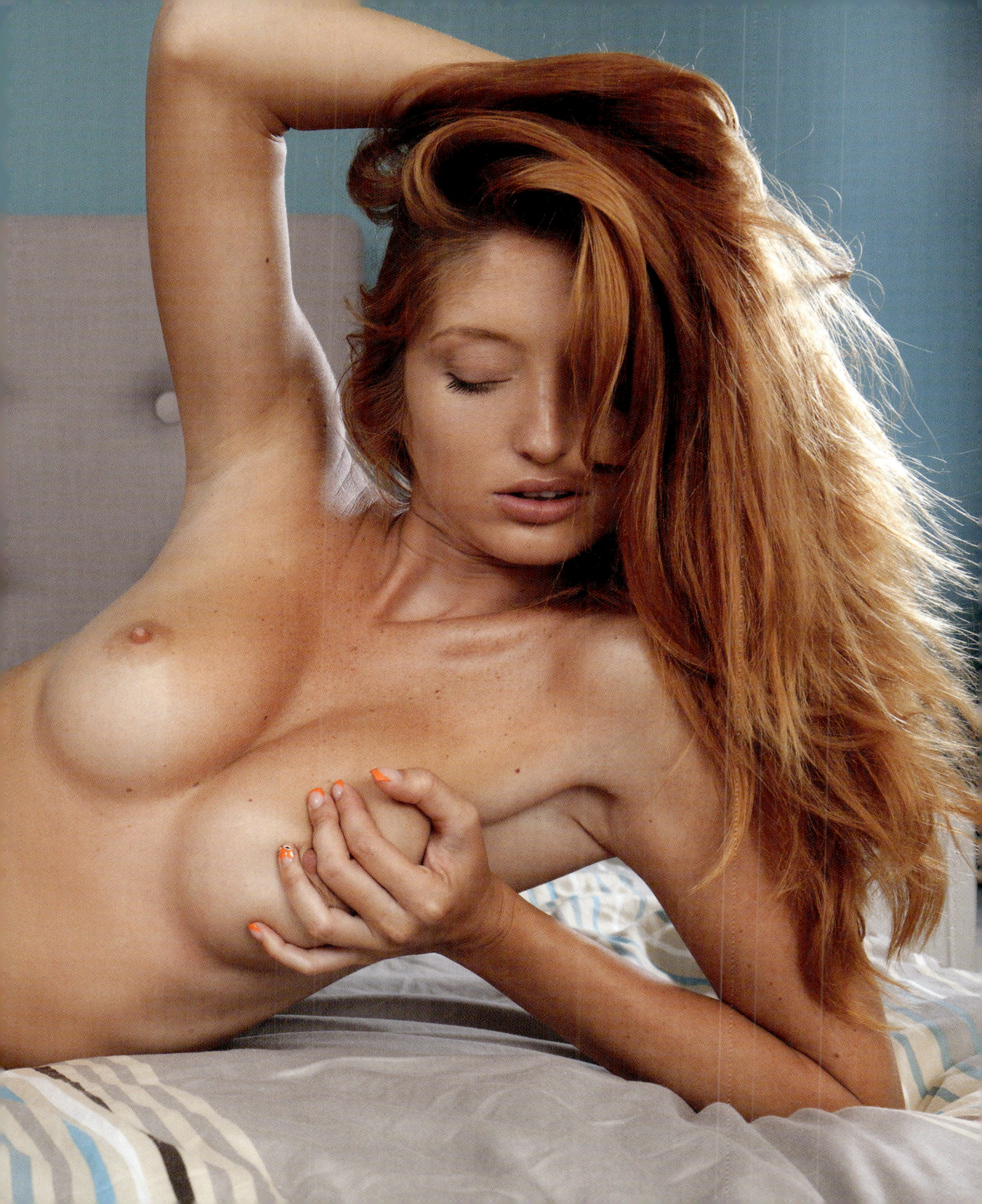

COLLECT THEM ALL: OUR MOST BEAUTIFUL

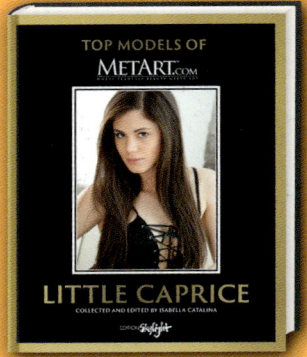

ISBN 978-3-03766-659-3

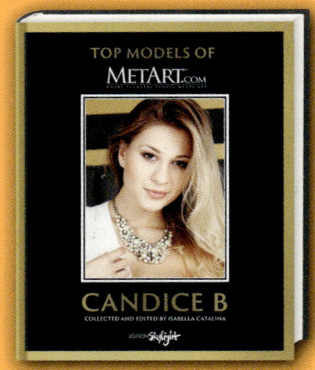

ISBN 978-3-03766-660-9

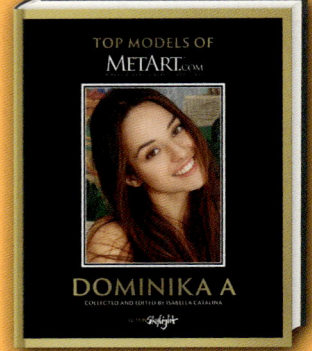

ISBN 978-3-03766-679-1

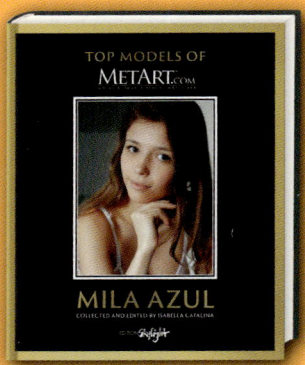

ISBN 978-3-03766-680-7

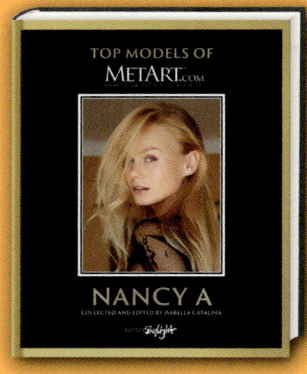

ISBN 978-3-03766-687-6

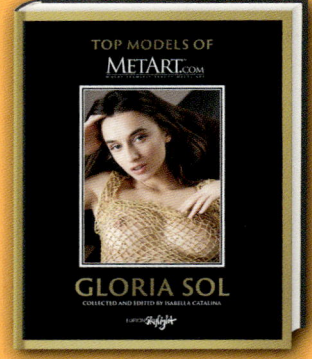

ISBN 978-3-03766-688-3

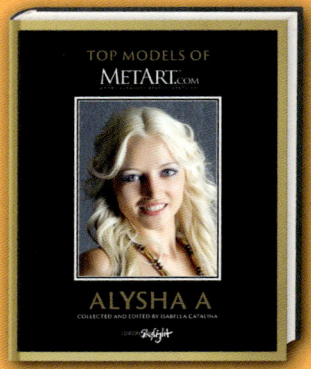

ISBN 978-3-03766-692-0

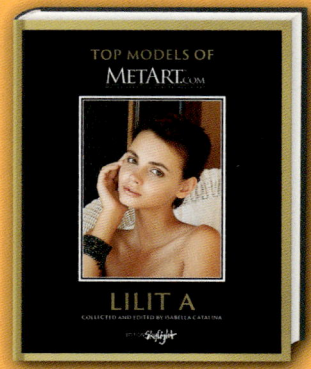

ISBN 978-3-03766-693-7

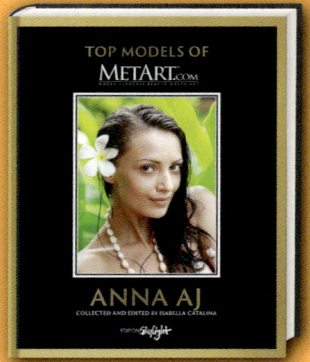

ISBN 978-3-03766-695-1